MUSIC, POLITICS,
AND THE ACADEMY

MUSIC, POLITICS, AND THE ACADEMY

PIETER C. VAN DEN TOORN

UNIVERSITY OF CALIFORNIA PRESS
BERKELEY   LOS ANGELES   LONDON

University of California Press
Berkeley and Los Angeles, California

University of California Press, Ltd.
London, England

© 1995 by the Regents of the University of California

Library of Congress Cataloging-in-Publication Data

Van den Toorn, Pieter C., 1938–
    Music, politics, and the academy / Pieter C. van den Toorn.
      p.   cm.
    Includes bibliographical references and index.
    ISBN 0-520-20115-9 (alk. paper) — ISBN 0-520-20116-7
(pbk., alk. paper)
    1. Musicology.   2. Musical analysis.   3. Music—
Philosophy and aesthetics.   1. Title.
ML3797.V26   1995
781.1'7—dc20   94-42446
                                                      CIP
                                                      MN

Printed in the United States of America
9 8 7 6 5 4 3 2 1

To my colleagues, students, and friends, past and present,
at the University of California at Berkeley and Santa Barbara,
Yale University, and the University of Washington

Contents

Acknowledgments

Ideas for this book arose several years ago in response to a number of accounts of Beethoven's Ninth Symphony published by Susan McClary, Leo Treitler, Maynard Solomon, and Richard Taruskin. I had wanted to rebut not only aspects of the accounts themselves but (as I thought) unsympathetic and sometimes erroneous assumptions about the aims and practices of various "technical" methods of analysis in music. It seemed to me that the latter were being slighted, misrepresented as "technically" distant and, as such, incapable of serving larger aesthetic ends. At the same time, a great divide seemed to be in the making, one between approaches that were characterized as liberal, democratic, multifaceted, sympathetically interdisciplinary, multicultural, open, feminist, caring, giving, literary, expressive, subjective, and poetic on the one hand, and conservative, elitist, specialist, insular, narrow, closed, masculinist, formalist, positivist, "technical," dry, objective, and mechanical on the other.

In the completion of this book I am indebted to the *Journal of Musicology* for permission to publish another version of "Politics, Feminism, and Contemporary Music Theory" (9, no. 3 [1991]: 275–299); revised and somewhat expanded, this appears here as chapter 1, "Feminism, Politics, and the Ninth." My thanks are also due the *International Journal of Musicology* for permission to publish a second version of "Context and Analytical Method in Stravinsky" (1 [1992]: 161–200); revised and expanded, this appears here as chapter 7.

For their assistance in reading portions of the manuscript and offering comments, I am grateful to Benjamin Boretz, Martha Hyde, John McGinness, Peter H. Smith, and Richard Taruskin. At the University of California Press, Doris Kretschmer offered invaluable advice at various stages in the completion and publication of the manuscript. With consummate skill, too, Jane-Ellen Long completed the editing and George Thomson set the musical illustrations.

Cattarina van den Toorn helped with the preparation of several drafts. I am also grateful to Anna-Marie and Linnea van den Toorn for their assistance on numerous occasions.

Santa Barbara, 1995

Introduction

As evidence of a consuming interest in music, why should we trust a facility with words, poetic expression, or sociopolitical comment rather than the methods of music theory and analysis, methods presumably more germane to the matter at hand? In an effort to draw ourselves closer to a musical context and enhance our appreciation accordingly, why should we turn to the former rather than the latter? And why should we judge the former to be warmly human or "humanistic," the latter coldly "technical," specialist, or formalistic in its appeal?

No doubt, complaints about the "technical" in music, the separation of its study from experience, have always been current. More specifically, however, the assumptions underlying the above questions stem from today's New Musicology, and reflect, as I understand them, a new impatience with the specialized knowledge of disciplines such as theory and analysis, the insularity of that knowledge, the difficulty of relating it to other branches of the humanities. Increasingly apparent, too, is the populism inherent in the complaint, although earlier versions appealed to the general public as well, claiming to represent the interests of that public in one way or another. (The latter are always presumed to be served by broader and more general discussion, never by closer engagement with the materials of music and their detail. Such engagement would require greater precision in the application of a method and its terminology, no doubt, but that precision would continue to rely on an underlying descriptive or metaphorical premise, one open to general understanding and use.) What can no longer be taken for granted, however, is a degree of familiarity with the canon of Western art music (Beethoven's symphonies, for example), indeed, a degree of musical literacy. The so-called informed or common listeners of yesteryear are beginning to disappear.

New economic realities have taken hold. In California, tax relief measures and a severe recession have combined to scuttle music education in the public schools; fewer and fewer students play an instrument or read music proficiently. The demands for greater diversity in the curriculum have had an effect as well: at the college level, there is less time for the complexities of sixteenth-century polyphony, the composition of Baroque fugues, "prolongation" in tonal music, or the study of various types of hexachords in the music of Schoenberg. What I am suggesting is that the arguments for and against certain kinds of "technical" knowledge in music education and scholarship are likely to become moot in the near future. Without elementary forms of instruction, forms widely accessible, the study and the appreciation of Western art music are likely to become wholly what many ethnomusicologists have claimed they have always been at least in part, namely, elitist and professional. (The strategy of the New Musicologists, that of promoting appreciation by encouraging more and more interdisciplinary study— retreating from "technical" matters, in other words, as part of a rearguard action to "save" music—will not work. Increasingly, Western art music will be transformed into something artificial, be experienced secondhand as an artifact—that is, solely as a means to ends apart from itself, as a way of understanding, if not those other disciplines, then larger cultural issues. Its immediacy, by which I mean its point, the consciousness it has awakened, passion stirred, curiosity aroused, will become more and more irrelevant to its study, performance, and composition. And the fact that various New Musicologists may already have envisioned such a fate, finding additional fault not with their own reactive strategies but with the methods of positivist musicology and theory and analysis, need not deter us here. We shall be contesting a good deal of their argument.)

But this would be to oversimplify the concerns of the New Musicologists, a large and varied group of humanists, multiculturalists, social critics, feminists, and postmodernists. Much "technical" analysis in music is eschewed because it would imply self-sufficiency, self-containedness on the part of single musical works —would imply, indeed, Carl Dahlhaus's "autonomy principle."[1] That principle would seem to question not only the existence of "external" forces in and about music (the "extramusical"), but, obviously, their study as well. Such forces include large-scale historical trends, social conditions, biography, criticism, reception, and, most recently, gender and sexuality. The alternative has been to view such forces as fully a part of the immediate experience of music; apprehended, they are subsumed by that experience. However unconsciously, they are a part of the attraction of music, of the ability of listeners to understand and respond "intuitively."

Of course, the two extremes of autonomy and experience of the "extramusical" are generally compromised. Few believe in complete autonomy, the complete detachment of music and its appreciation from a connecting environment. As Carl Dahlhaus has put it, "No-one—with the exception of scattered adherents of a rigorous aesthetic Platonism—denies that the autonomy of musical works is merely 'relative.'"[2] There are degrees of autonomy, in other words, high and low degrees. In the eighteenth century, much music was freed at least outwardly from explicit texts and external social and religious functions. Earning the right to be listened to for its own sake, it began to come into its own (as Dahlhaus might have expressed it). And the aesthetics that followed stressed the indefiniteness of musical expression, music's appeal to the infinite and, paradoxically, to the inexpressible. (Such ideas anticipated the "inner life" which, according to later figures such as Schenker and Schoenberg, music mirrored.) Becoming immersed

1. Carl Dahlhaus, *Foundations of Music History*, trans. J. B. Robinson (Cambridge: Cambridge University Press, 1983), p. 27.

2. Carl Dahlhaus, "The Musical Work of Art as a Subject of Sociology" (1974), in his *Schoenberg and the New Music: Essays by Carl Dahlhaus*, trans. Derrick Puffett and Alfred Clayton (Cambridge: Cambridge University Press, 1987), p. 238.

in a musical object for its own sake, listeners forgot both themselves and the world at large. In the immediacy of such a contemplation, inner and outer worlds were joined in a unity of experience; if only for a brief moment, alienation was overcome.
Dahlhaus seems to have viewed such transcending experiences and
the notions of autonomy and the inexpressible to which they were
linked as emancipating for both composer and listener; they were
viewed as an outgrowth of the process whereby music was relieved
outwardly of its dependence on texts and social functions.

Such a view is not ordinarily shared by the New Musicologists,
however. Instead, they have associated high degrees of autonomy
with self-sufficiency, the latter with positive knowledge in musicology (a preoccupation with music's factual environment, its
dates and chronologies), formalism in analysis (Schenkerian
graphs, for example, or the relating of abstract pitch-class sets). In
the face of the indefinite and the inexpressible, in other words, traditional scholars are accused of having retreated to what could be
defined and expressed plainly. According to the New Musicologists, such scholars have consistently ignored the more elusive
problems of expression and representation, emotion and meaning—ignored, indeed, the nature of their personal engagement
with music. Above all, they have shied away from critical involvement with the objects of their scholarship, which for many years
has been of concern to Joseph Kerman. Theory and analysis, inherently close to music and from which, therefore, an involvement of
this kind might have been expected, have failed to respond. Indeed,
they have become increasingly isolated. As with positivistic musicology, the aesthetic quality or worth of musical works has rou-
tinely been either ignored or taken for granted.

In a similar vein, Leo Treitler has condemned the "ideal of objectivity" which has in his view shaped music scholarship, an ideal he
characterizes further as "masculine."[3] Essentializing terms of this
kind—the opposite poles at which Treitler assumes males and females to operate, poles representing reason and rationality on the

3. Leo Treitler, *Music and the Historical Imagination* (Cambridge: Harvard University Press, 1989), pp. 4, 14–18.

one hand, passion and the irrational on the other—may be compared to the "models of sexuality" (male and female stereotypes) with which Susan McClary has examined the music of composers such as Beethoven, Schubert, Tchaikovsky, and Schoenberg. According to McClary, the relationship of males—white, heterosexual males, for the most part—to music has been marked by "aggression," "phallic violence," "domination," "rape," "rationality," and the need for climaxes and cadences; that of females, by "expression," "shared pleasure," "community," and "a desire to prolong the experience." With McClary, too, there is much bemoaning of the "hard-core" paths of theory and analysis, the failure of those paths to address adequately matters of expression, politics, sexuality, and personal engagement.[4] And under all these concerns lies the more general plea of the New Musicologists, namely, that music be judged more completely as a "product" or practice of culture, "an instance of social, political, discursive, and cultural action that traverses a larger field . . . of such actions."[5] In reaction to the idea of autonomy, they demand that music be studied, analyzed, criticized, performed, and composed by way of such a "larger field."

There can be no objection to a new openness in music scholarship, a broadening of its environment, a greater recognition of the sensing subject and his or her relationship not only to music but to specific musical constructions. Why not, then, also speculate more freely about the "technical" details of music, about possible connections to less definite qualities? Starting with intuition, why not pursue critical evaluation with the same care and rigor as one might the just-noted details? Why not attempt a merger of such separated areas, pulling them together for the sake of the exchange?

Problems with this approach surface, however, at least for this

4. See Susan McClary, "Getting Down Off the Beanstalk," *Minnesota Composers Forum Newsletter* (January 1987); and Susan McClary, "Terminal Prestige: The Case of Avant-Garde Music Composition," *Cultural Critique* 12 (1989).

5. Lawrence Kramer, "Haydn's Chaos, Schenker's Order; or, Hermeneutics and Musical Analysis: Can They Mix?" *19th-Century Music* 15, no. 1 (1992): 3. Or see Lawrence Kramer, *Music as Cultural Practice* (Berkeley: University of California Press, 1990).

observer. As with others, no doubt, a consuming interest in music may be taken for granted. Beyond the relationship itself, however, explanations are another matter. For there can be no certainty as to the matter of music, its underlying meanings or significances. Indeed, apart from the notion of music as a mirror of "inner life" or as a transcendence, and by way of the aesthetic experience described briefly above, this observer has little understanding as to why specific pieces of music should have the effects they do, why it should be those pieces and not certain others, him and not someone else (evidently), here rather than there, and so forth. The synthesis that is the whole of this complex web remains a mystery, however much individual pieces may be discussed either part by part or in terms of their general features or characteristics, separated analytically to be made whole again synthetically. (In analysis, parts are separated only to be assembled again, a process that permits a gradual assimilation, the acquisition of a familiarity, and for the purpose of enhancing what may be sensed and felt, adding to the pleasure that is to be gained from contemplation.) Perhaps the transcending circumstances of the relationship between music and the listener may best be compared to those of romantic love, individual musical works to single human beings or characters. The difficulties encountered in analysis are quite similar in the two cases.

But although music is ultimately nonexplainable, it can be performed, pointed at, and described. There are translations, ways of describing its behavior, of splitting it apart in order to test what may or may not be joined (segmentation into parts), even of determining the conditions under which that testing can take place. In the process, we can draw ourselves closer to the objects themselves, allowing those objects to become more fully a part of ourselves.

Can McClary's "models of sexuality" be of some use in this connection? Or are they based too overwhelmingly on the issues themselves, local considerations of personal-political cause and debate? Does attention shift too readily to the latter and the critic-scholar him- or herself rather than to the music? All human behavior may be colored sociopolitically, no doubt, with music and its appreciation no particular exception. Yet there are kinds and degrees of that coloring which need not prove overwhelming or monopolizing, kinds that can allow for a diversity of outlook and thought, the cultivation of a sense of focus and concentration.

A more significant objection to the use of such models may be that they cannot be pushed into the detail of music with any degree of regularity. As they are moved in the direction of greater musical particularity they collapse. In effect, the stereotypes become more stereotypical, their relationship to particular works more strained. The overall concept of sexuality or sexual desire may have applicability, of course, imagined as mirrored or reflected in one way or another. Ultimately, however, it proves too remote and abstract; further detail undermines both sides of the equation.

What are needed are terms and concepts of greater neutrality, ones that can flex with music, acquiring meaning as a result of that flexing. Such terms, ideally, are dependent on a "close reading" of the materials themselves; they invite and encourage that inspection. Although in this respect they are quasi-technical, they need never lose their ties to an initial and more general understanding and use.

What is to be gained from a close study of music, its harmony and counterpoint? Why should we concern ourselves with the principles of voice-leading in tonal music, phrases and their lengths, pitch-class sets and their properties, motives and their developing variations? A few general answers have already been provided. Addressing analytical approaches to various types of music, this book was conceived in large part as a response to some of the complaints and assumptions of the New Musicology. The sense here is that much established procedure has been misrepresented by that group, who often confuse the aims of analysis with those of the institutions in which it is taught, practiced, and debated.

Chapter 1 will introduce a number of aesthetic concepts having to do with analysis and the detail of music; more specifically, it will offer, by way of Beethoven's Ninth Symphony, a critique of McClary's feminist indictment of tonal music. Chapters 2 and 3 will deal with aesthetic immediacy and the role of much "technical" analysis in fostering a sense of intimacy with music, specifically by way of a close working with its materials. Also considered will be the relationship of scholars to scholarship and of various modes of scholarship to the institutions. The subject-object duality will be of concern as it relates to Treitler's polarity of reason and sensibility as, respectively, "masculine" and "feminine."

Schenkerian analysis and its underlying rationale will be the subject of chapter 4. I have wanted to defend Schenkerian practices against recent criticisms depicting them as cultist, elitist, insular, specialist, and formalistic, capable of verifying a theory but not of highlighting the individual qualities of the works considered. Complaints about the "technical" ways and means of Schenkerian theory and analysis will also be discussed.

Chapters 5 and 6 will be primarily analytical. In chapter 5, a return to the Beethoven Ninth, an approach featuring motives and their varied repetitions, orderings, and contents will replace the Schenkerian model; stemming in large part from Schoenberg, the rationale of this alternative approach will be discussed from both a historical and an analytic-theoretical perspective. Emphasis will again be placed on the uncovering of detail and on the manner in which, by way of that detail, a sense of intimacy is encouraged. (A prime assumption of the New Musicology is that intimacy—a feeling, sensing, caring relationship to music—is encouraged only with music standing as a "product of culture," a reflection of sociopolitical, economic, and sexual relations, never by way of the quasi-technical paths to which reference has been made here, and notwithstanding the ties that necessarily bind such paths to a more general understanding and use.) Crucial here as well will be the close identification of the motive and its development with the individual context and its making. Even the much-maligned pitch-class set can assume a tangible quality under these circumstances and, notwithstanding the high degree of its abstraction, can relate music of a great variety of idioms, practices, and periods. (We shall be availing ourselves of that advantage in moving rather swiftly from the Beethoven Ninth to Schoenberg's *Suite*, Op. 29.)

The notion of the individual context and its integrity—self-reference, to be exact—will again be of concern in chapter 6, although here from the standpoint of the neoclassical works of Stravinsky, *Pulcinella* in particular. The nature of the integration in these works will be questioned, as will the standard approach in analysis, one in which the old is separated from the new, tradition from the modern, classical procedure from Stravinsky's additions. Finally, chapter 7 will consider the oeuvre rather than the single work—more specifically, the identity of the oeuvre as a whole, its treatment in theory and analysis, relations to various immediate and nonimmediate traditions. Featured will be the problems of rhythm and meter and the octatonicism of several of Debussy's piano preludes.

An Epilogue will summarize the New Musicology and the debate in the later chapters of this book of a good many of that school's underlying assumptions. As was suggested already, the strategy will be one of exemplification: terms, concepts, and approaches will be introduced as a way of promoting experience, that close, personal contact with music so highly prized by the reforming critics themselves. A caution, however: like-mindedness in these and other matters of music and its study may not be the blessing often imagined or hoped for. There may be considerable advantage in maintaining a relatively high degree of independence when focusing closely on the materials of music, and not only for the discipline of theory and analysis, but for historians, critics, composers, and performers as well.

I

Feminism, Politics,
and the Ninth

The soul knew what it wanted. It had its own natural
knowledge. It sat unhappily on superstructures of explanation, poor bird, not knowing which way to fly.
Saul Bellow, *Mr. Sammler's Planet*

I

Is music inviolate? Can it withstand indefinitely our search for an
explanation of its appeal? Is there a point at which this scrutiny, directed not only at the structure and context of music or at the psychology of perception and cognition but also at our sociopolitical
and psychological profiles as listeners, might inhibit our ability to
respond freely to the stimulus? The kind of immunity referred to
here is not unlike that which may accompany religious convictions
and experiences of love, a blanket that insulates these forms of inwardness from arbitration, from the detours of reason and abstract,
conceptual thought. With varying degrees of intensity, musical
works can become objects of affection, faith, and love. They can
speak to us directly, cut through to the heart without deliberation,
without verbal approximation. And they can speak to us as individuals, single beings, not as representatives compromised by partisanship. Indeed, they may appear to serve no other purpose than
that of the relationship that is struck. And this would seem to be the

measure of their seriousness. Their worth would seem to hinge on the extent to which they are valued for their own sake, not for the outside uses to which they are put, the things or ideas they could be made to serve or represent. Each such work is valued for what it uniquely is, what it alone creates, its "peculiar, unrepeatable features."[1] It is judged according to its special appeal as a felt presence that cannot be duplicated or subjected to analytical reduction.[2] So, too, the relationship to such a work is neither willed nor forced but is entered into freely and spontaneously. Although not necessarily private, it is personal, inward, and spiritual. Music is a "language," as Eduard Hanslick observed, and composing is a "working of spirit in material fit for spirit."[3]

The assumption here is that the source of the attraction, the source of our conscious intellectual concern with music, is the passionate nature of the relationship that is struck. But this relationship is given immediately in experience and is not open to the inquiry that it inspires. Moments of aesthetic rapport, of self-forgetting at-oneness with music, are immediate. The mind, losing itself in contemplation, becomes immersed in the musical object, becomes one with that object. And the experience defines a bonding that would seem to transcend separation, the subject-object, inner-outer polarities, the rift separating consciousness from the world in which consciousness finds itself.[4]

1. Carl Dahlhaus, *Esthetics of Music*, trans. William W. Austin (Cambridge: Cambridge University Press, 1982), p. 15. For Dahlhaus, no doubt, consciousness of such unique, "unrepeatable features" and of the unrepeatable contexts of which such features were a reflection was symptomatic of a high degree of aesthetic autonomy, a degree that was linked to the canon of Western art music generally. To my mind, however, Dahlhaus placed too much emphasis on a historical definition, on works of a specific period of Western art music. An aesthetic orientation of this kind need not be confined historically or even culturally, but, once experienced, can become a part of a relationship to music of very different types, periods, and styles. Its confirmation can be sought and experienced more generally.
2. To rephrase this interpretation of the felt uniqueness of a musical work: if, for the sake of the pleasure that is to be derived, we wish to summon the presence of a particular musical context, then it is that particular context of which we wish to summon the presence, and not some other.
3. Eduard Hanslick, *Vom Musikalisch-Schönen* (Leipzig: Barth, 1854), p. 32, cited in Dahlhaus, *Esthetics of Music*, p. 53.
4. There are many such accounts of the aesthetic experience, accounts stem-

True enough, such moments of contemplation are but moments. Owing to an inability to hold fast, to the complexity of the stimulus, or to deeper, psychological inhibitions on the part of the listener, immediacy gives way to reflection. But periods of reflection need not signal a complete break with immediacy. Striving to regain a sense of rapport, the mind may remain suspended in music, seeking assistance not from the outside but from connections that may suggest themselves as part of the continuing musical context. No doubt immediacy and reflection are never experienced simultaneously. Thinking in and thinking about music may be mutually exclusive propositions, and the nature of their interaction may be indirect. Yet the two may coalesce in such strong mutual support as to suggest a thorough and intimate intermingling.[5]

Indeed, to suggest, as Carl Dahlhaus has suggested, that immediacy is a "thin abstraction," something that "knows nothing of itself," is to overstate the case for reflection.[6] Immediacy, the direct

---

ming from different sets of circumstances. See, for example, Lewis Rowell, *Thinking About Music: An Introduction to the Philosophy of Music* (Amherst: University of Massachusetts Press, 1983), p. 140. Pointing to the "traditional aesthetics of India," Rowell notes that the philosophy of yoga "describes the aesthetic experience as the achievement of zero-distance; an intense attachment (the literal meaning of yoga) to the illusion of music, loss of personal identity and absorption in experience, a fusion of self and object, and the achievement of a state of transcendental bliss."

5. *Immediacy* and *reflection* correspond to Edward Cone's "immediate apprehension" and "synoptic comprehension," respectively. Cone relates his own terms to "experience" and "contemplation." "Immediate apprehension" implies direct contact, while "synoptic comprehension" implies conceptualization, an attempt to realize "the form of what we have perceived." See Edward T. Cone, *Musical Form and Musical Performance* (New York: W. W. Norton, 1968), p. 89. It should be noted, however, that the opposition or duality implied by these terms, the extent to which immediacy is indeed unreflective, reflection nonimmediate, has been the subject of much debate, not least in the writings of today's postmodernists. For a brief comment on this, see Lawrence Kramer's review of Nicholas Cook's *Music, Imagination, and Culture*, "The Politics and Poetics of Listening," in *Current Musicology* 50, pp. 64–67; see also the discussion of immediacy and reflection in Dahlhaus, *Esthetics of Music*, pp. 72–73, 84–85.

6. Dahlhaus, *Esthetics of Music*, pp. 72, 85. In general, Dahlhaus is suspicious of immediacy, and especially of a "first immediacy" (pp. 72–73); he stresses, instead, the theoretical and historical assumptions that underlie a subsequent or "second immediacy" (p. 85), one informed and angled by reflection. In other ways, however, the account of the aesthetic experience given here is consistent

form of contact that is nonetheless open to revision by way of reflection, may not be unique to the aesthetic experience, but it is a necessary condition of that experience. And while its most conspicuous moments may be experienced during actual audition, an immediate sense of a musical context need never be lost to that which is held in memory. Indeed, such a sense may overwhelm memory. Reflection serves immediacy, and it is entirely instrumental in this respect. It follows immediacy in an effort to sustain immediacy. And while, on the side of reflection, we may be left with only an image of aesthetic pleasure, that image is a reflection of what is known in immediacy, what is felt and sensed accordingly. To cite Merleau-Ponty on this point, "Perception is a judgment which, however, is unaware of the reasons underlying its own formation. . . . The perceived object presents itself as a totality and a unity before we have apprehended the intelligible law governing it."[7]

What may be required of analysis from this perspective is that it serve as a foil, a means of articulating the details of a given context. Drawing those details into sharper focus, attending above all to those that would seem to have ignited the engagement from the start, analysis would seek to sustain the relationship, maintain contact. (It is from the standpoint of such action, not from that of pure knowledge, that the divisions of consciousness, of language and conceptual thought, become necessary and inevitable.)[8]

To this end, general terms and concepts may be introduced. In the case of tonal contexts this might consist of an implementation

---

with Dahlhaus's. And it is consistent as well with some of the earliest attempts at finding a rationale for wordless, functionless instrumental music. See, in this connection, Carl Dahlhaus, *The Idea of Absolute Music,* trans. Roger Lustig (Chicago: University of Chicago Press, 1989).

7. M. Merleau-Ponty, *The Phenomenology of Perception,* trans. Colin Smith (London: Routledge & Kegan Paul, 1962), p. 42. Merleau-Ponty adds the following remark from Descartes, *Meditations on First Philosophy,* "Meditation VI," AT, IX, p. 60: "I noticed that the judgments which I was accustomed to make about these objects were formed within me before I had time to weigh and consider any reasons which might have forced me to make them."

8. See Ernst Cassirer, *The Philosophy of Symbolic Forms.* Vol. 3: *The Phenomenology of Knowledge,* trans. Ralph Manheim (New Haven: Yale University Press, 1957), p. 36.

EXAMPLE I.   Beethoven, Symphony No. 9, III, opening.

of a number of Schenkerian terms, as demonstrated in Examples 1 and 2 from the opening theme of the Adagio of Beethoven's Ninth Symphony. In Example 2, the initial four measures of this theme are heard and understood as an arpeggiation of the tonic triad (B♭ D F), a prolongation of that triad with its third (D) on top. The A and E♭ of mm. 1–2 play a subsidiary role, embellishing the arpeggiation of the tonic triad as, respectively, a neighbor note and a passing tone. At the same time, the arpeggiation is tied to an overreaching third-progression that straddles the echo-like refrain in the woodwinds. The boxed-in areas in Example 2 outline motivic reiterations that tighten the context, motivating its parts with as individual or contextual a bearing as possible.[9] (The motivic and the

9. *Contextual* refers to the single instance and corresponds to "specific" or "individual." Its meaning in this inquiry is derived from Milton Babbitt, *Words About Music*, ed. Stephen Dembski and Joseph N. Straus (Madison: University of Wisconsin Press, 1987). There, *contextuality* refers to the extent to which a musical work is "self-referential," the extent to which aspects of structure are individual; *communality*, its opposite, refers to the shared basis of musical structures. Issues stemming from the interaction of these terms will be dealt with in chapters 5 and 6.

EXAMPLE 2.   Beethoven, Symphony No. 9, III, initial four measures.

contextual are closely allied in this respect, a matter to which we shall be turning in greater detail in chapter 5.)

The point here is that the application of these "technical" concepts (arpeggiation, prolongation, linear progression) need not be abstract. Quite apart from their broad metaphorical implications, they can be introduced with a record of prior applications, so that, at least initially, analysis can assume the character of a comparison. Understanding can become a matter of framing the sensed particular (the Adagio theme of the Beethoven Ninth, in this example) by what is known of the general (Schenker's terms and concepts); it can become a matter of the tension that is likely to emerge as a result of that framing. The fit, of course, is rarely complete; other concerns are likely to be raised in its wake, and in the direction of the individual context.

More specifically, understanding can become a matter of reading the relevant terms and concepts into a given passage and of testing the reaction to those terms. The analyst can move back and forth between the demands of the terms and those of the context. And, contrary to much recent criticism of Schenkerian analysis (indeed, of "technical" analysis in general), this process can enliven a sense of the foreground, heightening an awareness of its detail.[10]

10. For a similar description of the analytical process, see Scott Burnham, "Counterpoint: The Criticism of Analysis and the Analysis of Criticism," *19th-Century Music* 15, no. 1 (1992). Referring more specifically to Schenkerian theory and analysis, Burnham notes that, as part of the process itself, "the demands of an assumed background" are projected "onto the foreground" so that an attempt is made "to read the background into the foreground" (p. 73). In this way, the foreground "gains significance" as it is "shown to be part of a highly ramified contra-

Thus, in the graph of Example 2, the arpeggiation of (B♭ D F) and the descending third-progression D-C-B♭ are read into the foreground. In this way the reductions serve as foils, a way of highlighting the specific texture of the foreground, indeed, its *structure*. So, too, not all pitches or pitch-classes are heard and understood as fulfilling the same purpose. Each is in some way distinct. The function of the inverted dominant chords at mm. 1–2 is different from that of the dominant in root position at m. 4; although the $\hat{2}$ or second degree at m. 4 is attached to the over-reaching third-progression D-C-B♭, it remains a part of the theme and hence of the foreground as well. The functions it fulfills are multiple, in other words; a less determinate role does not eliminate the respect in which it operates more determinately at the surface.

In turn, an awareness of this detail can inflect experience. Indirectly, and however implicitly, such awareness can become a part of what is immediately sensed and felt. So, too, the more there can be to a specification of this kind, the more there can be to the context. And the more of the latter, what is sensed and felt in this vein, the greater the enjoyment, the pleasure that is to be derived from contemplation.

Such a perspective can prevail with frames of a more determinate character as well. Shown in Example 3 is the Adagio theme of Beethoven's *Sonate pathétique*. The first four measures of the bass line of this theme are identical to those of the bass line of the Adagio theme of the Ninth Symphony (Example 1). Yet this identity need

---

puntal process" (p. 74). Burnham's article was published as a response to Lawrence Kramer, "Haydn's Chaos, Schenker's Order; or, Hermeneutics and Musical Analysis: Can They Mix?" *19th-Century Music* 15, no. 1 (1992). Kramer had characterized Schenker's background structures as "faceless" (p. 5) and "independent of the expressive character of the foreground" (p. 6); their "foundational" status had seemed promoted at the expense of the "signifying surface" (p. 6). Yet Schenker tended to "devalue" the foreground only to the extent that its coherence and meaning were heard and understood as dependent on middle and background structures. Kramer overlooks the role of abstractions in music perception and analysis, it seems to me, conceiving of them only as impoverishments of the foreground or of what may be given immediately in experience. For a critique of his analysis of the opening "Chaos" episode of Haydn's *Creation*, see Charles Rosen, "Music à la Mode," *New York Review of Books* 41, no. 12 (23 June 1994): 55–57.

EXAMPLE 3.   Beethoven, *Sonate pathétique*, II.

not disturb a sense of the individuality of the given contexts. On the contrary, the purpose of the analysis would remain the same, namely, to pursue identity as a foil, a means of highlighting the individual in each case.

On the other hand, it would not ordinarily be the intention of the analyst to equate theoretical propositions of structural weight with aesthetic value and significance. In Example 2, the dominant in root position at m. 4 is distinguished in function from the dominants in inversion at mm. 1–2. From an aesthetic standpoint, however, the analyst would not ordinarily insist that, by virtue of its relative structural weight, the dominant at m. 4 was "more important" than the dominants at mm. 1–2, or "more important," indeed, than the embellishing tones A and E♭, tones for which the dominants at mm. 1–2 serve as harmonic support.[11]

And such is the path of analysis and of the sort of theory that analysis is obliged both to create and to depend upon in the elaboration of its detail. For attempts to specify, say, the functional behavior of pitches and pitch-configurations can do so only by way of a larger whole, a theoretical premise. In tonal music, the notion of a passing tone can be understood only in relation to the pitches between which that tone passes, just as the latter can be understood only as they relate to notions of consonance and dissonance, the triad, and so forth. The thread that joins these levels of understand-

11. For a revealing discussion of this issue, see David Lewin, "Music Theory, Phenomenology, and Modes of Perception," *Music Perception* 3, no. 4 (1986): 362–365.

ing is structure, the structure that is inferred from one context to the next. Questioned is the mind's ear, how it groups pitches and pitch-configurations, relates one such component to another; how, to reverse this sequence, pitches are held together, made to coalesce in one way or another. And to the extent that an analytic-theoretical pursuit of this kind guides and discovers as well as infers, it is dynamic in character.

Indeed, analysis may be prized as much for the process as for the results, for the doing as for the finished product; the latter can matter only to the extent that the process itself is undertaken. And it is with such considerations in mind that I have wanted to reexamine the sort of "technical" analysis to which brief reference has already been made here apropos of Schenker. Indeed, as part of the larger purpose of this inquiry, I shall be defending some of the traditions of music theory and analysis against recent depictions of those traditions as dry, lifeless, and mechanical in application. Preaching sensibility and its scholarly acknowledgment, couching their advice in a "rhetoric of liberation,"[12] groups identifying themselves variously as "humanists,"[13] "feminists,"[14] and postmodernists"[15]

12. Burnham, "Counterpoint," p. 71. Burnham remarks that the "epistemological authority" of theory-based analysis is being "challenged by a new kind of authority, an ideologically 'clean,' nonobjectivist, nonmasculinist discourse which itself is starting to bear the stigmata of orthodoxy" (pp. 70–71).

13. See Leo Treitler, *Music and the Historical Imagination* (Cambridge: Harvard University Press, 1989), pp. 1–18, 28–40; or Joseph Kerman, *Contemplating Music* (Cambridge: Harvard University Press, 1985), pp. 66–112.

14. See, especially, the critique of music theory and analysis in Susan McClary, "The Politics of Silence and Sound," Afterword to Jacques Attali, *Noise: The Political Economy of Music*, trans. Brian Massumi (Minneapolis: University of Minnesota Press, 1985), pp. 150–153. And see Ruth Solie, "What Do Feminists Want? A Reply to Pieter van den Toorn," *Journal of Musicology* 9, no. 4 (1991). In responding to a different, separately published version of this opening chapter ("Politics, Feminism, and Contemporary Music Theory," *Journal of Musicology* 9, no. 3 [1991]), Solie questioned the role of traditional theory and analysis, as opposed to literary, feminist, and cultural theory, in confronting immediacy and appreciation. Much of this inquiry, both here and in subsequent chapters, is an attempt to answer those questions, providing a more substantial rationale for many of the traditional practices of theory and analysis.

15. See Lawrence Kramer, "The Musicology of the Future," *Repercussions* 1, no. 1 (1992), which reads like a manifesto of the new creed. Listed among those practicing "postmodernist strategies of understanding" are "poststructuralists, neopragmatists, feminists, psychoanalytic theorists, critical social theorists, and

have sought to rescue music from the positivism of musicology and the formalism of music theory. Above all, they have sought to lecture theorists on the falsity of their scholarly ideals (those of personal detachment and objectivity, it seems), and on the evident resistance of those ideals to sensibility, to any discussion of the experience of music, of the personal and social aspects of that experience.[16] Reflecting an apparent shift in focus from the musical work to the experiencing subject, the bulk of these criticisms can be summarized as follows:

1. In positivistic or formalistic pursuit of objective, verifiable data, music theory and analysis have developed highly specialized, "technical" vocabularies.

2. In doing so, they have become increasingly "insular" (rather than sympathetically interdisciplinary),[17] cut off not only from the knowledgeable public but from related disciplines such as music history, literary criticism, and sociology.

3. In working with general notions and concepts, with the me-

---

multiculturalists" (p. 5). Kramer acknowledges the diversity of this group but insists that all are "radically anti-foundationalist, anti-essentialist, and anti-totalizing" and that all emphasize the "constructedness, both linguistic and ideological, of all human identities and institutions." Yet it is the diversity that prompts Kramer's avowal of "political correctness," in the form of a broadside against Western art music and its "aging, shrinking, and overly palefaced" audiences: by promoting the "autonomous greatness" of their music, those audiences are charged with "veiling and perpetuating a narrow set of social interests" (p. 6). It is evidently only the "palefaced" West, however, that is prevented from coveting the traditions and practices of its own music and that has spawned "social interests" that are necessarily "narrow" and unwarranted. The term "postmodernist music criticism" also appears in Kramer, "Haydn's Chaos, Schenker's Order," pp. 3–4.

16. This resistance has been judged to be a product of homophobia, "anxiety over masculine identity," and misogyny; to the extent that music appreciation has been judged "feminine," the male artist himself has been seen as "effeminate." Thus, the preoccupation with "hard-core" procedures of "academic music" and music theory, with notions of objectivity, rationality, and autonomy, has been viewed as a specifically male retreat from female concerns with "expression, pleasure, and community," indeed, as a repudiation of those concerns. See Susan McClary, "Terminal Prestige: The Case of Avant-Garde Music Composition," *Cultural Critique* 12 (1989): 71–73.

17. Kerman, *Contemplating Music*, p. 82.

chanical ("mechanistic" or "mathematical")[18] reproduction of
those notions and concepts from one musical context to the
next, they have ignored the "individual qualities"[19] or "salient
features"[20] of those contexts.

4. In ignoring individuality, they have ignored "presentness" as
   well,[21] the felt presence of individual works, the personal and
   social impact of those works.

Each of these points merits consideration. For the moment,
however, I have wanted to stress the detail that specialized, "technical" accounts of music are capable of eliciting, as well as the overall purpose of that elucidation. For, in the long run, that purpose
has less to do with the confirmation of general notions and concepts than with the testing of immediate experience. Analysis seeks
to draw the analyst into the detail of the materials of music. And by
drawing him or her into that detail, a sensed and felt awareness
thereof, analysis becomes a way of summoning the aesthetic presence of musical contexts, providing those contexts with a means of
articulation, with connections and associations that can assist in
that articulation. In this way, both theory and analysis serve ends
which they have only recently been accused of ignoring, ends
which critics of the combined discipline have tended to judge only
themselves capable of serving.[22]

As should be abundantly clear, however, no path can claim exclusive access to the heart of these matters. No approach, Schenkerian or postmodernist, can claim to be the sole reflection of those
who sense and feel music, the only way of summoning, sustaining,
and enhancing a sense of immediacy. The evidence of that which is
sensed and felt (and therefore true)—evidence of the personal self,

18. McClary, "The Politics of Silence and Sound," p. 150.
19. Treitler, *Music and the Historical Imagination*, p. 310.
20. Kerman, *Contemplating Music*, p. 82.
21. Treitler, *Music and the Historical Imagination*, pp. 37, 40.
22. See, for example, Kramer, "Haydn's Chaos, Schenker's Order," p. 4. According to Kramer, behind the inhibitions or "charmed circle" of the traditional
analytic-theoretical experience "there roams a subjectivity gone wild, a specter often feared but seldom seen." He suggests that the long-awaited task of unmasking
or unleashing that "subjectivity" has been left to the postmodernists.

in other words—cannot be allowed to rest with a claim, in any case, however passionately intoned. Those who would condemn Schenker for the formalism of his ideas (a misrepresentation), the tyranny of his "technical" apparatus, cannot have overlooked the passionate devotion of this theorist to a chosen repertory. The experiencing subject can seem very much alive in Schenker's accounts, a subject who listens and exhorts as well as guides. And my impression, indeed, is that many of the standard objections to Schenker's ideas have less to do with the ideas themselves than with the many practical difficulties that attend their analytic-theoretical application. At the same time, the exercise does not leave itself all that open to sociopolitical comment, to reflections of a world-historical nature or consequence, notwithstanding Schenker's own inclinations along these lines, his readiness to comment and reflect accordingly. This paradox, too, will be discussed in due course.

2

But to return to a question of musical aesthetics: why should moments of aesthetic contemplation, of the bonding that overcomes separation and alienation, be moments of rapture? How is it that music serves as a carrier of these privileged states? In seeking to answer these questions, contemporary philosophers and psychologists have often turned to the psychology of children and especially young infants. To follow Ernst Cassirer,

Separation into distinct spheres of sensation is not inherent in the original datum of perception, but rather vanishes more and more as we go back to the primitive configurations of consciousness. In fact, it seems to be a distinguishing feature of these configurations that they never show the sharp dividing lines which we tend to draw between the sensations of the different senses. Perception forms a relatively undifferentiated whole from which the various sensory spheres have not yet been singled out in any time sharpness.[23]

Jean Piaget has argued that, at the outset of mental evolution, "there is no definite differentiation between the self and the external

23. Cassirer, *The Philosophy of Symbolic Forms*, vol. III, p. 34.

world; impressions that are experienced and perceived are not attached to a personal consciousness sensed as a 'self', nor to objects conceived as external to the self."[24]

Finally, Susan McClary has suggested that music's privilege lies in its ability to create the illusion of "authentic communion," that of the nondifferentiation that characterizes early childhood.

A psychoanalytic model permits the following sort of explanation: music is able to simulate that state when the infant still feels itself to be coextensive with the mother's body, a state in which all sensation appears to be authentic before the alienating social codes of language and culture intervene, before one is even aware of being an individual separate from the mother. Musical patterns act upon most listeners in ways that are not rationally explicable, and it is as though one is connected to the subjectivity of another without mediation—as though still linked directly to the mother's body. The medium is therefore privileged above others (all of which bear more obviously the signs of their social, symbolic constructedness) because of that illusion of authentic communion.[25]

But McClary herself is contemptuous of this line of thought. She argues that American musicology has foundered on a "contradiction" involving opposing beliefs, a belief in transcendental significance ("the divine inspiration and ineffability of great music") and an opposing belief in positivism ("the obsessive search for facts").[26] And this "contradiction" has allowed students of the discipline to forgo questions of expressive or symbolic content as ultimately unanswerable and to take refuge, instead, in what can be trusted as fact, in objective, verifiable information, historical documentation, "technical" analysis, and the like.

In point of fact, of course, transcendental significance and posi-

24. Jean Piaget, *Six Psychological Studies,* trans. Anita Tenzer (New York: Random House, 1968), p. 12, cited in Thomas Clifton, *Music as Heard: A Study in Applied Phenomenology* (New Haven: Yale University Press, 1983), p. 285.

25. Susan McClary, "The Undoing of Opera: Toward a Feminist Criticism of Music," Foreword to Catherine Clément, *Opera, or the Undoing of Women,* trans. Betsy Wing (Minneapolis: University of Minnesota Press, 1988), p. xv.

26. McClary, "The Undoing of Opera," p. xv. The same argument appears in Susan McClary, "The Blasphemy of Talking Politics During Bach Year," in Richard Leppert and Susan McClary, eds., *Music and Society* (Cambridge: Cambridge University Press, 1987), pp. 14–19.

tivism need not be considered contradictory beliefs. It is quite possible to describe and study aspects of music and of the musical experience in ways that are openly—indeed, *necessarily*—representational without relinquishing a belief in "irreducible essences," in meanings that are not susceptible to reductive or comparative analysis and that are therefore spiritual. Many of Schenker's "technical" terms are expressive and metaphorical, yet their use would not contradict a belief in meanings that were beyond the reach of metaphors, analogies, and symbols. Music appreciation is itself a duplicity of sorts, in that elements of a common language or practice, elements shared and presumably open to analysis, are shaped in ways that are ultimately contextual, unique, and nonrepeatable. According to the conception introduced here, however, this duplicity is overcome in moments of aesthetic contemplation, moments of attunement with music. The common language can assume a transparency, be absorbed unconsciously as a medium through which the idea of a context, its whole, is transmitted. That idea transforms the language, rendering it individual and unique.

More specifically, McClary believes that the meaning of music is sexual-political, a meaning that embraces not just sex or sexuality but the sociology and politics of sex as well. Western art music, composed in large part by males, transmits a sexual image that is "male-defined," that is organized "in terms of the phallus."[27] Tonal forms rely on tension-and-release patterns that instill in the listener "an intense desire for the final tonal cadence," for closure in the form of a tonic or tonic triad.[28] At more local levels, techniques work to inhibit and delay this "artificial need" until the "climax," an eruption or "violent release of pent-up tension which is quite clearly to be experienced as metaphorical ejaculation."[29] (Here, "climax" has replaced "cadence" as the point of release, as the object of "intense desire" on the part of the male.)

---

27. Susan McClary, "Getting Down Off the Beanstalk," *Minnesota Composers Forum Newsletter* (January 1987): 7. A revised version of this article appears in Susan McClary, *Feminine Endings: Music, Gender, and Sexuality* (Minneapolis: University of Minnesota Press, 1991), pp. 112–131.

28. McClary, "Getting Down Off the Beanstalk," p. 5.

29. McClary, "Getting Down Off the Beanstalk," p. 5.

Familiar tonal terms can spring to mind in this context, terms such as "initial ascent," "prolongation," and "interruption." (Once ignited, the sexual image is not easily contained. It tends to spread like wildfire, in fact, a tendency that McClary is quick to exploit.) Of course, Schenker, the source of many of such terms, sought to project a comprehensive picture of motion and organic growth, one that encompassed images of necessity, of irreversible, hereditary codes (as his critics have tended to stress),[30] as well as images of spontaneity, of abundant and inexhaustible variety (as his critics have tended to overlook). For Schoenberg, too, the compositional process, perception, and tradition in music had all resembled organic life. "In an apple tree's blossoms," he wrote, "the whole future apple is present in all its details—they have only to mature, to grow, to become the apple, the apple tree, and its power of reproduction."[31]

The fundamental line *(Urlinie)* signified "motion, a striving for a goal," as well as the attainment of that goal.[32] But here again, Schenker's reference was to a larger conception of growth and evolution, one often linked to the inner, spiritual life of the individual. In this latter respect, tonal music was deemed an "analogy to our inner life," an "image of our life-motion."[33] Prolongations of various types, linear progressions and foreground diminutions, symbolized the dramatic course of that "inner life," its sensed obstacles, challenges, and renewals.

In the art of music, as in life, motion toward the goal encounters obstacles, reverses, disappointments, and involves great distances, detours, expansions, interpolations in short, retardations of all kinds. Therein lies the source of all artistic delaying.[34]

30. See, most recently, the critique of Schenker in Treitler, *Music and the Historical Imagination*, pp. 28–40, 50–54. Or see Joseph Kerman, "How We Got into Analysis, and How to Get Out," *Critical Inquiry* 7 (Winter 1980).

31. Arnold Schoenberg, *Style and Idea,* trans. Leo Black, ed. Leonard Stein (Berkeley: University of California Press, 1984), p. 165.

32. Heinrich Schenker, *Free Composition,* trans. Ernst Oster (New York: Longman, 1979), p. 4.

33. Schenker, *Free Composition,* p. 5.

34. Schenker, *Free Composition,* p. 5.

Thus, too, Leonard Meyer, when addressing questions of "value and greatness in music," [35] adopted a similar vocabulary, extending it to include the value judgment that had been at least implicit in Schenker's account. "Great" music, sophisticated art music, was distinguished from "primitive" or "sensual" music by its ability to circumvent easy "probabilities," inhibit "stylistic tendencies," create uncertainty, and delay "gratification."[36] "Value and greatness" could be measured in part by the "speed of tendency gratification."[37] And the willingness of the listener of Western, tonal music to inhibit tendency and withstand uncertainty, to delay "gratification," was viewed as a sign of maturity, not, as in McClary's account, a sign of the male's perverse (or sadomasochistic) desire to delay and intensify the "gratification" of sexual release. (Does perversity for the male lie in the impulsive lunge or in the act of inhibiting, delaying, or prolonging? The two are viewed as equally perverse in McClary's account, since her definition of goal-oriented, "male-defined" tonality encompasses both closure and the techniques that act to delay and intensify closure, that instill in the listener "an intense desire" for closure. But music as a symbol of sex and sexuality could take on a more telling complexion if explicit sex, the specifics of sexual conduct, were viewed less as a trigger in a vast causal chain and more as a reflection of how we as individuals think and act more generally.)

Meyer ignored the obvious sexual connotations of his argument, an omission that is likely to strike today's readers as implausible. Although informed in provocative ways with insights drawn from Gestalt psychology and information theory, parts of his 1959 essay can still read like a popish plea for celibacy. And the idea of ranking the Beethoven Ninth and Debussy's *L'Après-midi d'un faune* as, respectively, "great" and "sensual" (or "only excellent")[38] music can seem not only puritanical but simplistic and naive even to those

---

35. Leonard B. Meyer, *Music, the Arts, and Ideas* (Chicago: University of Chicago Press, 1967), p. 22. The essay first appeared as "Some Remarks on Greatness and Value in Music," *Journal of Aesthetics and Art Criticism* 17, no. 4 (1959).

36. Meyer, *Music, the Arts, and Ideas*, p. 33.

37. Meyer, *Music, the Arts, and Ideas*, p. 32.

38. Meyer, *Music, the Arts, and Ideas*, p. 38.

who might be inclined to sympathize with the taking of these kinds of critical stands, those who, like the present observer, have become somewhat put off by the opposite of what such stands represent, namely, the peculiar and—from the standpoint of music appreciation—unnatural neutrality of today's relativism, the noncommittal, leveling effect of today's officially sponsored ideologies of inter-, cross-, and multi-everything. Respect for the music and aesthetic beliefs of other cultures and societies need not require the proof of a conversion.

Indeed, when set against the so-called self-affirming (but often merely self-promoting) ways of today's me-generation, Meyer's blend of morality and aesthetic value can seem as if gapped not by a generation but by an entire civilization. Reference is made to personal sacrifice since, as Meyer insists, real maturity, real caring, is "a product of the resistances and uncertainties with which life confronts us."[39] And while suffering can lead to debilitation, it can also encourage "a higher level of consciousness and a more sensitive, realistic awareness of the nature and meaning of existence."[40] In sum, it is the personal, individual dimension of value that is stressed. Truth and reality are revealed humanely or "humanistically" in the experience of the single individual, the single instance. "Truth is inwardness," as Kierkegaard observed. It is not a product of philosophical, political, or "world-historical" debate.[41]

But McClary is in fact far from neutral from a critical standpoint. According to her, it is not just the male who defines the eroticism of Western, tonal music, but the "patriarchically invested male."[42] Tonal forms are concerned not just with "male-defined models of sexuality," but with the "exclusive control of sexuality by the phallus,"[43] a control that has led to "aggression" and "phallic violence."[44] Tonal forms are "a part of a larger cultural tendency

39. Meyer, *Music, the Arts, and Ideas*, pp. 34–35, 38.
40. Meyer, *Music, the Arts, and Ideas*, p. 35.
41. Søren Kierkegaard, *Concluding Unscientific Postscript*, trans. David F. Swenson and Walter Lowrie (Princeton: Princeton University Press, 1968), p. 71.
42. McClary, "Getting Down Off the Beanstalk," p. 7.
43. McClary, "Getting Down Off the Beanstalk," p. 7.
44. McClary, "The Undoing of Opera," p. xviii.

. . . to devalue and even to deny other erotic sensibilities (especially those of the female), to impose and maintain a hierarchy of power based on gender."[45]

In turn, female sexuality is passive and receptive. Indeed, "female erotic energy . . . need not be thought of as tied specifically to sexual encounter" but is an energy "that permits confident, free and open interchange with others."[46] In contrast to the erotic image of the male, that of the female "is one that combines shared pleasure and a desire to prolong the experience rather than lunging for closure."[47] (Earlier, "prolong[ing] the experience" had been linked to the delaying tactics of "male-defined" tonality, to tactics that had inhibited tendency and forestalled closure or release. This confusion can seem incidental at first, but my impression is that it underscores all too obviously the difficulty in getting the tonal repertory to connect not only to these generalized forms of sex and sexuality but to the sharp male-female oppositions that are a part of McClary's essentializing approach.)

And history is (re)written accordingly. Medieval culture, marked (like ancient Greece) by "the ideals of harmony, balance, and stability," fostered a music that "reveled in the present moment." It encouraged modal techniques that were "relatively nondirectional" and rhythms that were "grounded in the physicality and repetitiveness of the dance." Unfortunately, however, these dynamics were cast aside by the "thrusting" ways of the Renaissance. And in the wake of the religious and scientific revolutions of the seventeenth century, stability and balance in the arts gave way to "extravagant, individualistic assertion," "aggressive, rhetorical gestures," and a "secular spirit of passionate manipulation."[48] In turn, modern times have witnessed the catastrophe of man's ascent, the devastation of his folly, and the projection of a "postnuclear silence."[49]

It seems inevitable that the generalities would be allowed to flow

45. McClary, "Getting Down Off the Beanstalk," p. 7.
46. McClary, "Getting Down Off the Beanstalk," p. 6.
47. McClary, "Getting Down Off the Beanstalk," p. 8.
48. McClary, "Getting Down Off the Beanstalk," p. 6.
49. McClary, "Getting Down Off the Beanstalk." p. 7.

rather freely at points, given the massiveness of McClary's reductions. Beyond the capacities of this particular observer, however, are the mental gymnastics required in reconciling contemporary feminism—the "aggressive, rhetorical gestures" of that feminism, its "secular spirit of passionate manipulation"—with the socioeconomic stagnancy of the medieval era, a period in which at least half the population—McClary's half—survived socially, politically, and legally as little more than instruments of service and barter.

3

McClary's history reaches its culmination with the symphonies of Beethoven:

And if the thrusting impulse characteristic of tonality and the aggression characteristic of first themes were not enough, Beethoven's symphonies add two other dimensions to the history of style: assaultive pelvic pounding (for instance, in the last movement of the Fifth Symphony and in all but the "passive" third movement of the Ninth) and sexual violence. The point of recapitulation in the first movement of the Ninth is one of the most horrifying moments in music, as the carefully prepared cadence is frustrated, damming up energy which finally explodes in the throttling, murderous rage of a rapist incapable of attaining release.[50]

The offending passage from the first movement of the Beethoven Ninth is condensed in Example 4. And at issue here is the "point of recapitulation" at m. 301 and the return to the (D F A) tonic triad at m. 315.

The end of the development is marked by an unstable F-major

---

50. McClary, "Getting Down Off the Beanstalk," p. 8. In the revised version of this article in McClary, *Feminine Endings*, pp. 112–131, the wording of this passage is softened considerably. Although the "point of recapitulation" in the first movement of the Ninth is still regarded as "one of the most horrifyingly violent episodes in the history of music" (p. 128), the specifics of that "episode," the earlier references to "assaultive pelvic pounding," "sexual violence," and the "throttling, murderous rage of a rapist incapable of attaining release," are deleted. But there are problems with these deletions as well. For while the specifics of McClary's feminist argument against tonal music and the Ninth are implausible, they are at the very least the specifics of an argument. Without them, the point of her inquiry is that much more open to question.

EXAMPLE 4.   Beethoven, Symphony No. 9, I.

(III), in relation to which the C♯ in the bass at m. 295 appears to signal an applied dominant. However, the resolution of this application comes in the form of a (D F♯ A) triad in first inversion. Following a crescendo, the introductory material intrudes abruptly with (F♯ A D) at m. 301 to announce the beginning of the recapitulation.

In his early treatise on the Ninth (1912), Schenker reasoned that the Introduction "gave birth" to the principal theme, and that this was a function it was obliged to repeat at subsequent restatements

EXAMPLE 5.   Beethoven, Symphony No. 9, II.

of the theme.[51] (I am less persuaded as to this obligation than Schenker was.) He also treated the (F♯ A D) triad at m. 301 as yet another applied dominant, a function it gives every indication of assuming, at least initially. And he dismissed implications of a (D F A/D F♯ A) modal mixture at m. 301, implications that figure substantially in the lengthy discussion of this passage in Leo Treitler's collection of essays.[52]

The problem, however, is that the resolution of (F♯ A D) to the subdominant (G B♭ D) fails to materialize in the immediate context. (The F♯ is reclaimed at m. 322 and is resolved to the subdominant several bars later.) Instead, (F♯ A D) proceeds to (F A D), and by way of an augmented sixth chord that, from the standpoint of the voice-leading in the bass, is approached and resolved in a highly unorthodox manner. The omission of the dominant from the resolution of the augmented sixth is mentioned repeatedly in Treitler's account.[53] Yet it should be noted that omissions of this kind occur elsewhere in Beethoven's music—indeed, in the Scherzo movement of the Ninth itself. Reproduced in Example 5, the same augmented sixth chord appears at m. 256 in the Scherzo, where it is followed by the tonic six-four chord. The latter proceeds, without

51. Heinrich Schenker, *Beethovens Neunte Sinfonie* (Vienna: Universal Edition, 1912), pp. 3–4. An English translation has been published recently: Heinrich Schenker, *Beethoven's Ninth Symphony*, trans. and ed. John Rothgeb (New Haven: Yale University Press, 1992).

52. Treitler, *Music and the Historical Imagination*, pp. 23, 59.

53. Treitler, *Music and the Historical Imagination*, pp. 24, 33, 59.

EXAMPLE 6.   Brahms, Piano Concerto No. 1, I.

dominant resolution, to the root-positioned tonic triad and a re-statement of the principal Scherzo theme.

Indeed, shortchanging the counterpoint of this cadential cliché, circumventing its stylistic redundancy with inflections of a more immediately individual or contextual character, is fairly common in nineteenth music. It is what ultimately characterizes the "cadence" at m. 25 in the first movement of Brahms's First Piano Concerto (Example 6), a cadence that follows a lengthy D–C–B♭–A stepwise descent in the bass. (Brahms's First Concerto also relates in other ways to Beethoven's Ninth: in the role assumed by B♭ and the [B♭ D F] triad from the opening measures and, especially in the first movement, in the role assumed by the timpani.) Then, too, the resolution of the augmented sixth to the dominant was often delayed until well after the arrival of the tonic six-four and the initiation of a new phrase or section. The effect of this delay was to blur the distinction between cadence and renewed departure—to allow, in the manner of a "structural downbeat,"[54] for a convergence of these two functions at the arrival of the cadential six-four chord. In addition to the example from the Brahms Concerto, two pas-

---

54. See Fred Lerdahl and Ray Jackendoff, *A Generative Theory of Tonal Music* (Cambridge: MIT Press, 1983), p. 33. "Structural downbeat" is defined as a "convergence" at a single moment of "significant articulations" in grouping, metrical, and harmonic structure. "The structural anacrusis drives to its cadence, which simultaneously, by means of a grouping overlap, initiates a new impulse forward at the beginning of the following section."

EXAMPLE 7.   Beethoven, Symphony No. 9, III.

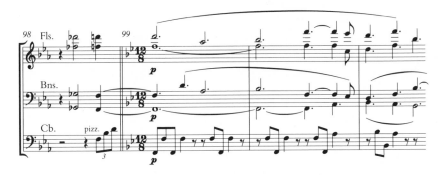

EXAMPLE 8.   Schubert, Sonata in B♭ Major, I.

sages that spring to mind in this connection are the return to the variation theme at mm. 98–101 in the Adagio of the Ninth (Example 7), and, in the first movement of Schubert's Piano Sonata in B♭ Major, the restatement of the principal theme at m. 36 (Example 8). Observe, in addition, that these techniques of delay are consistent with the processes alluded to above in connection with the tonal vocabulary of McClary, Schenker, and Meyer.

What tends to matter, then, is not the deviation itself, the omission or delay of the dominant resolution of the augmented sixth, but the specific manner of its articulation. Deviations of the kind that, à la McClary, Schenker, or Meyer, inhibit tendency and delay "gratification" remain meaningful only to the extent that they are a part of a developing train of thought, to the extent that they are perceived as motivated by that thought, felt as belonging to that thought. And modifications of common formulae, of the common language of tonality, can be exciting for precisely that reason, namely, for the obvious ways in which they can direct the ear to a contextual reading, entice it into an engagement with the individual context that can sustain a sense of immediacy.

Indeed, the contextual aspect of the augmented sixth chord in Example 4 is not all that difficult to discern, at least locally: as the brackets indicate, the F–B♭–F descending line in the lower strings at mm. 312–315 imitates the falling D–A–D lines of the introductory material. In other words, the definition of that contextual aspect is motivic; the F–B♭–F bass line that supports the augmented sixth at mm. 312–315 bears a motivic relationship to the D–A–D lines of the opening material. And it is by way of such a motivic relationship that the context itself can be heard and understood as modifying the augmented sixth and its resolution. The context modifies the convention, a modification that itself motivates context. The latter is motivated by rendering it motivic, in other words; and it is made motivic by modifying the common language accordingly.

More globally, too, the dramatic F♯–F slip at m. 312 echoes the earlier slip at the end of the exposition at m. 160, where the closing section in B♭ major (VI) slips back abruptly to the dominant A and a return to the introduction. The forte outburst at the "point of recapitulation" at m. 301 echoes this earlier return of the introduction, and especially the crescendo passage at m. 186, with F♯ in the bass. Indeed, it projects a large-scale formal association that tends to dampen, at least for this observer, its potential for alarm, the effect of "horror" or "murderous rage" felt by McClary. And following the initial blast at m. 301, the hollow, rhetorical character of this fourth appearance of the introduction, all forte, can seem formal and forced even when, at mm. 312–315, its point is revealed by the dramatic F♯–F slip in the bass, a point which Tovey, in connection with a loosely designed psycho-drama for the symphony as a whole, characterized as "catastrophic."[55]

According to the specifics of this drama, (F♯ A D) at m. 301 is heard to anticipate the key of D major, to reach out prematurely for its sunny, joyful rays; at m. 314, it slips back abruptly to the grim struggle of (F A D) and D minor, and by way of an augmented

---

55. Donald Francis Tovey, *Beethoven's Ninth Symphony* (Edinburgh: James Thin, 1927), p. 19.

sixth that is modified in order to accommodate the falling motive of the introduction and the semi-tonal slip encountered at m. 160. Such a profile is consistent with the idea of a "quest for Elisium" in the Ninth, as has been suggested by several recent commentators.[56] But it contradicts Schenker's earlier assertion, which was that the applied dominant (F♯ A D) at m. 301 surfaces without implications of a (D F A/D F♯ A) modal mixture.

On the other hand, McClary's sexual politics are alien to my understanding of this music, as they are to my understanding of the "sensual" in Western, tonal music generally. A sexual premise could be granted, no doubt, but, as I see it, only if it were part of a larger, more comprehensive premise. And it would remain merely a premise, something subterranean and largely ineffectual above ground. To envision anything more is to tyrannize music, it seems to me, to subject it to uses of an imposed character, robbing it of its invitation to transcend such uses. A premise of this kind can be appropriate only when kept at bay, harnessed with the understanding that it cannot be taken as the whole of the matter, that it is but one aspect of a much larger entanglement.

More specifically, that which is being simulated operates at too great a distance from the real and actual details of music. Even when supplemented with male- and female-defined "models of sexuality" (as in McClary's case), images of sex and sexuality are too remote (indeed, I sometimes imagine, too blunt and corny) to be of much assistance in coming to terms with the inexhaustible details of musical structure and expression. One could argue, no doubt, that the overtly political use to which McClary's "models" are put undermines the premise itself; it tends to shrink music's potential. But my impression is that the sexual premise would not be greatly enhanced were the politics less overt and the approach less one-dimensional.

Nor, it seems to me, could such an approach benefit from greater specificity. For the world of sex and sexuality, of desire and

56. See Maynard Solomon, *Beethoven Essays* (Cambridge: Harvard University Press, 1988), pp. 11–12; Treitler, *Music and the Historical Imagination,* pp. 59–61; and Richard Taruskin, "Resisting the Ninth," *19th-Century Music* 12, no. 3 (1989).

its politics, is too richly developed in itself, too powerfully defined, to serve as a foil for music, a world very nearly as rich in its definition. Drawn into greater and more explicit detail, the one side could only disappoint the other, become the distraction of the other. It would be diminished, reduced to a form of silliness.

This happens with McClary's analysis of the Ninth. The sort of detail outlined above concerning the augmented sixth chord and its irregular resolutions, the musical sense that was made of that detail, is not available to her approach. On the contrary, following its initial point of contact, the beginning of the recapitulation in the first movement, additional detail undermines the alleged relationship between music and sex or sexual politics; the two sides are pulled further apart, with the sexual stereotypes becoming more stereotypical, the music less focused. Worked to any appreciable extent, in other words, the connection cannot be sustained. (Such is the fate of much interdisciplinary study as well, of course; too often required of at least one of the several disciplines is far too great a sacrifice in the sophistication of its detail.)

But the irony here concerns not only the nature of McClary's "models of sexuality," but the use of models in analytic-theoretical discussion more generally. For it can readily be seen that, from a strictly methodological standpoint, the use of such models by McClary is no different from their use by more traditional forms of theory and analysis. (I refer to the "prototypes" or "archetypes" that typically encompass, for example, the sonata form or the Schenkerian *Ursatz*.) In each case, the individual is dealt with by way of the general. Yet it is the models and types of the more traditional forms that the new humanists and postmodernists have singled out for rebuke, and in large part because of their generality, the fact that they deal with parts rather than wholes, that they reduce concrete reality to abstraction, the sensed uniqueness of individual works to general terms and concepts. And so, here again, the assumption would seem to be that the new models of sex, gender, and sexuality can overcome the paradox of analysis, the separation of immediate experience (the individual) from conscious analytic-theoretical pursuit. At the very least, in contrast with the older models, they can place the general usefully at the service of the individual.

So, too, at issue here is not the existence of the sexual or socio-political forces to which McClary refers (patriarchal society and its ills, for example), however crudely those forces may be drawn, however simplistic and one-sided may be their modeling and typing. (The crudeness of the application is a reflection not only of the stridency of the ideology, of McClary's feminism and its essential-izing character, but also of its forced juxtaposition with music.) At issue, rather, is the extent to which music exists as a way of reflect-ing and transmitting such forces, the extent to which it makes its point accordingly, or the extent to which, on the contrary, it exists as a way of resisting and transcending such forces, with its pulls and attractions felt and sensed as such.

At the same time, deep, psychological tension, the fear and ap-prehension that underlie all emotion, need not be sexual in origin. For those inclined toward such signification, the psychological im-pact of the tension-and-release patterns of tonal music can be un-derstood in ways unrelated to sexual conflict. The dynamics of ten-sion, of the departure that signals a departure-and-release pattern, can refer to any number of elementary and even biological needs and functions. Sex and sexuality are one; death and the emotions that accompany our perception of mortality are another.

Much of Beethoven's music, much of the stubborn, driven char-acter of its timing and motivic manipulation, can suggest an ear-nestness or seriousness of purpose (indeed, a "sententious moral earnestness," as Charles Rosen has put it),[57] that is difficult to rec-oncile with McClary's sexual imagery. The effect of struggle can seem heroic in this context, the messages of hope and joy, pursued with such tenacity, superhuman and even a bit crazy at times. But quite apart from the validity of these familiar representations, I would cite Tovey's opinion on this subject, which is that the scope of Beethoven's music, what that music can suggest as expression,

57. Charles Rosen, *The Classical Style* (New York: W. W. Norton, 1972), p. 385.

is far too vast for it to succumb to the formation of an "anti-Beethoven aesthetic."[58]

4

Beethoven the Pornographer. Beethoven the Sexist. What are the merits of this case, and how could a determination of those merits work to the advantage of music and its appreciation? Specifically, how could these claims be made to connect not just with an image of that which ignites music, *any* music ("Man the Music Maker," in other words),[59] but with music's finished products, the details that distinguish individual tonal works, details that elicit the affective responses that stand, when all is said and done, as the target of McClary's feminist indictment?

For it is not tonality as such that is likely to elicit such responses, the system that is inferred and processed as a common language or practice, but individual instances of tonality. And even then, and in contradiction to science and scientific method, it is not as instances of tonality that tonal works are likely to take hold as objects of aesthetic attraction, but as individually motivated instances, "singular, individuated accomplishments."[60] And the expectation, of course, is not that a Schenkerian or feminist analysis will reproduce individuality, but that it will provide for the means of its articula-

58. Tovey, *Beethoven's Ninth Symphony,* p. 9. "No artist of such range as Beethoven has ever set up a tyranny from which revolt is possible," Tovey writes.

59. See John Blacking, *How Musical Is Man?* (Seattle: University of Washington Press, 1973), p. 4. The quotation is as follows: "In the long run, it is the activities of Man the Music Maker that are of more interest and consequence to humanity than the particular musical achievements of Western man." But there is in fact no moral, aesthetic, or intellectual (or "humanistic") reason why Western listeners, musicians, and scholars should find greater consequence in "Man the Music Maker" than in the music of man; or, indeed, in any and all music, in the phenomenon of music, than in the specific and uniquely shaped constructions of the art music of their own particular culture. Only in relation to such primary objects of attraction, to an active and passionate engagement with those objects, are "Man the Music Maker" and a universal definition of the phenomenon of music and its "maker" likely to be of interest and consequence. See footnote 62, below.

60. Babbitt, *Words About Music,* p. 4.

tion, will serve as a way of familiarizing the observer with its detail, thereby sustaining and enhancing its immediacy.

Analogous to "vulgar Marxism," in which man is reduced to "economic forces," ceaselessly scrambling for food, shelter, and reserves, McClary's feminism reduces him to his sexual needs, to a groping about for release, as it were, and then to the socioeconomic arrangements by which that release is secured. And my sense is that the difficulty in getting the sexual-political motive to connect in meaningful ways to the superstructure of music, a difficulty likely to touch on the question of music's autonomy, its aesthetic presence or "space," is roughly of the same kind and magnitude as that which accompanies the Marxist reduction.[61]

Fairly standard as a line of rebuttal in cases of this kind is the one that focuses not on the merits of the case but on the ulterior motives of the sponsor. By these means, an attempt is made to turn the tables in an about-face. Thus, having cited Western, tonal music for sexist or elitist tendencies,[62] for the harboring of antisocial thought artfully concealed under a cloak of spiritual, transcendental mumbo-jumbo, the issuers of these citations, upholders of down-

61. See, for example, McClary, "The Undoing of Opera," pp. xv–xvii; and John Shepherd, "Music and Male Hegemony," in Leppert and McClary, eds., *Music and Society*, pp. 151–172. See also the critique of Marxist criticism and musicology in Carl Dahlhaus, *Foundations of Music History*, trans. J. B. Robinson (Cambridge: Cambridge University Press, 1983), pp. 112–129; or, indeed, Carl Dahlhaus, "The Musical Work of Art as a Subject of Sociology" (1974) in his *Schoenberg and the New Music: Essays by Carl Dahlhaus*, trans. Derrick Puffett and Alfred Clayton (Cambridge: Cambridge University Press, 1987), pp. 234–248.

62. Leveled against Western art music in general, the charge of elitism is repeated occasionally in Blacking, *How Musical Is Man?* pp. 3–4. Blacking comments on the complexity of Western art music, its commercialization, professional class of musicians, and so forth. But my sense is that he misrepresents the substance of that complexity as well as the problem of access. For if individual examples of Western art music are defined not so much by these conditions of transmission as by the nature of the relationship that is formed with the individual listener, the passionate nature of the engagement, then elitism ceases to be a musical issue, and Western art music and its appreciation become no more elitist in character, no more socially or politically motivated in this respect, than the music of the Venda of the Northern Transvaal and Blacking's evident enthusiasm for that music. For a critique of ethnomusicology and its study of African music in particular, see Kofi Agawu, "Representing African Music," *Critical Inquiry* 18 (Winter 1992).

to-earth, see-through-'em realism, of the primacy of naked self-interest, are asked to reveal something of their own particular motivations. (In the long run, such an about-face cannot work wholeheartedly to the advantage of adherents of Western art music, since their position would tend to stress the autonomy or transcending independence of music and its appreciation, music's resistance to, or aesthetic freedom from, purely local considerations of sex, gender, and politics.)

In the present case, the suggestion might be that Beethoven's music, or tonal music in general, is being placed at the service of an unrelated personal animosity. Fanned by an aversion for male sexuality, which is depicted as something brutal and contemptible, feelings of distaste are read into the music. In due course, these feelings are made to connect with a larger critique, a comprehensive feminist argument. There, they are made the experience not just of McClary but of women in general; they are made symbolic of all women, their victimization or plight in a world seemingly conditioned by the sexual inclinations of the male. And tonal music is made one of the many instruments of their oppression, a part of the dark conspiracy of men in their relations with women.[63]

63. See Solie, "What Do Feminists Want?" pp. 406–407. Solie remarks at length that feminists disagree on the essentialist issue, the extent to which "innate gender traits" exist, the extent to which women are genetically different from men in their moral outlook, sensibilities, and perception. But this would be difficult to gauge, it seems to me, since the issue is seldom met head-on in McClary's work or in feminist literature in general, notwithstanding its relevance to many feminist arguments. Thus, it is often assumed that women are more caring and nurturing than men (who bother more about reason, rationality, and abstract principles), that they are more empathetic, trust their emotions more, and so forth. Such a thesis is supported by interviews and analysis in Carol Gilligan, *In a Different Voice* (Cambridge: Harvard University Press, 1982). In turn, Gilligan draws on the theories of early mothering in Nancy Chodorow, *The Reproduction of Mothering: Psychoanalysis and the Sociology of Gender* (Berkeley: University of California Press, 1978). According to Chodorow, "From very early, then, because they are parented by a person of the same gender . . . girls come to experience themselves as less differentiated than boys, as more continuous with and related to the external object-world." As a consequence, girls emerge with a "basis for 'empathy,'" attachment, and intimacy, while men are defined by processes of separation and "individuation" (p. 167). Chodorow's ideas are cited approvingly (but with little comment) in McClary, *Feminine Endings*, p. 47, and in Fred Everett Maus, "Hanslick's Animism," *Journal of Musicology* 10, no. 3 (1992): p. 288. Leo Treitler has

Indeed, without at least the skeleton of such a scenario in place, there would be no reason to suppose, as McClary supposes, that the diverse cadences, crescendos, and climaxes in Beethoven's symphonies were all uniquely or particularly symbolic of male rather than female orgasms; that the mood of the Adagio of the Ninth reflected the sexual sensibilities of women rather than men; or that the rhythms in Beethoven's scherzos and finales signified "pelvic pounding" on the part of the male rather than the female, or, indeed, "pelvic pounding" rather than drunkenness, boisterousness, laughter, athletic exercise, aerobic dancing, or the like. The nature of many of these connections is so vague and abstract that I suspect that the mere hypothetical substitution of a female for the male composer in question would have been enough to tilt the verdict insofar as the music is concerned.

The crusading ideology turns tyrannical. Like a giant, runaway metaphor, it takes root and begins to envelop everything. The environment of music is mobilized accordingly; indeed, it becomes meaningful only in relation to the central cause, its significance determined solely by the uses to which it is put in the service of that cause. Music and its appeal are judged overtly sexual-political in order that they may serve the overtly sexual-political cause. Beethoven's music, deprived of its aesthetic "space," a measure of autonomy, ceases to be seen as distinct, unique, and transcending. And for the listener, too, it is no longer permitted to allow this music to speak to some degree for itself, to allow himself or herself to

---

also made much of the mother-daughter bond: "The outlook for the female child is for continued bonding," he writes, "whereas for the male child the outlook is toward separation." See Treitler, *Music and the Historical Imagination*, p. 15. Treitler relates these opposing "outlooks" to opposing "ideals of truth and knowledge that are polarized according to gender" (p. 15): the sensitive, passionate model, in which there is a sympathetic "bonding of the knower with the known," associated with the female, and the rationalist model of the male. Here again, the report of the female is in glowing contrast to that of the male, although there is no specific reference to Chodorow's work. See also, in this connection, Gayatri Chakravorty Spivak, *The Post-Colonial Critic*, ed. Sarah Harasym (New York: Routledge, 1990), pp. 10–12. Spivak suggests that an essentialist stance may be necessary strategically for feminists, as a means of countering sexism, for example, even if it is theoretically unsupportable.

be enticed spontaneously, to allow for an immediate, intuitive response. Rather, the verbal, intellectual conjecture, embodying the meaning and purpose of music, is to precede the response.

No doubt, the foregoing is what might well have been expected as a reaction to McClary's argument. Challenges to deep-seated convictions are likely to be met with objections that address not the argument itself but its particular motivation. But how else could a rebuttal have been managed in the present case? Given that the issues in question do in fact involve ulterior motives in music and music appreciation, how else could the merits of this case have been assessed?

Of course, to characterize McClary's interpretations as sexually and politically manipulative, as examples of feminist propaganda, is merely to invite circularity. In her view, music is inherently and essentially sexual-political. Notions of transcendent meaning are therefore the means by which male composers and listeners have concealed the real, underlying sexual-political motives for their engagement with music. Western society is patriarchal, Western art music reflects that structure, and listening to Western art music reinforces the idea of that structure.

Indeed, to extend the feminist side of this argument: on the matter of our musical affections generally and particularly on the intensity with which those affections are felt, who can claim immunity from outside reference and circumstance? Who can claim isolation from eventful and emotive life? No doubt our sexualities reach into every crevice of our beings; their pulls and attractions are a part of daily life. But this, too, may be precisely the point. Diffuse and reaching everywhere, sexuality is potentially a part of everything. But this truth should not suggest that everything is therefore only an undifferentiated, unintelligible mass. It should not suggest that our powers of concentration are so feeble—indeed, so ungenerous—as to discourage the separate parts of this entanglement from taking shape, from acquiring a sense of focus, identity, and distinction.

Indeed, only as a form of representation do musical works become vague and imprecise. As objects of affection, they are likely to be specific and highly contextual. (In fact, the greater the affection, the greater the sensed contextuality.) Even very slight changes in their details are likely to bring about a reversal in response.[64] When all is said and done, then, it may be that music and music appreciation are no more inherently (or revealingly) sexual or sexual-political than countless other human endeavors and activities, including athletics, cooking, and card-playing. Sex and sexuality may be of no more assistance in coming to terms with music than they are in dealing with these other works and activities. They may explain no more of Beethoven's Ninth, in other words, than they do, say, of the game of tennis. And we may seek no more of their detail in describing the Adagio of the Ninth than we do in describing the form, structure, dynamics, sense, and feel of a two-fisted backhand.

64. As it concerns the "work of art" in general, see the discussion of this in Frank Sibley, "Aesthetic Concepts," *Philosophical Review* 68 (1959). "The aesthetic quality depends upon exactly this individual or unique combination of just these specific colors and shapes so that even a slight change might make all the difference" (p. 432). Or see, more recently, Jerrold Levinson, *Music, Art, and Metaphysics: Essays in Philosophical Aesthetics* (Ithaca: Cornell University Press, 1990), pp. 107–112.

2

In Defense of Music Theory
and Analysis

I

As a commentator on current trends in music scholarship, Leo Treitler harbors political sympathies that are both current and "correct." Or so it would seem from the lengthy introduction to *Music and the Historical Imagination,* a collection of his essays.[1] I mention the sympathies because of Treitler's insistence that music scholarship acknowledge more fully and openly the mundane social and political attitudes that, in his opinion, lie just beneath its surface. Such attitudes are viewed as informing scholarly research in pivotal ways even when the prevailing winds would seem to favor an objective knowledge of observation and fact processed in detached and impersonal tones.

Hence, as with Susan McClary, the complaint becomes focused not just on so-called positivist or formalist discourse but on the failure of that discourse to confront underlying sociopolitical, sexual, and critical biases. And the assumption is that the failure to confront such biases, to "come clean" on matters of personal bent and circumstance, is political. For it has fostered the myth of a hard and fast currency in the humanities, an unassailable body of knowledge

1. Leo Treitler, *Music and the Historical Imagination* (Cambridge: Harvard University Press, 1989).

indifferent to human intervention and accessible only to trained experts, to professional scholars and their scholarship. It has served as a guarantee, in other words, a justification of the profession; it has given rise to a "trained priesthood," in McClary's words.[2]

My impression, however, is that Treitler steers clear of the logical conclusion to this train of thought. He avoids the larger entanglement, and hence also the subversive heart of the argument, its anti-academic implications.[3] While he pleads for a new form of humanistic scholarship in music, one that would acknowledge more fully the subjective presence of the scholar, he ignores the academic institutions and programs of which scholarship is a part.[4] Hence,

---

2. Susan McClary, "The Politics of Silence and Sound," Afterword to Jacques Attali, *Noise: The Political Economy of Music*, trans. Brian Massumi (Minneapolis: University of Minnesota Press, 1985), p. 150.

3. The argument is treated with greater consequence in McClary, "The Politics of Silence and Sound." McClary writes as follows:

The tendency to deal with music by means of acoustics, mathematics, or mechanistic models preserves [music's] mystery (accessible only to a trained priesthood), lends it higher prestige in a culture that values quantifiable knowledge over mere expression, and conceals the ideological basis of its conventions and repertories. In our society [listeners] are told that they cannot know anything about music without having absorbed the whole theoretical apparatus necessary for music specialization. But to learn this apparatus is to learn to renounce one's responses, to discover that the musical phenomenon is to be understood mechanistically, mathematically. Thus, non-trained listeners are prevented from talking about social and expressive dimensions of music (for they lack the vocabulary to refer to its parts) and so are trained musicians (for they have been taught, in learning the proper vocabulary, that music is strictly self-contained structure). (p. 150)

Some of this is well taken, of course, even if, like Treitler, McClary overlooks the obvious connection between institutions, process, and objective, "quantifiable knowledge." Beyond this, some of the conditions she describes are exaggerated to the point of nonrecognition. Obviously, "talking about social and expressive dimensions of music" has been a part of scholarship as represented by many diverse journals and publications. Moreover, almost to the point of caricature, McClary exaggerates the role of academic scholarship (including her own) not only in the world of music but in the experience of music as well. She exaggerates the dependency of this engagement on academic training and scholarship, on the "theoretical apparatus" that she condemns, and on her own brand of sociopolitical, feminist argumentation. Like Treitler, she underestimates the transcending independence of the engagement, its (merciful) separation from the uses of education and its system—its separation, indeed, from use pure and simple.

4. On the matter of the scholar's subjective presence, see Treitler, *Music and the Historical Imagination*, pp. 12–18; or Leo Treitler's review of Joseph Kerman's *Con-*

too, he ignores the dependency of those institutions on systematic process, as well as the extent to which that dependency reflects the complex reality of mass education. Indeed, in matters of higher education generally, he ignores large-scale interests that are economic and sociopolitical as well as academic or intellectual.[5] And the implication is that, like the positivist and formalist approaches he decries, his own approach can operate at a distance, free and clear of the entanglement of interests that link scholarship to economics, institutions, the professions, and education in general.

In the introduction to *Music and the Historical Imagination*, academic programs in the humanities are viewed as having fallen short only to the extent that, prior to the student, hippie, and peace movements of the 1960s and 1970s, large numbers of women and minorities were excluded from participation.[6] In reality, however, it is not the composition of transient student bodies that is on the line in Treitler's argument, but the system of higher education and research, that system of which he himself is as much a part as are his fellow teacher-scholars, be they positivistic or humanistic in orientation. To an extent far greater than does the makeup of student bodies, the system itself compels the scholarly product. Style, number, and content are affected by administrative priorities, competitive strategies of "excellence" and prestige that reflect the socio-

templating Music in *Journal of the American Musicological Society* 40, no. 2 (1987). The considerable gains of Treitler and other reforming humanists, it seems to me, include a new awareness of the musically sensing subject, the social aspects of music, and the new avenues of inquiry that are suggested accordingly. Less satisfactory, as examined in these opening chapters, are their critiques and outright dismissals of many of the traditional concerns of musicology and music theory and analysis.

5. Needless to say, the concerns that govern higher education need not be academic or intellectual, especially when, as with today's generations, the socioeconomic alternatives to "getting" such an education can seem less and less plausible. The case for higher education as the privilege of academic standing is argued elegantly in Eugene Genovese, "Heresy, Yes—Sensitivity, No," *New Republic* (15 April 1991). The conflict in today's schools between traditional academic standards and the sociopolitical pressures of diversity and multiculturalism is discussed in Daniel J. Singal, "The Other Crises in American Education," *Atlantic Monthly* (November 1991). The latter is cited in Robert Hughes, *Culture of Complaint: The Fraying of America* (New York: Oxford University Press, 1993), p. 63.

6. Treitler, *Music and the Historical Imagination*, p. 8.

economic pressures of the real world. And those pressures reach into academic life by way of the "publish or perish" syndrome, a syndrome that has had the effect of encouraging the narrow, specialized, and positivistic approach to which Treitler takes exception.

Indeed, the mundane effects of that syndrome, effects that reach into the lives of individual teacher-scholars, are inconsistent with Treitler's humane or humanistic values, the values of sensibility, empathy, and personal identification that he would promote not only in scholarship but in the social and political life of the community. In effect, relations among teachers and students, between scholars and their scholarship, are discussed without reference to the academic system of which those relations are a part, without reference, indeed, to the enveloping forces at work, those that relate to the more tangible business of "making a living." And this, notwithstanding the fact that it is to "secular, mundane politics" that the appeal is made for openness, and for the very purpose of rendering the system more humane for teachers and students alike, scholarship itself a more honest, personal endeavor.[7]

In essence, then, ideals may be championed in the face of hardened realities. But in seeking to lay bare the realities of idealistically framed superstructures (in this instance, those of our colleges and universities), Treitler cannot overlook the messy ironies that can spring just as easily from his own idealist contentions. The "publish or perish" syndrome, for example, began its heated trajectory not before but after the protest movements of the 1960s and 1970s, in the wake of the liberal and egalitarian causes that are adopted by Treitler as the backbone of his populist beliefs. And the trajectory came as a result of the massive new enrollments in public education that are welcomed by Treitler as potentially supportive of his pleas for a more humanistically inspired scholarship. Those increased, more diversified enrollments may carry overriding advantages, of course. Yet I would estimate the potential for miseducation in the feverishly competitive circumstances that have accompanied this expansion to be far greater than at any time prior to the 1960s.

7. Treitler, *Music and the Historical Imagination*, p. 8.

A realist cannot overlook the socioeconomic purpose of education, a purpose served most persuasively not by the humanities but by areas of study with a more immediate stake, areas such as business, technology, and the law. And the more massively education stands at the service of immediate socioeconomic ends, the less are its ways and means likely to reflect the humanist ideals advertised by Treitler. If the contemporary equation lacks an essential ingredient, then it is not academic humanism (of which, I would contend, there is already a great deal), but a stimulus capable of resisting a meritocratic way of life that has become all-consuming and abusive. New, supposedly more humanistic scholarship in higher education, being a part of the meritocratic shuffle to begin with, can hardly be trumpeted as a means of furthering the deeply spiritual, personally liberating causes underlying Treitler's concerns. It is not, of course, that those causes are misplaced in a larger sense. An answer to our current woes—an alternative, as I see it, to the meritocracy, to a consciousness consumed by considerations of competitive worth and standing—may well lie in a concern for the spiritual resources of the individual. My point is that, in addressing such concerns within the context of academic research, Treitler ignores the professions and institutions of which that research is a part. And he therefore misreads the ability of these components to resist, let alone stand apart from, the socioeconomic pressures of which all are a part.

But it is not scholarship alone but music too, the music of the past as well as of the present, that has been left without a social context. Treitler argues that musicologists and theorists have insulated scholarship not only from sociopolitical concerns but from the "presentness" of music, from the experience of music, the emotional ties that are linked to that experience.[8] He concludes that humanism, conceived as the harmonious union of sense and sensibility, of reason and sensuality, would be better served if scholarship were to focus its attention on the expressive impact of music, and if it were to do so in a style that is personal and subjective, one more

8. Treitler, *Music and the Historical Imagination*, pp. 37, 40.

reflective of the true, experienced reality of music and its appreciation. The cited culprits in his chronicle of failure and omission are, first, style history, history that emphasizes the general at the expense of the particular, and, second, the "technical" analysis of contemporary music theory.[9] (Schenkerian analysis is included in the latter category, a category that is referred to as the "methodologies of formalist analysis being taught and practiced in North America today.")[10] In each case, individual works are said to be of interest only to the extent that large-scale abstractions of style, period, and compositional method are substantiated. Overlooked are the intrinsic qualities of such works, qualities that, according to this argument, are the focus of the immediate, subjective response, that response toward which Treitler's more humanistic scholarship would be directed. And it has been in the interests of scholarship not to pursue questions of aesthetic immediacy but to concentrate instead on materials of historical fact, circumstance, and "technical" analysis. The assumption is that such materials merely surround the musical object and its immediate impact or "presentness."

Thus, too, the positivistic approach has been accompanied by a determination to maintain a neutral, objective presence. Along pseudo-scientific lines, scholars have distanced themselves from the objects of their scrutiny, have maintained a "posture of aloofness" in the face of those objects.[11] Their aim has evidently been the exercise of control, control not only over the musical objects but over their sensing selves as well.[12] Stemming in part from the socio-

9. Treitler, *Music and the Historical Imagination*, p. 66.

10. Treitler, *Music and the Historical Imagination*, p. 66.

11. Treitler, *Music and the Historical Imagination*, p. 4.

12. See Treitler, *Music and the Historical Imagination*, p. 17. The traditional scholarly relationship to music, masculinist as well as positivist, as Treitler insists, has been "one of control by the knower over the known—to put it bluntly, a relationship of power." But whatever the approach, humanist, feminist, positivist, or formalist in design, scholars are bound to seek control in their work, even "power" in this regard, so that the issue becomes one not of control per se but of the nature, purpose, and use of such control. Control may be sought in scholarly work for a variety of reasons both internal and external to an inquiry. More generally, the external motivations for scholarly work are of a kind already referred to

economic pressures alluded to above, the exercise of that control can mask timidity, a shying away from that which moves, from that which may well have moved the scholar to scholarship. Scholars protect themselves from exposure in this respect, from their vulnerability to the sensation of music, from ties that are personal, emotional, and, in just these respects, unprofessional. For it is not sensation but knowledge that separates and distinguishes the scholar. And it is knowledge of a kind that, isolated from the individual subject, lends itself to process, to a form of expertise that is open to large-scale evaluation. Within the entanglement envisioned by this argument, moments of aesthetic immediacy are the products of innate sensitivity, not of scholarship or scholarly learning. They are available randomly, without benefit of the system, and thus cannot serve a process of accreditation. And it cannot, therefore, be for such moments that at the most sensitive link of the entanglement, that linking disinterested scholarship to the world at large, programs are initiated, credits are amassed, degrees are conferred, and university payloads are met.

As indicated already, however, Treitler ignores these more subversive implications of his argument. Although he lobbies for greater personal and sociopolitical involvement on the part of the scholar, an end to the scholar's "civil tone of reflective writing" and the "insulating distance that scholars aim to keep between their work and the conditions under which it is done," he skirts the issues of conflict that any such involvement would entail, issues stemming from his humanistic values and their clash (as I see it) with real-life conditions.[13] No mention is made of the academic system of which scholarship is a part, or of the socioeconomic factors that envelop and motivate that system. And although a connection is made between the scholar's "ideal of objectivity" and his or her ex-

---

by way of the larger entanglement; in large part, they involve socioeconomic, institutional, professional, and educational pressures. The larger point here is that, while misrepresenting the intrinsic (and eminently humanistic) purpose of many traditional forms of musicology and music analysis, Treitler ignores the external motivations altogether. In so doing, he implies that his own approach can remain untouched by such motivations.

13. Treitler, *Music and the Historical Imagination*, p. 4.

ercise of "control" or "power," the motivation for that exercise, lying both within and outside the discipline, is left unexamined.[14] In sum, Treitler overlooks the symbiotic nature of the relationship between the system (any system, really) and the positivistic approach to teaching, learning, and research, the practical, systematic, and intellectual pressures that encourage the objective methods of which he disapproves. And the effects of this oversight are not trivial. For he assumes that his own brand of scholarship, one supposedly more humanistic in style and content, one with a "human face," as it were, can escape the entanglement of the older brands, the complex web that joins education, research, and socioeconomic purpose with accreditation. He assumes, indeed, that, by virtue of its subjectivity, its special concern for the intrinsic qualities of individual works, his own brand can escape the subject-object battles of old, those that are a part not only of scholarship but of everyday life, of the effort to seek an accommodation and to *communicate*.

Indeed, it is in its underlying assumptions that his argument seems most vulnerable. A sociopolitical attitude, properly "correct" in its sympathies, is made to reflect the caring individual, the one who identifies closely with humankind, the sensing, feeling instincts of that kind, its true spiritual needs. (The value judgment entailed by this identification is also left unexamined.) Such an individual is made the rationale for a new, humanistic form of scholarship, one that is personal in style (nonspecialist and therefore literary and sympathetically interdisciplinary; "poetic," as it were), one that is expressive of the immediate impact of music on the individual listener or scholar, of the feelings and emotions of that impact, of the possible sociopolitical or sexual ramifications of those emotions. And this mode of scholarship is placed in opposition to positivist and formalist modes, to what are regarded as the twin scourges of traditional musicology; "positive knowledge about the contexts of music—its notation, provenance, performance venues and practices, material and mechanical reproduction," and "techni-

14. Treitler, *Music and the Historical Imagination*, p. 4.

cal" knowledge about "style and structure," knowledge that can be absorbed with a "minimum of misrepresentation."[15]

At the same time, the implication is that humanistic study of this newly enriched kind is pursued by those who do in fact sense and feel music, scholars whose engagement with music is immediate and therefore passionate, not by those who sense and feel little in this regard and whose scholarly pursuits are therefore positivist or formalist. In other words, the connections are drawn squarely. The new humanistic study both reflects and encourages a passionate engagement with music, while positivist or formalist approaches (including Schenkerian analysis) lead to a mechanical (absent-eared and disengaged) reproduction of received formulae or "methodologies." The latter are not undertaken with the idea of sustaining a sense of aesthetic immediacy or encouraging a sense of intimacy with the materials themselves. Only the new brand can serve such ends.

---

15. Lawrence Kramer, "The Musicology of the Future," *Repercussions* 1, no. 1 (1992): 8. The tone of Kramer's essay is different from Treitler's, no doubt, yet the politics and targets (traditional so-called positivist musicology and music analysis) are very much the same. The larger labels can be defined in straightforward fashion, it seems to me, even if they are not hard and fast. Humanists, old or new, tend to view themselves as preoccupied with the human dimension in history, with questions of human value and significance. They tend to identify positivists with a concern for objective truth and the scientific model of explanation, formalists with a concern for the formal relationships that may be inferred from music, models of general application and the mathematics of those models. Still more popularly, humanists see themselves as struck by the expressive force of music; they are suspicious of the measurements of positivists and formalists and of the significance that may be attached to those measurements; and they are sensitive to any apparent neglect of questions of expression and aesthetic value. Positivists, in search of the facts and circumstances of music, the sources, texts, and data that may be open to objective verification, are viewed as alert to the personal voice, of course, but only to the extent that that voice may encompass opinion and propaganda, the opinion that may be concealed by scholarship or the literary effort generally. Such attitudes can carry moral assessments, however implicitly. Humanists see themselves as Mensch-like; they sense and feel music, are true believers in this respect, caring individuals, and so forth. Positivists, nerd-like creatures indifferent to such sensing and feeling, care only for a truth that can be arrived at objectively. In a more sensible but at the same time still popular vein, see Victor F. Weisskopf, *The Privilege of Being a Physicist* (New York: Freeman, 1989). "Science is an important part of the humanities," Weisskopf writes, "because it is based on an essential human trait: curiosity about the how and why in our environment" (p. 33).

So, too, in the new humanism attention shifts from an appreciation of the music to one of the scholar himself or herself. What begins to matter is not the music and its interpretation but music as a means of interpreting the interpreter, a way of celebrating his or her special affinities, whether social, literary, political, or sexual. And the pathway to this new emphasis is to be laid by the meritocratic institutions, which reduce to large-scale process, test, screen, and credit on a level that is necessarily general, detached, and impersonal.

No doubt, the traditional role of the humanist has been one of countering such pressure. Featuring a bonding of sense and sensibility, humanistic study has ideally been informed by an aesthetic sensitivity as it has sought to heighten that sensitivity. But what criteria are to be applied by the credit-bearing institutions? Is that which has stood beyond measurement, humanistically beyond utility, purpose, or reward, to be measured nonetheless (in positivistic fashion)? Is the intangible to be made tangible? Is the true self to become known after all, and for the sake of the meritocracy? (Sociopolitical notions of freedom and democracy have always been dependent on the intangible, the idea that, sensed and felt, true individuality exists, and that not everything can be known—and hence controlled—in this respect.)

My worry is that, officially installed with its own "priesthood," the new subjectivity will constitute a greater imposition on the individual aesthetic than anything that might have emerged from positivist or formalist thought. So, too, in the name of passion, or the scholarly pursuit of passion, music is likely to be reduced to something wholly sociological, passion itself to the humdrum or vulgar.[16] Ironically, this is of course not unlike the complaint that has surfaced against positivist and formalist approaches to the study of music.

---

16. See Kramer, "The Musicology of the Future," p. 9. Kramer assures us that, according to the new humanist or postmodernist creed, immediacy will not be "deconstructed" as something "spurious and pernicious." "The last thing a postmodernist musicology wants to be," he writes, "is a neo-Puritanism that offers to show its love for music by ceasing to enjoy it." I remain skeptical nonetheless.

2

But what can be said of the passionate nature of the relationship that is struck with music? For those who, like Treitler, lament an academic purpose increasingly detached and neglectful of the intellectual and spiritual values of humanistic study (the values of the human soul and its salvation, in their best light), has the transcending character of the relationship to music, the separation of that relationship from the uses of education and its system, become a source of disbelief? Have we not always believed in music's transcendence, its separation not just from educational use but from use pure and simple, from that which is derived, functional, or purposeful?

The ongoing assumption has been that music appreciation is a form of inwardness that, like love or religious faith, is relatively immune to critical persuasion. The implication has been that musical works can speak to us directly. Free and spontaneous rather than willed or forced, the relationship is personal, inward, and spiritual, an essential truth about which there can be an essential certainty.[17] ("Truth is inwardness," as Kierkegaard observed; "spirit is inwardness, inwardness is subjectivity, and subjectivity is essentially passion"; "all decisiveness, all essential decisiveness, is rooted in subjectivity.")[18]

Moreover, the passionate nature of the relationship is not open to the inquiry that it inspires. As was detailed in the preceding chapter, moments of aesthetic contemplation are immediate; they define an at-oneness with music that transcends the familiar subject-object, inner-outer dualities. What follows, however, are periods of reflection, periods that yield an image of aesthetic pleasure, of that which is sensed and felt in immediacy. Reflection serves immediacy in this way, following in an effort to capture and sustain immediacy.

17. See Søren Kierkegaard, *Concluding Unscientific Postscript,* trans. David F. Swenson and Walter Lowrie (Princeton: Princeton University Press, 1968), p. 71.
18. Kierkegaard, *Concluding Unscientific Postscript,* p. 33.

A similar case can be made for music theory and analysis. An extension of the reflective process, analysis, too, follows experience in an effort to sustain immediacy. In doing so, it provides a great many foils (general terms and concepts, as a rule) against which the details of a given musical work can be set. And it is in the setting of those details, in the discovery and rediscovery of their significance in relation to an imagined whole, that the relationship is sustained, a sense of immediacy renewed. Using the general as a foil for the sensed particular, the tension that is likely to emerge in the process of this dialectic, reflection and analysis act to kindle and, if possible, intensify the aesthetic presence or "presentness" of a given work.

Thus, too, few limits may be placed on the subject matter of an inquiry, on that which, however removed from the immediacy of an aesthetic presence, may nonetheless act to stimulate that presence. As with the experience of love, that of music extends outward, affecting much that is external to it. Such a fanning outward is relatively indeterminate in what it may encompass, what it may touch and enliven. Similarly, what may prove helpful in igniting a point of contact is largely indeterminate.

In his criticism of style history and contemporary music theory, Treitler distinguishes between subjective and objective, humanist and nonhumanist modes of scholarship. He associates the subjective with individuality, uniqueness, and the particular in music, and the particular, in turn, with inwardness and spirituality, with sensibility and humanistic value. And he implies that applications of his own abstractions of style, genre, form, and rhetoric can elude the usual difficulties of abstraction, can penetrate individuality and, by implication, that which separates analytical description from experienced reality.

What [Schenker's] restrictive definition of "content" amounts to, in effect, is that again and again individualizing features of the work are neutralized by placing them under general concepts that apply across the tonal system or the symphonic form, or both. The effect is to head off just those questions that can lead to an illumination of the qualities of the particular work. *What is accomplished is the demonstration that the work exemplifies a system or a class, or a theory about one or the other.*[19]

Schenker's purpose was to demonstrate the unity of the work and the necessity of its constituent moments, and to display it as exemplification of a theory. . . . *My purpose . . . was the illumination of the work in its individuality.*[20]

My sense, however, is that many of these distinctions are more elusive than allowed. Even if the subjective or humanistic could be isolated and hailed as the cure for an assortment of scholarly ills, such a determination could never be pursued on the basis of content, of what is actually studied in relation to a given musical context. Quite naturally, Treitler assumes that his own experiments in this direction, his ideas about "style and genre" and his literary-poetic descriptions of his experiences of the Beethoven Ninth,[21] are more empathetic with the sensing subject, more true or real to that subject than conventional style history or the "methodologies of formalist analysis" of contemporary music theory. But another, equally passionate and subjective response to the Beethoven Ninth could take flight in the direction of musical biography, manifesting itself in the form of an appetite for the most incidental details of the life and times of the composer. And still another response, no less passionate and subjective, could gravitate toward those more specific, "technical" terms and concepts of theory and analysis, terms that permit a "close reading" of the music at hand, that permit attention to be directed not at "style," historical context, or the self in aesthetic contemplation, but at the ignition itself, the immediate source of the attraction. Why, indeed, would anyone passionately engaged with a given work find a study of that work's social con-

---

19. Treitler, *Music and the Historical Imagination,* p. 30 (italics added). Reference here is to Schenker's early monograph *Beethovens Neunte Sinfonie* (Vienna: Universal Edition, 1912). The recent English translation of this is *Beethoven's Ninth Symphony,* trans. and ed. John Rothgeb (New Haven: Yale University Press, 1992).

20. Treitler, *Music and the Historical Imagination,* p. 32 (italics added).

21. Treitler, *Music and the Historical Imagination,* pp. 36, 19–28.

text, a study treating that work as a "product of culture,"[22] to be more supportive of the engagement (or of the humanist cause generally, as Treitler interprets that cause) than a "technical" analysis of the details of musical structure? In what way would the former be more useful in renewing and sustaining a sense of the work's immediacy, the pleasure that is to be gained from immediacy? And if the value of an analytical method is to be assessed on the basis of its nonabstractness from immediate experience (a highly problematic contention, obviously), would such a standard bar logic and mathematics from the study of music? Would the latter be judged too removed from the musically experiencing subject to be of analytic-theoretical assistance?

We may grant the potentially misleading implications of much systematic theory and analysis. We may grant the "sins of Positivism," just as we grant those of relativism and "metaphysical solipsism."[23] But Treitler seems to believe that theorists and analysts are absolutists in the most trivial sense, believers in a musical "play" without outside reference and, therefore, without meaning. My understanding, however, is that theorists as a group are guided not by unbelief (by which I mean the absence of a belief in larger meanings or significances, however unspecified) but by a desire to familiarize themselves with the workings of musical structures. And that desire is prompted not so much by a need to control those workings, to treat them mathematically as a means of control for the sake of control (reflecting, as Treitler would have it, a typically masculinist, positivist, or formalist relationship to music, a "relationship of power")[24] as it is by a desire for intimacy. Working closely with the materials of music, theorists and analysts seek a more detailed knowledge of those materials, and for the purpose of adding to the attraction itself, intensifying the felt presence of a

22. McClary, "The Politics of Silence and Sound," p. 150. See also Lawrence Kramer, "Haydn's Chaos, Schenker's Order; or, Hermeneutics and Musical Analysis: Can They Mix?" *19th-Century Music* 15, no. 1 (1992): 3–6, 17.

23. See Benjamin Boretz, "Meta-Variations: Studies in the Foundations of Musical Thought (I)," *Perspectives of New Music* 8, no. 1 (1969): 9.

24. See footnote 12, above.

given context. What they seek are images ever more intimate in their detail, and as such, ever more capable of yielding pleasure.

No doubt, theory and analysis are subject to the outside pressures to which the profession as a whole is subject, the larger entanglement alluded to above. But it cannot be argued, it seems to me, that the role of "music appreciation" in higher education has been any less problematic in this respect. To the music appreciator may go the humanist's laurels, and in opposition to groups chided as "donkey people," those with systematic rigor on their minds, plodders who would commit to systems, theories, and graphs the givens (however flabby) that others would take for granted. Yet the appreciator is compromised as well, and if not by the marketing of a spiritual message, then by the giant socioeconomic testing device at whose service that message is placed. In the interests of sensibility and the human soul, of culture and the contending "good life," scholars teach, profess, promote, test, and evaluate "appreciation."

Indeed, viewed idealistically, the teacher-appreciator can recall the lover or religious believer who would persuade an audience (in the case of the appreciator, a socioeconomically captive one, of course) of the merits of his or her case, the merits of inwardness and spirituality. The greater the inwardness and hence truth of that individual love or religious belief, the more anxious the dilemma: to teach what cannot be taught, only praised, to guide where guidance slips into misguidance. That which defies direct expression, that which is only to be sensed and felt, must be made narrowly purposeful. And in the futility of this arrangement it is the appreciator who is put to the test, who becomes an object of scrutiny. Attention shifts from the musical objects themselves and the relationship of those objects to each and every sensing individual; it becomes fastened on the persuasive powers of this official music appreciator. Mired in contradiction, the implications are farcical. And it cannot be otherwise, because speaker and audience are locked in the same embrace, in the same shadow undertaking. They teach and profess what is in essence a secret, what can be no more than an assumption.

In the relationship of the sensing subject to academic institutions, it is not so much the materials that can alienate as the manner in which those materials are processed. And that manner is, as has been indicated already, a reflection of a competitive environment, a prodding system of credits, rewards, and privileges, one of sorting, selecting, and excluding of which reforming critics such as Treitler and McClary are both products and beneficiaries (as I continue to insist), a system that is itself enveloped by a larger socioeconomic purpose.[25] It is unrealistic to expect such a system to respond to the humanities or the study of music all that differently than it does to, say, computer science or business management, categories with more immediate ties to that larger purpose. And I would submit that to expect as much is to tempt deception still further, to surrender that much more of the promise of a spiritual life to the uses of that purpose.

My argument with the reformers stems from their belief that it can be had both ways, that the personal can be combined with the conveniences of the crediting apparatus. To combat the overly detached, rational, and objective in contemporary methodology, they would mix the personal and the spiritual in more completely with the apparatus, a marriage of longstanding convenience, of course, but one in which the interests of the latter have always taken precedence. In effect, the apparatus is to assume greater responsibility for the mix (the correct mix correctly displayed, of course), to sit more fully in judgment of the mix (of the subjective, in other words, the condition of "being oneself"), to be *trusted* more completely in these respects. A more humane and humanistic approach is to be achieved, the spiritual in music reclaimed, passion and inwardness restored, by means of the credit-bearing institutions, the system and its purpose, a properly rehearsed "priesthood."[26] All

25. In their habitual complaints about the impersonal character of academic institutions, critics who are themselves academics tend to overlook their own practical dependence on that impersonality, on a system that processes on a massive scale independently of their own personal intervention. And they overlook their socioeconomic dependency as well, the degree to which the system, by way of its sorting and crediting, generates the demand for their services.

26. McClary refers to academic music faculties, or at least those engaged in the teaching and publication of impersonal, objective, "technical" knowledge, as a "trained priesthood." See, in footnote 3, above, the quotation from McClary, "The Politics of Silence and Sound," p. 150. My point here, of course, is that such

this is to be achieved by way of the meritocracy, in other words. McClary's feminist indictment of current objective, positivistic scholarship is a case in point. Much is made of the irrational and the passionate in music, of the role of the sensing, experiencing individual. Inevitably, however, the indictment celebrates neither passion nor the irrational but a new reduction, a new rationalization of music and its appreciation. Its appeal is not to aesthetic immediacy, to an effective (or affective) means of sustaining immediacy, but to an intellectual argumentation, a new way of objectifying the musical experience. And the effort (or the system it builds) is far more driven from an ideological standpoint, more *controlling* vis-à-vis music and its appreciation, than is, say, Schenker's *Free Composition*. Yet Schenker's treatise is condemned because of its attempt to control tonal music, to rid tonality of its irrational "transgressions," which are associated with passion.[27] (In my view, Schenker's methods are distinguished not by their "technical" means but by their study at close range, their determination to come to grips with the details of tonal structures; the "technical" angle—which, necessarily, is descriptive and metaphorical, notwithstanding the label— is symptomatic of that intimacy, of an overriding focus and determination in the direction of detail. I shall return to this point in chapter 4.)

As a critic of tonal and twentieth-century music, McClary prizes musical excess, of course, but at the expense of those normative procedures (harmony and counterpoint à la Schenker, for example, the ways and means of a "common language" or "grammar") *that define that excess,* that allow structures (tonal structures, in this instance) to acquire depth in their commonality and hence in their transcending intrinsic qualities as well, rather than to stand as instances of a self-indulgence that is merely shallow, isolated, and fitful. At the same time, her reductions are invariably of the same sys-

---

a "priesthood" is unlikely to disappear once it is populated by agents of an institutionalized subjectivity. Indeed, the prospects of a tyranny of ideology, of a truly politicized environment, are likely to grow more sinister.

27. Susan McClary, *Feminine Endings: Music, Gender, and Sexuality* (Minneapolis: University of Minnesota Press, 1991), pp. 104–105.

tematic sort, namely, to sexual conflict and a form of victimization borne exclusively by the female. Excess itself is always reduced to the same dreary predicament: men, in their rationally, objectively constructed world (of diatonicism, controlled dissonance) are threatened—or feel themselves threatened—by female sexuality and the abyss (of chromaticism). This formula is applied not only to tonality but to atonal and twelve-tone music as well.[28]

With less of a belief in the transcending powers of music, in the ability of music to speak to some degree for itself, musical structures are not more but less free, less able to affect us spontaneously, to stand apart from the material or the materially purposeful. Drawn more and more into the uses of the world, into forms of ideological and personal-political manipulation, they are less able to function as an alternative to those uses or to awaken a capacity for that alternative. Deprived of focus and concentration, of a measure of aesthetic autonomy, they lose all significance in and of themselves. Rather, they are valued solely as sociopolitical comment and for the opportunity they afford for such comment. And in the current balancing act between object and subject, musical structure and sensing subject, attention shifts not from music to the musically experiencing subject but from music to the experiencing subject as such, the subject and his or her needs, wants, desires, and concerns (whether musical or not), the self and its preoccupations, with the study of music transforming itself—at least for Mc-Clary—into a kind of *musicology of resentment*—personal resentment. Music and its study serve ends neither musical nor musically experiencing, in other words, but personal-political. As a means of interpretation, of gaining access to music, the effort is ungenerous. And it is ungenerous not only to music (and to our own capacities as experiencing individuals), but to music as a "product of culture" as well.

Thus, too, the objective spirit, pegged repeatedly in Treitler's essays as an "evil empire," a source of aesthetic, sociopolitical, and linguistic ills, is not without its place and value. Here again, it seems to me, the distinctions Treitler draws are more subtle and

28. See, especially, McClary, *Feminine Endings*, pp. 105–109.

difficult than allowed. Consider briefly in this connection—and with a view toward a contemporary "social context"—the narcissistic tendencies of the current age. The latter has been described as unduly absorbed with images and reflections of itself, its prototypical individual as obsessed with the analysis, projection, celebration, and "instant gratification" of the self. And the evidence for this assessment is everywhere within reach, it seems to me, from the latest in health foods to the exotic in group therapy; laid out in these terms is a contemporary being very self-consciously aware of or "into" himself or herself. (Therapies stress the need for "staying in touch" with the self, of course, but their more pragmatic and merciful strategies feature the familiar escape routes all the same, the ways of "getting rid" of the over-heated self.)

But these unflattering circumstances are nowhere taken into account by Treitler. Instead, it is the objective spirit which is made the source of all that is misguided and unfortunate. And given a sufficiently apocalyptic vision of that spirit, of the exercise of reason and rationality, the self can no doubt be made to appear neglected and pitiful in its attempt to assert itself, to force the issue of itself in one way or another. My own view is a good deal less sympathetic, however, even if the two sides of this equation are not easily kept separate. Angled differently, the self can be made to appear neither neglected nor pitiful but impatient with its transparency as spirit, open to the easy affirmations of the real world, to its own conscious manipulation, its promotion as something tangible. And the consensus has tended to favor this less sympathetic view, in fact, the idea of a massive confusion between subjectivity and vanity. The subjective is everywhere, of course, but it is everywhere merely transparent and passive. Its conscious projection is therefore perverse, futile, and symptomatic of impotence.

The point here, however, is not the validity of one or the other of these two views but their complexity, the depth of the issues to which Treitler alludes. Thus, were we for a moment to acknowledge the less sympathetic view, would our sense of the subjective remain unaffected by this acknowledgment? Would we be inclined to trust the subjective any more than we do the objective? And is there indeed a reasonably accurate point at which the difference could be told? The problem with Treitler's subject-object argument is that it lacks the means of preventing his favored subjective tones from becoming as abusive as his deplored objective ones. As such, it is only half an argument. More to the point, the issues with which he deals are moral and ethical rather than merely sociopolitical or psychological. And his reluctance to recognize and treat them as such is ideological, as ideological, in fact, as anything that could be found lurking behind the positivistic impulses of contemporary methodology. Running counter to today's relativism, such issues could, more readily than the subjective voice or academic humanism, be identified as the modern taboo, as that which is most anxiously sidestepped in contemporary intellectual life.

Can the objective voice be the voice of fairness as well as of impartiality and detachment? Can it represent the search for that of which we can be reasonably certain? Or is it, as Kierkegaard thought, inherently uncertain and approximate? Does it merely reflect the subjective as that which is essentially true and decisive? Obviously, the cold, heartless, objective tones deplored by Treitler, the scholarly "restraints" of which he makes such a mockery,[29] are a necessary part of a larger framework. As such, they can offer an occasional way out of the dilemma, a way that is genuinely aware and hence expressive. There are in any case no guidelines for the emergence of the expressive voice, no specific standards or methods.

So, too, squeamishness in the face of passion, a reluctance to give vent to the passion of a musical engagement, can signify timidity. The scholar may be unwilling to break with the dry, impersonal tones of scholarship, to risk his or her personal self in a profession that would seem intent on just the opposite. Such are the tones of authority, after all. Signifying distance and the ability to stand above the fray, they distinguish the profession as a profession, are a part of its sociopolitical and economic legitimacy in this respect. But the same tones can signify perspective, a sense of focus and concentration. And restraint can signify an unwillingness to engage the public in matters that may indeed be personal. The scholar

29. Treitler, *Music and the Historical Imagination,* p. 9.

may deal circumspectly so as not to constitute an imposition in matters of personal appropriation; he or she may not wish to be mistaken for the objects themselves, indeed, the confusion that is to be avoided above all others. And seeking therefore not to stray from those objects, he or she may indeed stand somewhat aloof. (The advantage of committing matters of personal experience to analysis rather than, say, poetry or musical composition, is not always clear. In Treitler's case, the effort is often poetic or *literary* rather than musical or musically analytical.)

Moreover, paradoxically, in suppressing that which is only human, that which is sensed and felt irrespective of what may be said or written, restraint can have its own expressive appeal. In a larger sense, restraint *is* expression. And we all restrain ourselves. Coming to terms with his audience, even Treitler must adopt a civil tone, a proper distance. He too must become an observer, strike a compromise, and wrestle with the problems of translation. He too must deal with the beast within, so to speak.

In matters of musical intimacy, then, the tendency has been to ignore the role of privacy in cradling inwardness, that form of essential truth without which no sensibility of the kind Treitler cherishes would be possible. In an age given to overexposure and confessional junk, privacy has had to defend itself not with rules of etiquette but with deflections more and more improvised and stressful in implication. And it remains an open question, it seems to me, whether this erosion of private life has made for a more just and open society or whether, on the contrary, or at the same time, it has added to the barriers behind which the individual, in a bid for composure, for a sense of what may indeed be true and real, is forced to take refuge.

3

Politics Ho!

No doubt the plea for a new approach to music scholarship, one that would place greater emphasis on the personal and social aspects of music and its appreciation, has struck a sympathetic chord with a great many musicologists and theorists. The argument for such an approach is encountered in Joseph Kerman's *Contemplating Music*,[1] for example, and is shared by the present observer as well, notwithstanding the many reservations expressed here. According to Leo Treitler, the approach would aim for a more realistic balance between sense and sensibility; above all, it would not "draw the blinds before music's expressive force."[2] Treitler's views touch on issues that are consistent with Susan McClary's point of departure, her idea that positivism has conspired with a belief in "transcendental significance" to discourage inquiry into the nature of the aes-

1. Joseph Kerman, *Contemplating Music* (Cambridge: Harvard University Press, 1985). See also Stanley Cavell, *Must We Mean What We Say?* (Cambridge: Cambridge University Press, 1976); Peter Kivy, *The Corded Shell: Reflections on Musical Expression* (Princeton: Princeton University Press, 1980); and Fred Everett Maus, "Music as Drama," *Music Theory Spectrum* 10 (1988). Maus prefaces his study with a lengthy summary of the problems of integrating theory and analysis with questions of affect and expression and refers at length to both Kerman and Kivy.
2. Leo Treitler, *Music and the Historical Imagination* (Cambridge: Harvard University Press, 1989), p. 46.

thetic experience.[3] Treitler even characterizes the opposing forces of this conspiracy in essentialized masculine and feminine terms: sense, reason, rationality, objectivity, positivism, and the collective as well as vested authority of the foregoing are associated with the male; nature, passivity, sensibility, subjectivity, sensuality, and passion are associated with the female.[4]

More problematic than this voguish appropriation, however, is the subject-object dichotomy to which it is linked. As was discussed in the preceding chapter, the two sides of this ancient, epistemological divide are locked in isolation. Subject and object—inner and outer, the spiritual and the rational—may be treated in absolute terms, of course. But Treitler's concerns are sociopolitical and aesthetic and tend therefore to imply varieties of subject-object interaction. Here again, however, the stand against all things of an "objective nature" is wholly without compromise.

Indeed, as Treitler describes it, the subject–object division seems an inhuman construction, "not natural" to man.[5] It does not appear to devolve from the symbolic forms of music and language, forms that have arisen in recognition of ultimate commonality, the very focus of Treitler's essays. The passions of aesthetic contemplation, of "great" music in the form of the Beethoven Ninth, are, after all, the passions of the divided self struck by a momentary release from that division. For how could the rapture of self-forgetting at-oneness with the world through music be experienced without the underlying division of which the self rids itself in moments of

---

3. Susan McClary, "The Undoing of Opera: Toward a Feminist Criticism of Music," Foreword to Catherine Clément, *Opera, or the Undoing of Women*, trans. Betsy Wing (Minneapolis: University of Minnesota Press, 1988), p. xv.

4. Treitler, *Music and the Historical Imagination*, pp. 14–18. The division of these opposing forces, a separation of "the knower from the known," is characterized as Western and masculine in origin; it is pursued as two "ideals of truth and knowledge that are polarized according to gender" (p. 15). And it is pursued in psychological terms as well, with the bond between the mother and her daughter contrasted with that between the mother and her son: from early on, Treitler writes, "the outlook for the female child is continued bonding, whereas for the male child the outlook is toward separation" (p. 15). These and other issues relating to feminism, and in particular to the feminism of Susan McClary, were discussed in chapter 1.

5. Treitler, *Music and the Historical Imagination*, p. 10.

attunement? Such moments reverberate and can become a part of thought and action more generally, no doubt. Yet aesthetic immediacy brings with it an awareness not only of the spiritual world of attunement but of the separation from that world as well.

Within Treitler's polarized framework, with the two sides of the duality wholly divorced from one another, all virtue is assigned to the subjective. And he compounds the problem with gender assignments, whereby goodness and the subjective are characterized as feminine, badness and the objective spirit that breeds division, masculine. A weakness for constructions of this kind lies at the heart of what has been described as "feminism's unacknowledged problem."[6] Few would wish to quarrel with parts of Treitler's argument, specifically with the notion that music scholarship, in positivistic pursuit of fact and circumstance, has too often neglected that which ignites our intellectual concerns, namely, the aesthetic experience. Such are the gains of Treitler and other reforming humanists, it seems to me, a new awareness of the musically sensing subject, of the personal and social implications of music and of the areas of inquiry that are opened up accordingly. But it is one thing to campaign for a thaw in subject-object relations, an easing of tensions in favor of the subjective, and quite another to misconstrue the nature of those relations in fundamental ways. Many years ago, in a response to Treitler's essay on "The Present as History,"[7] Benjamin Boretz commented on the one-sidedness of Treitler's approach. That comment is still very much apropos:

In [Treitler's] rejection of an "objectivity" based on an elusive empirical Given, he seems unaware of any middle ground worth considering short of a complete retreat into "subjectivity." What he fails to take account of is the possibility of intersubjectivity, linguistically dependent to be sure but cognitive in the only sense that word has. Yet, of course, the assumption of such intersubjectivity must underlie any effort at explicit communication such as Treitler's own essay. The trouble appears to be that Treitler, along with many other writers, is so overwhelmed by the sins of Positiv-

6. Helen Vendler, "Feminism and Literature," *New York Review of Books* 37, no. 9 (31 May 1990): 22.

7. Leo Treitler, "The Present as History," *Perspectives of New Music* 7, no. 2 (1969); reprinted in Treitler, *Music and the Historical Imagination,* pp. 95–156.

ism that he is blinded to the residual virtues of empiricism, and, in advocating a restriction of the function of rational discourse to the merely *persuasive*, he is evidently, and in my view, unnecessarily, throwing the
cognitive baby out with the dogmatic bathwater. For while he accounts
for intellectual activity as "constructing" rather than "discovering truth,"
his radical subjectivism would hardly permit him to know what it is that
has been constructed, or whether the "constructed things" can be scrutinized (in thought, observation, or both) or only regarded as verbal placeholders without cognitive content. By the same token, Treitler's position
would make it impossible to suppose that any argument, even if purely
persuasive, could be reasonably insured to extrude a *particular persuasive
content*: for persuasive discourse is not "less cognitive" than other discourse, but merely locates its relevant "field of cognitivity" elsewhere.
. . . So Treitler's effort to attain a radical relativism actually reverts, because of his failure to recognize some vital distinctions, to a metaphysical
solipsism, as impossible of realization as the "objectivity" it purports to
supplant.[8]

It is unfortunate, too, that Treitler's politics should suffer from
this same tendency to reduce legitimate complexity to black-and-
white oppositions. Initially a traditional scholar, Treitler appears to
have found his mark with the student demonstrations of the late
1960s, with the calls at the time for "relevance" in the curriculum,
increased student participation, the introduction of ethnic studies,
and an end to the draft and the war in Vietnam. During this period,
students and faculties confronted live sociopolitical issues in immediately pressing ways. And what seems to have struck Treitler
in all this was the insularity of scholars and scholarship. He condemns the scholar's "ideal of objectivity" as a fetish of white, upper-middle-class males, a mere reflection of the socioeconomic advantage of that group, its privileged detachment from want or real
material concern. He notes, for example, that for many years during the 1960s "students . . . could not easily integrate lectures on the
forms of Haydn symphonies with their forced awareness that their
presence in the lecture hall was a privilege granted them in a society
that was just then making such a display of its barbarity."[9]

8. Benjamin Boretz, "Meta-Variations: Studies in the Foundations of Musical
Thought (I)," *Perspectives of New Music* 8, no. 1 (1969): 9.
    9. Treitler, *Music and the Historical Imagination*, p. 6.

"Barbarity" is a reference to the American intervention in Vietnam. One wonders, however, whether the interference he describes with the study of Haydn is of a kind that is being recommended more generally. (The matter is left unclear from the context of his remark.) Indeed, one wonders if replacing "the forms of Haydn symphonies" with those of the *Eroica* and the Ninth would have made a difference. It cannot escape my attention, in any case, that the image of Papa Haydn that would seem to underlie the point of Treitler's remark is one that Schenker the Formalist sought to dispel much earlier in the century.[10] And the image of a schematically applied *Formenlehre*, as also implied here, is precisely that against which Schenker directed the whole of his mature theoretical writing, the whole of his ideas about organic growth, prolongation, and "directed motion" in tonal music.

The cleansing spirit of the 1960s is evoked briefly by Treitler in terms of the civil rights marches, the riots in the Watts section of Los Angeles, and the student demonstrations at Berkeley, the University of Chicago, and Columbia University.[11] Missing from his account, however, is a sense of irony, a sense of the many potentially positive developments that ran aground or turned sour. The mostly liberal, egalitarian causes are recited as if the intervening years had provided no new perspective from which to assess deeper and less incidental causes and effects. No mention is made, for example, of the drug culture of the 1960s, the stone's throw that separated the Flower Children from the Weathermen, the self-indulgent posturing of so many leaders on both sides of the aisle (liberal and conservative, dove and hawk alike), and the endless sloganizing that managed to obscure or trivialize so much of what was said and done. (The truly politicized environment is a tyranny of which the radical should be obliged to remain cognizant at all

---

10. See Heinrich Schenker, *Haydn: Sonata in E-flat Major*, trans. Wayne Petty, *Theoria* 3 (1983); first published in *Der Tonwille* 3 (1922).

11. Treitler, *Music and the Historical Imagination*, p. 5. My own mixed feelings about the student uprisings derive in large part from the demonstrations at the University of California at Santa Barbara, 1968–1970. Those seeking an antidote to Treitler's cheery interpretations should consult the account of the events at Cornell University in Allan Bloom, *The Closing of the American Mind* (New York: Simon & Schuster, 1987), pp. 313–335, 347–356.

times.) Among Treitler's good/bad oppositions are the following: the Peace Movement vs. Johnson the Warmonger, Southeast Asia vs. American "barbarity," Truth-in-Advertising vs. the American Military, and, of course, Emotion and Meaning in music vs. Schenker the Formalist (or Absolutist).

The delusions of the war in Vietnam, however, were hardly those of the Johnson administration alone. At the time, American liberals and peace activists tended to view North Vietnam's Ho Chi Minh as a benign father of his country or a Lincoln of Southeast Asia, Mainland China as a mecca of communal interests holding sway harmoniously over the greed of the capitalist individual. Those images seem far removed indeed from those of postwar Southeast Asia or from those that were to emerge from the Cultural Revolution and the events in Tienanmen Square in May and June 1989. (Translations of Mao Zedong's *Little Red Book* were circulated widely during the 1960s, even at magazine counters of national airports. The details of Mao's particular "barbarity" have now also become known, of course.)[12]

No doubt, the escalation of the war in 1965 was a colossal failure, irrespective of the question of its legality and the unimaginable suffering it caused. My own view of the war is close to Treitler's, namely, that the American intervention was indeed "barbaric" and possibly illegal. But how many in academia today, or indeed in the popular media, would dispute that view? And why such a banner now, if not to ignite the easy oppositions of the 1960s, and as a way of fanning those of the author himself? The atmosphere of the sixties is called up to suffuse Treitler's one-dimensional approach to the causes of the Left, causes which now seem to include the harsh partisanship of academic feminism and multiculturalism.[13] Re-

12. See, for example, Dr. Li Zhisui, *The Private Life of Chairman Mao*, trans. Tai Hung-Chao, foreword by Andrew J. Nathan (New York: Random House, 1994).

13. The ills of today's multiculturalism, which often becomes an extreme form of social objectivity, have been recounted before, and include pan-relativism, the tendency to bless all cultures, even those that are ethnocentric in the most absolutist fashion. Indeed, because of the difficulties of such a universal blessing, multiculturalists tend in practice to be selective along "politically correct" lines. So, too, it seems to me, the multicultural banner often hides sociopolitical attack

duced and simplified in this form, liberal views of the past and present can be readily identified with the instincts of sensing, feeling, and caring people everywhere, and the latter in turn with sensing, feeling, and caring relationships with music, now seen as uniquely the concern of the New Humanists. By means of such connections, in many ways as old as politics itself and stretching here from music scholarship to gender characteristics and personal character, an overriding moral high ground is claimed. In support of his humanistic approach to music study, Treitler points to himself, in other words, to his overall goodness and sense of humanity. It is he and his fellow humanists who, sensing and feeling generally, have managed to encourage such capacities in the study and appreciation of music. It is they who have provided for the scholarly cultivation of such relationships.

But even were we to accept the form of such an argumentation, the selective character of the sympathies themselves would remain too heavy a burden. For why ignore the complicity of others, including Southeast Asians, in the "barbarity" of the war? And was the American cause, that ostensibly of preserving the independence of South Vietnam, wholly unjust? Such was not the view of the South Vietnamese, in any case, the majority of whom, ex–colonial sympathizers and all, feared and despised the Viet Cong and the regime to the north. As it happened, South Vietnam was left to the indoctrination camps of the North, while Cambodia was abandoned to the genocidal whims of its own Khmer Rouge and the invasion and occupation of the Vietnamese army. Few would be so bold as to credit American "barbarity" with the horror of these subsequent events.

Echoing the psychedelic, street-theater cant of the times, Treitler

---

under the appearance of an embrace. See the revealing and subtle discussion of the double standards that can often accompany the cause, as they relate to perceptions of North Africa, colonial and postcolonial, in Ernest Gellner, "The Mightier Pen?" a review of Edward W. Said's *Culture and Imperialism* in the *Times Literary Supplement*. In a lighter but no less revealing vein, see Robert Hughes, *Culture of Complaint: The Fraying of America* (New York: Oxford University Press, 1993), pp. 84–151. Both of these accounts are balanced, in my view, and show both the advantages of multiculturalism and the unreality of its extremes.

wonders how he and others avoided jail while "Lyndon Johnson was at large."[14] Here again, of course, the record is far from cut and dried. On the domestic front President Johnson was a New Dealer, something for which, in different circumstances, a few words of appreciation might have been forthcoming from Treitler. Johnson lobbied for and signed the Civil Rights Act of 1964. As the instigator of the War on Poverty and Great Society extravaganzas, he pushed for and signed the legislation that created Project Head Start, food stamps, guaranteed student loans, and the National Endowment for the Humanities. He was a tireless advocate of education, equal opportunity, civil rights, and, indeed, "affirmative action." But Johnson, vain beyond measure (as well as droopy-faced and Texas-drawled), tended to distrust himself in public. In ways that could have made a difference, he proved unable to communicate enough of his tough and immensely influential self. The public grew suspicious of his magnanimity which, in combination with a Texas-homespun approach, could seem fairly ludicrous on the television screen.

The larger point is that a better account of the 1960s would not necessarily have been a more "objective" one. And it would not necessarily have been supportive of the peace movement, to judge from the following highly personal remarks of John Updike. Setting the latter apart as sociopolitical comment is neither expressed opinion nor subjective or objective content (the two sides are fairly meshed), but the richness of their reference. Mercifully, too, Updike swims upstream against the tide of orthodoxy, against the current "correctness" that is all too unswervingly a part of Treitler's recollections. He suggests that the causes of the protesters and the American Left could be no less self-serving than those of the Johnson administration and its "hirelings."[15] He suggests, indeed, that, for all its shrill appeals to conscience and higher principle, the Left in the form of an "Eastern establishment" held no monopoly on principle or the better, caring instincts of Americans.

14. Treitler, *Music and the Historical Imagination*, p. 6.
15. John Updike, *Self-Consciousness: Memoirs* (New York: Knopf, 1989), p. 120.

The protest, from my perspective, was in large part a snobbish dismissal of Johnson by the Eastern establishment; Cambridge professors and Manhattan lawyers and their guitar-strumming children thought they could run the country and the world better than this lugubrious bohunk from Texas. These privileged members of a privileged nation believed that their enviable position could be maintained without anything visibly ugly happening in the world. They were full of aesthetic disdain for their own defenders, the business-suited hirelings drearily pondering geopolitics and its bloody necessities down in Washington. The protesters were spitting on the cops who were trying to keep their property—the U.S.A. and its many amenities—intact. A common report in this riotous era was of slum-dwellers throwing rocks and bottles at the firemen come to put out fires; the peace marchers, the upper-middle-class housewives pushing baby carriages along in candlelit processions, seemed to me to be behaving identically, without the excuse of being slum-dwellers.[16]

Just as with contemporary issues of music scholarship, in which the cause of the subjective is pursued categorically and without reference to the "residual virtues of empiricism," so, too, with the politics of the Left of the 1960s, a single, pat position is embraced without so much as a nod in the opposite direction. The union of these positions is meant to convey righteousness, the special concern of the New Humanists for the sensing subject and with the liberation of scholars and scholarship from objectivity, above all from the division and bias that are alleged to spring from objectivity. But with respect to the musical issues at hand, neither side, whether humanist or positivist in implication, can do without the other. Each must adopt terms and concepts that lend themselves to a form of underlying agreement and hence communication. Each must apply those terms and concepts to experienced reality, allowing what is musically unique to stand in relief. And in the case of the analytic-theoretical work of Heinrich Schenker, any attempt at categorization along one or the other of these lines can lead only to confusion and misunderstanding.

Here again, Treitler's essays can serve as illustration, and in the

16. Updike, *Self-Consciousness*, p. 120.

form of "conventional wisdom," as representation of much of the criticism of the past several decades. Treitler's appraisal of Schenker is negative, but in ways that are not altogether closed to interpretation and dissent. The point here, above all, is that the processing of a theoretical framework needs to be seen in a more positive light.

4

Schenker and His Critics

Must not pure instrumental music itself create its own
text? And is not the theme in it developed, confirmed,
varied, and contrasted in the same way as the object of
meditation in a philosophical series of ideas?

Friedrich Schlegel,
Fragment 444, Athenäum, 1798

Like the great majority of those who share his opinion,
Becker gives a detailed account of the [Ninth's] four
movements and the profound symbolism of their content without even mentioning the actual music; and this
is absolutely characteristic of this whole school of music
criticism, which prefers to avoid the issue of whether a
work is beautiful by referring to the grandeur of its
significance.

Eduard Hanslick,
Vom Musikalisch-Schönen, 1854

Schenker-bashing comes in many different forms, uninformed as
well as modestly informed, but the variety to which Leo Treitler
falls prey in his discussion of the Beethoven Ninth is entirely ordinary.[1] He accuses Schenker, apropos of Schenker's monograph
Beethovens Neunte Sinfonie,[2] of ignoring the "individual qualities"
of the Ninth so as to frame the piece under cover of his "analytical
theories."[3] In Treitler's view, the Ninth is of interest to Schenker

1. Leo Treitler, *Music and the Historical Imagination* (Cambridge: Harvard University Press, 1989), pp. 19–66.
2. Heinrich Schenker, *Beethovens Neunte Sinfonie* (Vienna: Universal Edition,
1912). The recent translation of this is Heinrich Schenker, *Beethoven's Ninth Symphony,* trans. and ed. John Rothgeb (New Haven: Yale University Press, 1992).
3. Treitler, *Music and the Historical Imagination,* pp. 28, 310.

only to the extent that it can be shown to exemplify and confirm Schenker's "theories":

What [Schenker's] restrictive definition of "content" amounts to, in effect, is that again and again individualizing features of the work are neutralized by placing them under general concepts that apply across the tonal system or the symphonic form, or both. The effect is to head off just those questions that can lead to an illumination of the qualities of the particular work. *What is accomplished is the demonstration that the work exemplifies a system or a class, or a theory about one or the other.*[4]

Schenker's purpose was to demonstrate the unity of the work and the necessity of its constituent moments, and to display it as exemplification of a theory. This amounts to the *explanation* of the work in the strict sense that its events are seen to follow with the force of deductive logic. *My purpose . . . was the illumination of the work in its individuality.* I take this to be a permanent difference between analysis and criticism.[5]

Musical analysis has been a thing separate from criticism because it is mainly practiced by theorists whose ultimate concern it is to determine the nature of the system underlying the event. . . . The [theorist's] task is not to study [works] for their own sake; they are of interest to him only in so far as they provide evidence about the nature of the underlying system.[6]

An analysis is a demonstration that, and how, a particular piece is an instance of a sound system whose conceptual structuring is described in a theory (it would correspond more or less to an explanation in science). . . . It is my impression that Schenker's shortfall in dealing with the individual qualities of the Ninth Symphony remains characteristic of much writing and teaching in what is called analysis.[7]

But such, of course, is the case whenever the theoretical assumptions underlying analysis are brought to the fore and put to the test. Had Treitler submitted his own assumptions to anything like the same scrutiny, he would, I suspect, have reached much the same conclusions.

More serious is Treitler's assumption that the difficulties of the individual context and its analytic-theoretical description can be

4. Treitler, *Music and the Historical Imagination*, p. 30 (italics added).
5. Treitler, *Music and the Historical Imagination*, p. 32 (italics added).
6. Treitler, *Music and the Historical Imagination*, p. 34.
7. Treitler, *Music and the Historical Imagination*, p. 310.

avoided in applications of his own favored "general concepts" of style, genre, form, and key. He seems to believe that, in these latter cases, "individualizing features" are not "neutralized" when placed "under general concepts that apply across the tonal system or the symphonic form, or both." Yet the reality is that analysis, theoretical or critical, is a coin with two sides to it, those of relatedness and distinctiveness. Taking commonality into account, theoretical frames can highlight idiosyncrasy. And while some accounts stress the covering frame itself, its exemplification and confirmation, others take the frame more or less for granted, focusing instead on points of distinction.[8] (Obviously, *true* distinction, *true* individuality or uniqueness—the *sensed particular*, as I have called it—is merely sensed and felt and pertains to imagined wholes rather than analytically abstracted parts or traits. Parts may retain a sense of the whole of which they are a part, of course, and their analysis and description, by comparison to like parts, can spur and shape the sensed whole. But the whole itself is not ordinarily open to analysis. A form of approximation that approximates by means of foils, knowing in analysis is knowing in relation to something else.)

But the larger point here is that the consequences of *not* putting underlying assumptions or concepts adequately to the test can be equally hazardous. And a case in point is Treitler's discussion of key

8. Best viewed as extremes, the two types of analysis are labeled "theoretical" and "aesthetic" in Carl Dahlhaus, *Analysis and Value Judgement*, trans. Siegmund Levarie (New York: Pendragon Press, 1983), p. 9. "Theoretical" analysis aims at the exemplification or verification of a theory, with the result that "the single case . . . appears as an interchangeable example of a rule" (p. 8). "Aesthetic" analysis, by contrast, attempts "to do justice to the particular and unrepeatable; the general, the theory, is but a means and instrument for the attempt to understand the unique individual case. The effort exhausts itself in approximations but nevertheless deserves to be stubbornly repeated." At the same time, Dahlhaus stresses the "close reciprocal relation" of analysis to theory, the fact that, for each analysis, the starting point is often "a piece of theory"; "the notion of a description without assumptions is phantom" (p. 10). Elsewhere in *Analysis and Value Judgement* he traces the rise of the "aesthetic" mode of inquiry from a variety of perspectives. By the turn of the century, evidently, general patterns and genres were used regularly as a means of confronting individuality. See, in this connection, Carl Dahlhaus, *Esthetics of Music*, trans. William W. Austin (Cambridge: Cambridge University Press, 1982), p. 15.

relations in the Ninth.[9] The individualizing understanding toward
which the discussion is purportedly drawn is undermined repeatedly by the permissiveness with which the term *key* is applied, the
absence of a working definition, in other words, any definition.
Key becomes equated with *chord* and *harmony*; it loses its distinction
and becomes a "verbal place-holder without cognitive content."[10]
Thus, for example, at mm. 70–74 in the first movement, in a
stretch of some five measures just prior to the B♭- major section of
the exposition, Treitler identifies four different keys, D minor (implied), F minor, F major, and B♭ major.[11] This extravagance of
keys, illustrated in Example 9, is never reconciled with the larger
understandings to which reference is made, understandings that are
accompanied by explicit narrative or psychological description
nonetheless.[12] And it is just such distinctions, distinctions brought

9. Treitler, *Music and the Historical Imagination*, pp. 56–66.

10. Benjamin Boretz, "Meta-Variations: Studies in the Foundations of Musical Thought (I)," *Perspectives of New Music* 8, no. 1 (1969): 9.

11. Treitler, *Music and the Historical Imagination*, p. 58: "The prolongation of V
[in D minor] from m. 63 onward plays with B-flat first as an accented neighbor
note (m. 67 ff.), then as a prolonged passing tone from A to C as the bass establishes F minor, then F major (mm. 70–74). That is identified in turn as V of B-flat."
Most dubious in this description is the "establishment" of F minor and F major as
keys, given, among other prominent features of this passage, the augmented sixth
chord in B♭ at m. 72. Treitler eschews the distinctions that are usually drawn between concepts such as *applied dominant, modal mixture, key,* and *modulation*; he fails
to appreciate the extent to which "technical" distinctions of this kind can lead to
greater subtlety in the description of our experience of this music. Indeed, given
Treitler's concern with individuality and with the difficulty of "technical" terms
and concepts, the opposite might have been expected from his analysis, namely, a
determined effort to apply the necessary terms with as much specificity as possible, taking advantage of the distinctions they have come to embody. Since all
terms of this kind are of a general nature, treating them specifically in order to
highlight that much more of the individual might have been more appropriate.

12. Obvious reference could be made to Schenker's later abhorrence of casual
use of terms such as *key* and *modulation*. See *Free Composition*, p. 8: "Nothing is as
indicative of the state of theory and analysis as is this absurd abundance of 'keys'.
The concept of the 'key' as a higher unity in the foreground is completely foreign
to theory: it is even capable of designating a single unprolonged chord as a key."
But discussion of such terms and the processes designated is central to virtually all
discussion of tonality in the works of the so-called common-practice period. In
connection with Schenker's ideas, see Schoenberg's discussion of "monotonality"
in Arnold Schoenberg, *Structural Functions of Harmony*, ed. Leonard Stein (New
York: W. W. Norton, 1954), pp. 19, 57.

EXAMPLE 9.   Beethoven, Symphony No. 9, I, transition.

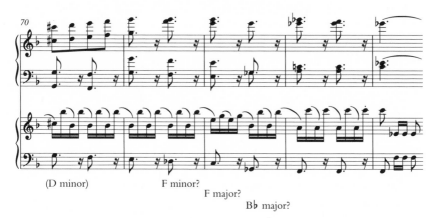

to light by the practical, individual application of general terms and concepts, that can add depth to a study of a piece such as the Ninth, do justice to a perception of that depth, and ensure a renewed sense of its immediacy.

More specifically, Treitler's account of this brief passage of transition lacks an adequate theoretical framework, one which could clarify the meanings of the required terms. As it stands, keys are everywhere with no central focus, no orientation that can be distinguished from more local phenomena. Indeed, distinctions implied by terms such as *dominant, applied dominant, modulation,* and *key* are not acknowledged. Nonetheless, it is by such means that, in opposition to Schenker's "theories," Treitler proposes to scale the individuality of the Ninth. Small wonder, then, the aversion for specialized knowledge and "technical" means, Treitler's sense of an irreconcilable detachment of that knowledge from experience. For the terms and concepts of theory and analysis are never given a chance in his account, never thought through musically to become a part of experience; they are never allowed to activate the material and be activated as a result. They are used as labels and "verbal place-holders." Unaffected by the context, they remain strictly "technical" in this respect.

And that Schenker forsook individuality for the sake of a theory and its confirmation is at least a half-truth, of course. The theorist is guilty as charged, even if the circumstances of his guilt are a good deal more complex than Treitler allows. Since Schenker's theory embodied a value judgment, pieces exemplifying the theory were "organic," "coherent," and so forth. To the extent that the theory stood fully engaged, in other words, exemplification carried with it a recognition of aesthetic worth—masterpiece-status as a rule, tonal coherence at the very least. And while links of this kind between aesthetic judgment calls (which presuppose immediacy) and abstract theoretical propositions can seem naive and simplistic, there is no mistaking the depth of Schenker's convictions along these lines. Immersed in the experience of tonal (mostly German instrumental) music from Bach to Brahms and convinced of the special status of this music, he set about trying to discover the common denominators in terms flexible enough to accommodate diversity yet taut enough to deflect unworthy pretension. And this has been his legacy: the referential basis of the tonal music with which he dealt has been given a sharper, more determinate focus.

At the same time, Schenker's methods were undeniably circular. Over a period of some twenty years, he inferred the theory from the same body of works that were called upon to exemplify the theory. And his analyses do often consist of a demonstration of how concrete musical phenomena fit the theory, how such phenomena can be heard and understood as instances of, for example, dominant prolongations, third-progressions, neighbor-note motions, and "initial ascents." (Given a comprehensive theory with such promise, how else but with its terms are we to expect Schenker and Schenkerians to have confronted the structure of tonal music?) But this is by no means the whole of it. In application, the terms of the theory stretched and contracted, assumed different shapes as a result of the individuality of each instance. Schenker's analyses could be understood as an explanation not only of how "individualizing features" submitted to the theory, but of how the theory submitted to those same features, how it reacted to those features in an engagement that was reciprocal rather than one-sided.[13] And this is an

13. See, for example, Heinrich Schenker, "Organic Structure in Sonata

aspect of Schenkerian analysis—indeed, of the practice of all analysis, the *doing* of it—that Treitler repeatedly ignores. And while the distinctions Schenker revealed were distinctions revealed according to the terms of his theory, they constituted a form of distinction nonetheless. Here, then, Treitler's criticism reduces to its most glaring half-truth, one whose truthful side can be shown to reflect little more than the difficulties that are inherent in all analysis.

And these rebuttals are applicable to Joseph Kerman's critique of Schenkerism as well, where the covering generality of Schenker's "theories" is likewise taken to task for its inability to address individual or "salient" features of the single work.[14] (Indeed, they are applicable to Peter Kivy's criticisms as well, to the extent that Kivy too confronts the individual tonal work and the problems of its general analytical-theoretical description.)[15] Like Treitler, Kerman assumes that favored "general concepts" (those pertaining to tonal form, for example, terms such as *key* and *modulation*) can be introduced without the engagement of a theoretical framework, without attending to the status of their generality. He assumes that such concepts can be applied with only the most "informal" ties to theory, and yet all the while for the purpose of pursuing individuality, very specific musical relations.[16] (How else but against the back-

---

Form," trans. Orin Grossman, in Maury Yeston, ed., *Readings in Schenker Analysis* (New Haven: Yale University Press, 1977), pp. 38–53; first published in *Das Meisterwerk in der Musik*, Jahrbuch 2 (Munich: Drei Masken Verlag, 1926), pp. 45–54. Schenker's discussion of the opening movements of Haydn's Piano Sonata in G Minor, Op. 54, No. 1, and Beethoven's Piano Sonata in E Major, Op. 109, illustrates precisely this form of reciprocity, where the theory is made to react to the musical details as much as vice versa.

14. Joseph Kerman, *Contemplating Music* (Cambridge: Harvard University Press, 1985), p. 82. "Schenkerian analysis repeatedly slights salient features," Kerman writes. "In the service of his idealistic vision, Schenker was ready to strip away not only salient details of individual compositions, but also distinctions between compositions, composers, and periods" (p. 85).

15. Peter Kivy, *Music Alone* (Ithaca : Cornell University Press, 1990), p. 126.

16. "While some sort of theory has to support the analysis," Kerman writes, "it is significant that this can be of the most informal sort. It can be so informal as to practically dissolve out of the usual range of reference of the word 'theory'": Kerman, *Contemplating Music*, p. 66. Analysis can proceed without acknowledging theoretical premises, of course, but only up to a point. And with the music of

drop of a working theoretical premise are individuality and "salience" to be discussed and defined?) And so the relationship between theory and the concrete object to which it is applied,
between general and abstract concepts and the musical experience,
is misunderstood. For the whole point of a theoretical model such
as Schenker's, one that attempts to pin down as much of the detail
of a general process as possible, is that it serve as a foil, a means of
angling the specific terms of a given work. And the greater the sophistication of the model, the more discerning is its role likely to be
in this respect.[17]

In this connection, specific reference can be made to Example 2
in chapter 1, the graph of the Adagio theme of the slow movement
of the Ninth. There, voice-leading reductions were read into the
foreground of the music; an arpeggiation and a descending third-
progression were used as foils, a way of setting the foreground in
relief, highlighting its detail, distinguishing the functions of various pitches, pitch-classes, and triads. And while each such reduction or level could be read independently of the others (each made
tonal sense in and of itself), its purpose was served not in isolation
but in relation to the other reductions or levels. The point was
made not by the reduction itself, the Schenkerian "tautology," as
Kerman has phrased it,[18] but by providing a backdrop for the specificity (indeed, the "salience") of more foreground levels.

Like Treitler, then, Kerman depicts the analytical process as an

---

the tonal era, music whose established theoretical premises are subtle and refined,
I would estimate that point to be a superficial one indeed.

17. See, in this connection, Carl Dahlhaus, "The Musical Work of Art as a
Subject of Sociology" (1974) in his *Schoenberg and the New Music: Essays by Carl
Dahlhaus*, trans. Derrick Puffett and Alfred Clayton (Cambridge: Cambridge
University Press, 1987), p. 236. Principally as a result of the theoretical work of
August Halm and Schenker, Dahlhaus writes, "in analysis worthy of the name the
individual shape no longer appears as representation of a pattern; rather, it is the
pattern that serves as a means with which to arrive at a description of the individuality of the work. The 'real' musical reality is sought in the individual entity, not
in the genre." Here, of course, the "aesthetic" type of analysis is stressed; see footnote 8, above. And it is stressed at the expense of sociological approaches, especially Marxist approaches, which, according to Dahlhaus, typically fail to move
beyond a merely generalizing and exemplifying mode to an individualizing one.

18. Kerman, *Contemplating Music*, p. 82.

exercise in classification, a labeling that serves only to exemplify and confirm a theory, a theory, moreover, that is little more than passively received. Here again, however, such a process need not be one-sided. Not just the individual work but the theory, with all that the theory implies, is subject to modification. The analyst can move back and forth between a sense of the specific terms of a given work and the theory that is being applied to those terms; knowledge gained of the former can affect the theory and its understanding. (The theory is assimilated accordingly, of course, not as a detached "scheme" but in close contact with the diverse, concrete objects to which it is applied *and from which it is inferred.*) By these means, a given work can illuminate the larger context of which it is a part, not just vice versa. And that Schenker was conscious of this reciprocity is evident from his remarks on various nineteenth-century concepts of the sonata form, which he judged ineffectual because of their inadequate attention to detail:

In order to reduce the world of appearances to only a few concepts, knowledge must seek general truths. At the same time, one must examine the particulars to the last detail, in all their secrets, if one wishes to grasp correctly these general concepts, which are, after all, supported by particulars. The task is difficult because generalities, however arrived at, easily mislead men into a premature satisfaction which spares any further effort concerning specifics. Through continuous disregard for detail, knowledge of general truths is impaired; it does not ripen into truth but remains limited to a schema.[19]

Schenker argued that earlier approaches had reduced the sonata to a patchwork of themes and keys, a "collection of individual parts and motives" without the unification of a "temporal background."[20] They had lacked a sense of the dynamics of the form, of the motivation of the "individual parts," which he likened to "organic structure." The latter could be achieved compositionally only by means of improvisation, spontaneous acts that transcended momentary effect, the "present moments" of the foreground:

19. Schenker, "Organic Structure," p. 38.
20. Schenker, "Organic Structure," p. 39.

Only what is composed with the sweep of improvisation guarantees unity in a composition. . . . The whole must be discovered through improvisation if the piece is to be more than a collection of individual parts and motives in the sense of a schema.[21]

Impressions of the foreground were thus owing to the larger whole of which they were a part.

More specifically problematic from the standpoint of Treitler's criticism, however, is the 1912 date of Schenker's monograph. For at no point in *Beethovens Neunte Sinfonie* is the "unity" of the Ninth, the "necessity of [the Ninth's] constituent moments," displayed as "exemplification" of Schenker's theory—indeed, of any theory other than that loose, hand-me-down assortment of contrapuntal and harmonic functions associated with figured bass and Roman-numeral analysis. Many of the "assumptions and premises" that guided the "development of the analytical theories" were present at an earlier stage, no doubt.[22] Conspicuous among these—at least by 1912—was a ferocious dedication to the so-called technical content of music, to a close and detailed reading of, above all, pitch-structural relationships; *Am Anfang was der Inhalt*, is Schenker's battle-cry in the monograph's introduction.[23] Yet it is not so much these "assumptions" as the later "analytical theories" and the man-

---

21. Schenker, "Organic Structure," p. 39. It should be noted that Schenker was snobbish, moralistic, and authoritarian in these views. A preoccupation with the "themes and melodies of a sonata" was associated with the pursuit of life's "superficial aspects." "Laymen" and the "masses" were so preoccupied; they preferred "melody" to true organic structure, the underlying linear progressions that were "melodies in a higher sense." See Schenker, "Organic Structure," p. 51. His remarks grew harsher: "The masses . . . lack the soul of genius. They are not aware of the background, they have no feeling for the future. Their lives are merely an eternally disordered foreground, a continuous present without connection, unwinding chaotically in empty, animal fashion." See Heinrich Schenker, *Free Composition*, trans. Ernst Oster (New York: Longman, 1979), p. 3. Sociopolitically, it seems possible that, fearful of the dangers of communism in the 1920s and 1930s, Schenker overlooked those of his own German nationalism. For further comment on this, see Richard Taruskin, "The Dark Side of Modern Music," *New Republic* (5 September 1988). And see William Drabkin, "Felix Eberhard von Cube and the North-German Tradition of Schenkerism," *Proceedings of the Royal Musical Association* 111 (1984–1985).

22. Treitler, *Music and the Historical Imagination*, p. 28.

23. Schenker, *Beethovens Neunte Sinfonie*, p. vii.

ner of their "exemplification" that spark Treitler's polemic. His concerns are with the "theories" themselves, "the *Ursatz* and its constituents," with the fact that, for Schenker, "an investigation of these things constituted the proper study of music."[24] And those concerns come by way of an early treatise in which an illustration of the "theories" is nowhere to be found.

It was not until the early 1920s, in fact, with the publication of the *Erläuterungsausgabe* of Beethoven's Op. 101 and the first issues of *Der Tonwille* that the first fundamental lines were drawn.[25] The latter were very different from those of *Free Composition*, but they encompassed inherently the notion of prolongation and that in turn of structural levels. And it was not until considerably later that Schenker attempted to reconcile, by means of the notion of "interruption," large-scale voice-leading with the regular repeat structures, the periods and parallel structures, of tonal form.[26]

Yet the early monograph is not without its "constituent moments." Although marred by a reliance on strict formal outlines (not as yet enlivened by the later "analytical theories") and by a play-by-play description that quickly becomes tiresome, the book has not outlived its usefulness. Corresponding to the four movements of the symphony, four giant chapters are prefaced by large form-key outlines. And, at least in profile, the play-by-play account is not unlike Tovey's more familiar guide,[27] even if it is more detailed and lacks Tovey's penchant for incidental narrative and psychological chit-chat. There are interesting comments on thematic types, modulation, and orchestral size and balance; many subsections conclude with hefty excerpts from Nottebohm's early study of the sketches and chronology. All in all, the impression it gives is that of an overextended program note, certainly not that of

---

24. Treitler, *Music and the Historical Imagination*, p. 28.
25. Heinrich Schenker, *Erläuterungsausgabe der letzten fünf Sonaten Beethovens: Opus 101* (Vienna: Universal Edition, 1920), 2d ed., ed. Oswald Jonas (1970–71).
26. For a discussion of the problems and ambiguities of the concept of "interruption" in Schenker's theory, see Allan Keiler, "On Some Properties of Schenker's Pitch Derivations," *Music Perception* 1, no. 2 (1983–1984).
27. Donald Francis Tovey, *Beethoven's Ninth Symphony* (Edinburgh: Thin, 1927).

a policy statement on contemporary practices in music theory and analysis.

But equally misleading is the implication that Schenker was indifferent to questions of meaning and symbolic content. Many of Schenker's publications, pre- and postdating the monograph in question, address critical and aesthetic issues at considerable length.[28] Even *Free Composition*, the decisive theoretical statement, is not at a loss in this respect. "Music mirrors the human soul in all its metamorphoses and moods," Schenker writes.[29] "Striving" toward its goal, the fundamental line signifies "our own life impulse" and is a "full analogy to our inner life":[30]

In the art of music, as in life, motion toward the goal encounters obstacles, reverses, disappointments, and involves great distances, detours, expansions, interpolations, and, in short, retardations of all kinds. Therein lies the source of all artistic delaying, from which the creative mind can derive content that is ever new. Thus we hear in the middleground and foreground an almost dramatic course of events.[31]

As the image of our life-motion, music can approach a state of objectivity, never, of course, to the extent that it need abandon its own specific nature as art. Thus, it may almost evoke pictures or seem to be endowed with speech; it may pursue its course by means of associations, references, and connectives; . . . it may simulate expectation, preparation, surprise, disappointment, patience, and humor.[32]

28. See, for example, Heinrich Schenker, "The Spirit of Musical Technique," trans. William A. Pastille, *Theoria* 3 (1993). The original text, *Der Geist der musikalischen Technik*, was published in the *Musikalisches Wochenblatt* of Leipzig in 1895. See the discussion of this in William A. Pastille, "Heinrich Schenker, Anti-Organicist," *19th-Century Music* 7, no. 1 (1984). For a different interpretation of Schenker's text, see Allan Keiler, "The Origins of Schenker's Thought: How Man Is Musical," *Journal of Music Theory* 33, no. 2 (1989).

29. Schenker, *Free Composition*, p. xxiii. Schoenberg's views were no different from Schenker's in this respect. "In its most advanced state," Schoenberg wrote, "art is exclusively concerned with the representation of inner nature." See Arnold Schoenberg, *Theory of Harmony*, trans. Roy E. Carter (Berkeley: University of California Press, 1983), p. 18.

30. Schenker, *Free Composition*, p. 4.

31. Schenker, *Free Composition*, p. 5.

32. Schenker, *Free Composition*, p. 5.

Music is never comparable to mathematics or architecture, but only to language, a kind of tonal language.[33]

In the foreground, coherence lies behind the tones, as, in speech, the coherence of thought lies behind the words.[34]

It seems unlikely that Schenker would have endorsed a narrative approach to analysis, above all one with ties to relatively undefined notions of style, genre, form, and key. Yet the case for an analogy between tonal music and language or narration could hardly have been argued more explicitly in the above quotations. If Schenker was absolutist in his aesthetic convictions, he was hardly trivially so. From what may be gleaned from his work as a whole, meaning in "pure instrumental" or "absolute" music stretched beyond the mechanics of pitches, intervals, and their relations. Transcending simple analogy and metaphor as well (however indispensable they may be to analytic-theoretical discourse), direct and tangible associations of one kind or another, such meaning seems ultimately to have embraced conceptions of nature and the eternal, the infinite, and the absolute. And categories of this kind are difficult to assess apart from the larger picture, the "idea of absolute music" in the nineteenth century and the evolution of that idea in the writings of such figures as Friedrich Schlegel, E. T. A. Hoffmann, Schopenhauer, Eduard Hanslick, and Nietzsche.[35] Indeed, they are difficult to manage apart from the strains of organicism and Gestalt psychology that manifest themselves more overtly in the theoretical work, or apart from the many ideas that seem to have been absorbed more casually during Schenker's formative years as a student, composer, pianist, and music critic in fin-de-siècle Vienna.[36]

33. Schenker, *Free Composition*, p. 5.
34. Schenker, *Free Composition*, p. 6.
35. See Carl Dahlhaus, *The Idea of Absolute Music*, trans. Roger Lustig (Chicago: University of Chicago Press, 1989), and cf. Carl Dahlhaus, *Between Romanticism and Modernism*, trans. Mary Whittall (Berkeley: University of California Press, 1980), pp. 19–39.
36. For the latter, see Keiler, "The Origins of Schenker's Thought." For a list of Schenker's early essays and reviews, see Nicholas Rast, "A Checklist of Essays and Reviews by Heinrich Schenker," *Music Analysis* 7, no. 2 (1988). And see Heinrich Schenker, "Three Essays from *Neue Revue* (1894–7)," trans. Jonathan Dunsby and Horst B. Loeschmann, *Music Analysis* 7, no. 2 (1988).

In sum, both the personal relationship and the larger picture are distorted when Schenker's absolutist aesthetics are equated with a concern for "technical" process *in and of itself*, when the theoretical work is depicted as "technically" detached in this respect. Myths of ideological purity are brought into service to sell a supposedly humanist argumentation, one, in Treitler's case, that can too easily be shown to have had no place in the real scheme of things.

Often forgotten in the humanist's polemic against "technical" or specialized accounts of music, the positivism that such accounts are presumed to exemplify, is the vulnerability of the alternatives—poetic-narrative approaches, in the present case—to sentiment, triviality, propaganda, and display. The assumption would seem to be that, in contrast to positivistic impulses, narrative descriptions of the kind favored by Treitler are sympathetically human and democratic (because non-"technical" and interdisciplinary), as well as reflective of the passion of the immediate response to music. Yet those descriptions are subject to the same problems of abstraction as are the accounts of the so-called formalists. They too must meet the challenge of translation, groping with the problems of a common language. More to the point, they are as capable today as they were during the nineteenth century of distracting the listener, diverting attention and its appreciation away from the music and onto the agendas, musical and other, of the writers in question.[37] They can discourage as well as encourage a sense of rapport.

And the sensing subject is saved from that confusion only by the music itself, it seems to me, only by the ability of a musical object to create a focus of its own, doing so by imparting something that is in fact its own, something that, if not necessarily static or fixed, is essential and inviolate. The subject is saved, in other words, by the ability of such an object to invite attention for its own sake, and by his or her capacity to respond to that invitation. And the greater the intensity of the attraction, the greater the fidelity to what that

37. For a survey of nineteenth-century interpretations of the Ninth, see Ruth A. Solie, "Beethoven as Secular Humanist: Ideology and the Ninth Symphony in Nineteenth-Century Criticism," in Eugene Narmour and Ruth A. Solie, eds., *Explorations in Music, the Arts, and Ideas: Essays in Honor of Leonard B. Meyer* (New York: Pendragon, 1988), pp. 1–42.

object is for its own sake, not for what it could be made to represent culturally, historically, or sociopolitically:

Confronted with the supreme revelations of music, we even feel, willy-nilly, the *crudeness* of all imagery and of every emotion that might be adduced by way of an analogy. Thus Beethoven's last quartets put to shame everything visual and the whole realm of empirical reality. In the face of the supreme deity revealing himself, the symbol no longer has any significance; indeed, it comes to be seen as an insulting externality.[38]

Reaching into the heart of absolutist aesthetics, such an attitude can apply to all forms of analysis, all attempts to come to terms with music intellectually. Yet the *literary* effort is especially vulnerable in this respect, subject to the ways and means of its persuasive purpose, open to its own eloquence, as it were. It struggles both with vanity and with the futility of that struggle, the struggle to overcome vanity.

Treitler's purpose would have been better served had he submitted the relevant passages of the Ninth to a Schenkerian analysis. In this way, Schenkerian ideas pertinent to his discussion, whether sympathetically pertinent or not, would have been met at least halfway. And instead of relying on key schemes and traditional formal outlines, he could have availed himself of a more finely tuned analytical instrument, one with a greater sense of the detail of tonal music.

For it is a mistake to regard Schenkerian theory as a "technical" matter, as if its understanding were out of reach of most listeners, musicians, and scholars, its "technical" terms, the processes to which they refer, of no use to the concerns that motivate Treitler (those of the individual context and its "presentness"), of no use to a close, active engagement with the musical materials, the sort of engagement that seems, indeed, to have marked their inception.[39]

38. Friedrich Nietzsche, "On Music and Words," trans. Walter Kaufmann, in Dahlhaus, *Between Romanticism and Modernism*, pp. 106–120.

39. This is Peter Kivy's opinion as well, of course, namely, that the practice of Schenkerian analysis is cult-like and elitist, too "technically" isolated for the average listener or musician. See Kivy, *Music Alone*, pp. 126–127, 137. But Kivy criticizes the methods of Rudoph Reti nonetheless, methods he associates with Schenker, without taking into account the large-scale dismissal of Reti's analyses

Here, of course, the notion of a severed "technical" content of or in music is elusive and problematic. Apart from acoustical data and the conventions of notation, analysis, and certainly Schenkerian analysis, confronts music as heard, the experience of music, and can articulate a measure of that experience, ignite or sustain a sense of immediacy, only by means that are representational, by means, in other words, of symbols imposed from without. And in this respect Schenker's vocabulary is no more "technical" or "specifically musical" than Treitler's. Terms such as *prolongation, neighbor note, reaching-over (übergreifen)*, and *initial ascent* are openly descriptive of tonal phenomena and were obviously intended to describe such phenomena by means of a physical imagery that was related to Schenker's two central metaphors, those of motion ("directed motion") and organic growth.[40] There is little reason why such a vocabulary, even when displayed graphically ("specialization"), should prove inhospitable to anyone with a need for expressive analytical discourse, for an overt metaphorical presence.

Indeed, one could argue that, in allowing for a closer and more intimate reading of tonal structure, Schenker's "technical" terms are more democratic than Treitler's "poetical" ones. From the standpoint of the "extra-musical," their metaphorical content is less explicit and hence less intrusive; more explicit images are left to the imagination of the individual beholder. But as has been suggested already, the connections that underlie arguments of this kind are so

---

of thematic unity by scholars of every conceivable bent: see, for example, Leonard B. Meyer, *Explaining Music* (Chicago: University of Chicago Press, 1973), pp. 59–79; and see the thematic analysis of the Beethoven Ninth in Rudolph Reti, *The Thematic Process in Music* (London: Faber and Faber, 1961), pp. 1–29. Thus, Kivy is unable to appreciate the extent to which his criticism of Reti, having to do with Reti's failure to consider musical structure, would have been met by taking Schenker into account.

40. For a discussion of the origins of the metaphor of organic life, see Ruth A. Solie, "The Living Work: Organicism and Musical Analysis," *19th-Century Music* 4, no. 2 (1980): 147–156. See also Pastille, "Heinrich Schenker, Anti-Organicist"; and William Pastille, "Music and Morphology: Goethe's Influence on Schenker's Thought," in Hedi Siegel, ed., *Schenker Studies* (Cambridge: Cambridge University Press, 1990), pp. 29–44.

tenuous that their construction is apt to impress as little more than a front for empty polemic.

There is little reason, in any case, why Schenker's description of the passing tone, metaphorical from the standpoint of "directed motion," psychological from that of the experience of that "motion," should prove "technically" removed as an interpretation of its application at various levels of structure:

Alongside all of the corporeality (which is always to be understood as independent) of the intervals available in strict counterpoint, the first appearance of the dissonant passing tone produces a curious intrusion of the imaginary: it consists in the covert retention, by the ear, of the consonant point of departure that accompanies the dissonant passing tone on its journey through the third-space. It is as though the dissonance would always carry with it the impression of its consonant origin, and thus we comprehend in the deepest sense the stipulation of strict counterpoint, which demands of the dissonant passing tone that it always proceed only by the step of a second and always only in the same direction [as that by which it was introduced].[41]

Indeed, Schenker's methods are distinguished not by their "technical" emphasis—in the sense of a lack of passion or denial or neglect of an expressive, symbolic, or spiritual equation in music—but by their attention to detail, by the lengths to which they resort in pinning down the specifics of a process, the particular realizations of a fairly determinate model of that process. The "technical" angle in his work is but a manifestation of that attention, of study at close range, in other words; the "technical" terms themselves are but a reflection of the sorts of distinctions that are brought to the fore by way of such study.

At the same time, questions of ideology need not impinge on an analytical application of the theory. The latter can be applied to the music for which it was intended generally, can contribute to an understanding of that music, irrespective of Schenker's critical judgments—his nationalist tendencies, for example, or his distaste for Wagner's music, Italian opera, and early twentieth-century

41. Heinrich Schenker, *Counterpoint*, Book 2, trans. John Rothgeb and Jürgen Thym (New York: Schirmer, 1987), pp. 57–58.

trends.[42] And his characterizations of specific tonal processes— those that relate to the organic metaphor, for example, with their emphasis on unity, spontaneity, and internally motivated development—can be understood analytic-theoretically, weighed in terms of their specific relevance to individual cases, without regard to absolutist criteria and without embroiling the scholar in sociopolitical debate, in contemporary issues of class conflict and gender bias.[43] As Dahlhaus puts it:

> It is quite defensible in methodological terms to isolate an object so long as we do not question the reality of the connections from which it has been extracted. . . . (It is a cheap rhetorical trick to talk about "false abstractions" without at the same time pointing out—in addition to the indubitable fact that they are abstract—precisely why they happen to be false.) We can always leave the social context of musical works out of consideration without belittling its importance; doing so only means that we consider social context irrelevant to the particular end we have in view, i.e. understanding those inner workings of a piece of music that make it art.[44]

Schenker's insistence on the involuntary character of the creative act and its appreciation placed the musical object at a certain distance from the sensing as well as from the intellectualizing subject. The two sides of the interaction, subject and object, were kept apart, the one in no way a substitute for the other. Schenker looked inward, of course, but inward as a means of reaching out to an ob-

---

42. For an interesting counter-argument to this, see Richard Littlefield and David Neumeyer, "Rewriting Schenker: Narrative–History–Ideology," *Music Theory Spectrum* 14, no. 1 (1992). The authors argue that Schenker's theories can be understood only with reference to their narrative and epic implications as well as to Schenker's "ideological agenda."

43. In this context see, especially, Susan McClary, "The Politics of Silence and Sound," Afterword to Jacques Attali, *Noise: The Political Economy of Music,* trans. Brian Massumi (Minneapolis: University of Minnesota Press, 1985), p. 150. McClary accuses the "academic priesthood" of having "concealed" the ideological background of current methodologies (including, presumably, the background of Schenkerian theory). But while ideology may have been ignored or taken for granted, it was rarely "concealed," in my estimation. On the other hand, McClary is quite right in taking the editor of *Free Composition,* Ernst Oster, to task for relegating many of Schenker's extravagant philosophical and sociopolitical asides to an appendix. See McClary, "The Politics of Silence and Sound," p. 151.

44. Carl Dahlhaus, *Foundations of Music History,* trans. J. B. Robinson (Cambridge: Cambridge University Press, 1983), p. 27.

ject "out there," to something not entirely of his own making, his own design or purpose. The source of an attraction that attracted freely and spontaneously rather than willfully or forcibly, it attracted out of a sense of its own particularity. It attracted not as an extension of the willful self, not for what it could be made to represent along such lines, but out of its relative freedom from that self. It attracted not out of ideology but out of its ability to resist ideology. And the engaged individual could feel himself or herself not constrained by such a purpose, but, on the contrary, released temporarily from its hold, that of the separation of alienation and division.

Resembling in all these respects a human soul or spirit, "inner life" or life's "impulse," the musical object could trigger considerations of faith and belief as well as reason and abstraction, could project itself as a transcending whole with an essential core, not as a collection of detachable parts valued solely for the external uses to which those parts could be put. And it is here, it seems to me, that the humanistic can be located in Schenker's work. It can be located not in the passion with which theoretical or critical issues were argued, not in the precise character of its metaphorical assumptions, but in the degree to which musical objects were valued for what they were in and of themselves, cherished for their own sake. Here, too, the appeal of an absolutist aesthetic can be understood, the granting of a measure of aesthetic autonomy. For a sense of humanity cannot rest with passion alone but must to some extent reflect the capacity to love. And love is loving a thing for what it is, not for what it could, should, or might possibly represent.[45]

45. I am reminded of Wagner's depiction of what is commonly understood as romantic love in his *A Communication to My Friends* (1851): "Lohengrin sought a woman who would believe in him: who would not ask who he was or whence he came, but would love him as he was because he was what he appeared to her to be." Romantic love is essential love, in other words, love irrespective of lineage, tradition, or social circumstance. Wagner's depiction is cited in Leonard B. Meyer, "A Pride of Prejudices; Or, Delight in Diversity," *Music Theory Spectrum* 13, no. 2 (1991): 248. Pertinent to the present discussion is the relation Meyer draws between romantic love, organicism, and formalist notions of self-contained, autonomous structure, notions of "art for art's sake," in other words, the appreciation of a given work for itself alone, appreciation as an innate rather than learned experience. But the distinctions Meyer draws between innate and learned responses,

Even for the tonal repertory for which they were intended, Schenker's methods are not invariably appropriate. Few would insist that they invariably make an insightful fit, or that other methods or modes of inquiry do not address issues of an equally compelling nature, issues in relation to which the particulars of Schenker's theory may figure only peripherally or not at all. In the music of the nineteenth century, third relations can make for a very uncomfortable fit indeed. When deeply seated, they can challenge underlying assumptions of the Schenkerian model, pointing to the difficulty of that model in coping with tonal implications in works that are just as obviously transitional and altered structurally.

Treitler and Kerman caution against theoretical prejudgment, against preempting the immediate response with received analytic-theoretical hardware. The music, they say, must be allowed to speak to some degree for itself, to suggest its own terms of reference and inquiry. They encourage the scholar to remain in touch with his or her aesthetic bearings, the personal relationship that is struck. And they deplore oversophistication, a music theory or "formalist analysis" grown insular and cut off not only from considerations of emotion and meaning but from related fields of inquiry as well, fields that include history, criticism, aesthetics, psychology, and performance practice.

But apart from these general cautions, which are well taken and applicable to theory and analysis in principle, the musicological complaint against Schenker and "Schenkerism" has had little to do with the merits of the case but has touched instead on concerns that are professional and institutional. Ignoring the advantages of a sophisticated model of tonality, a way of hearing and understanding tonal voice-leading and harmony that does at least partial justice to the richness and complexity of the repertory, the complaint has focused on what the theory in turn ignores, overlooks, or takes for granted: the vocal texts, dramatic plots, or "narrative strategies" it

---

essence and context, subject and object in this respect are drawn far too categorically, in my estimation. A belief in "irreducible essences," in the possibility of creation, need not overrule a belief in context, in the workings of history, culture, and society.

fails to consider. Since it is the materials themselves that are under discussion, misconceptions arise not only about the analytical process but about the nature of the musical engagement that the process presupposes, the benefits it bestows. The larger context of the theory is not taken into account; the focus is on the finished products, the single applications and their brief and selective commentaries, not on the means by which those ends are met, the larger purpose served. Product is favored over process, in other words, the ends over the means; the effort is treated as a closed literary-intellectual endeavor rather than as an applied discipline, one whose benefits—musical enlightenment and intimacy, presumably—lie in a detached pondering of the relevant ideas and concepts rather than in their application, the actual doing of it. Assumptions about the necessarily general and incomplete nature of analysis—all analysis, taken by itself—are also ignored. The result thus becomes inundated with unreasonable expectations. Either that result must succeed on its own, succeed by *reproducing* a given work in all its sensed uniqueness, or it is judged to fail altogether. Unless it manages to cover all interpretative bases, it is believed unworthy of its "technical" effort.

More to the point, Schenker deals with the intricate weighing of pitches and intervals, their relations at inferred local and global levels of structure. Drawing on the "technical" traditions of species counterpoint and figured bass, he conveys the results of that weighing by means of another "technical" language of slurs, beams, and the like, superimposing the latter over the more familiar "technical" language of musical notation, itself often realized in the form of a reduction. And it is especially this style of graphic analysis that has worked against the theory and its application, that has served to isolate it as a specialized form of study outside the mainstream of scholarly research in eighteenth- and nineteenth-century music.

The irony of that isolation is that it is just what the analysis and its graphic representation sought to overcome. Schenker's intention had been to engage the mind's ears and eyes more completely in the analytical process, to ensure that a sense of the materials was not lost to that process. That intention is in line with scholarly ideals generally, it seems to me, as those ideals surround the pedagogical commitment to "appreciation." The problem, however, was that the intention could be pursued only at the expense of language, only by slighting and in certain instances bypassing direct verbal communication. And this is how Schenker himself viewed the graphics of his analysis as an advantage. Circumventing verbal entanglement (as well as verbiage), he hoped to reach the mind's senses more directly and faithfully. The solution has stood, instead, as a "technical" barrier.

No doubt the musical detail to which he referred would have required a form of analytical notation. Yet there is no overstating the underlying contradiction. For it is to the word and its audience that scholars in the humanities are committed, not only intellectually but professionally and institutionally as well. That commitment prevails even among those who would champion human sensibility above all else, those who fight for the cause of the neglected soul, Schenker's "inner life," essential being. It prevails among those who would celebrate sensibility over the tendency to rationalize, to come to terms conceptually and to communicate accordingly. And it prevails among those who would draw the distinction along moral, philosophical, and sociopolitical lines, those who equate sensibility with humanity and virtue, rationality with the possessive exercise of control and the wielding of intellectual and professional authority.

Over and above these and other contradictions, the official view of humanism and humanistic value has held fast: in struggling with words, with *literary* forms of description, expression, and explanation, we enhance our ability both to understand conceptually and to experience aesthetically. Applying ourselves verbally, assuming in this way a measure of intellectual control over the process, we contribute to the experience itself, to our ability to respond to music as sensing, feeling, throbbing beings.[46] And we serve the larger

---

46. In recent years, the element of control in scholarship, control over the self as well as over the materials upon which the scholar directs his or her rationalizing gaze, has become associated negatively with repression and denial and with professional pressures that inhibit acknowledgment of the subjective in music, that to which the humanist scholar attaches humanistic value. Typically, however, the association is made only in relation to the "technical" methods of formal anal-

interests of the profession as well. Contact is maintained with the larger intellectual community and public upon which the profession depends for its recognition and support, its educational and socioeconomic standing and legitimacy.

For what is accomplished by way of a Schenker graph and its commentary? The product is meager and unglamorous when set against the literary-intellectual ambitions of the profession—the grand issues of musicology, for example, issues that relate more directly to historical placement, social context, musical biography, and, most recently, gender and sexuality. It can smack of the rudimentary, in other words, of chalk and erasers. My sense of much of this debate, in fact, is that the imagined insularity of both the analytic-theoretical process and its product has had less to do with technicality as such, with problems of "technical" access and humanistic value, than with the mundane fact that the effort is not sufficiently public, that it does not lend itself readily to sociopolitical comment, advocacy, self-analysis, and considerations of "world-historical" status, of the worldly significance of its subject matter. More modestly (and a good deal less presumptuously), it lends itself to the study of tonal music.

And there can be no mistaking the difficulty of the theory, the problems that beset its application. It is a complex theory for complex music; acquiring a working facility with its terms can be arduous and time-consuming. Schenker devoted nearly a lifetime to the task, of course, and seems to have condemned his adherents to the same fate. For at the heart of the matter is not the acquisition of a "technical" skill or facility but a means of drawing oneself into the workings of musical structures. Each application is undertaken with a history of prior applications; each qualifies and redefines the meaning of Schenker's terms, as it qualifies the meaning of those

---

ysis and systematic theory and to the historian's "obsessive search for facts," not to the more overtly persuasive, critical, ideological, and sociopolitical rhetoric of today's breast-beating humanists. In this way, the exercise of control in the effort to make sense out of anything at all is left unexamined. (The quotation is taken from Susan McClary, "The Undoing of Opera: Toward a Feminist Criticism of Music," Foreword to Catherine Clément, *Opera, or the Undoing of Women,* trans. Betsy Wing [Minneapolis: University of Minnesota Press, 1988], p. xv.)

prior applications as well. It is an operation of give and take, of moving back and forth between an evolving general understanding and the particular interpretations of that understanding. A vast comparative maneuver on the one hand, it is a way of weighing the details of individual contexts on the other. And what counts are the musical issues that are brought to the fore, not the product itself, its "solution" of a musical puzzle, or the fact that alternative readings may suggest themselves as equally valid. The latter are, indeed, encouraged as an essential part of the process.

But music historians are not adverse to specialization as such. Some historians devote their attention to the theories of Roland Barthes, for example; others, to newly found Beethoven portraits or to the familiar story of Beethoven's nephew. Many are experts in the study of music reception, music institutions, or the intricacies of musical patronage in the eighteenth and nineteenth centuries; others, in the study of sketches, watermarks, and chronology. (Our delight in sketches stems less from the imposing musical questions they raise, it seems to me, than from the psychological effect of their contact, the sense of intimacy they bring to an engagement with the materials.)

And why not? Passion can touch just about anything in its wake, and there is little reason why the above-noted occupations should not reflect, nourish, and sustain a passionate appreciation of music. And yet when the same rigor and concern for detail are brought to bear on the subject matter, when it is the materials themselves that are subjected to close scrutiny, complaints surface about the "technical" insularity of the results. When musical intimacy is sought by way of the music itself, by working closely with its pitches, intervals, and rhythms, the manner in which vast quantities of such components are structured by the mind's ear, the issues become "technical" as opposed to humanist, the problems those of the reductive process, of the poverty of analysis, and so forth.

Of course, the technicality of analytical methods may be a matter of degree. If the metaphorical content of Schenker's terms is relatively general and inexplicit, then those terms may depend to a greater extent on the musical phenomena to which they refer. The advantage here, however, is that, in seeking to clarify the meanings of those terms, it is with the music itself that the observer is brought into ever closer contact. Moreover, if the metaphor of organic life can appear overly deterministic in its application to Schenkerian theory, suggestive only of underlying unity while neglectful of features of contrast, diversity, and "salience,"[47] it can also point to varieties of connectedness that are no less crucial to a sympathetic hearing and understanding of the individual tonal work. To suggest that a unity is organic is to suggest that its parts adhere naturally rather than artificially or arbitrarily. It is to suggest that those parts are motivated by the specific unity of the whole, notwithstanding the common language of which they partake, the common functions they assume as, for example, dominants, arpeggiations, and neighbor-note motions. And it is to suggest that those parts are dynamic rather than static, lifelike rather than mechanistic. Such understandings are hardly at odds with the humanist's concern for the special qualities of the individual work or with the humanist's tendency to associate those individual qualities with the subjective response to music, with that which is immediate and essential to the experience of music.[48]

47. In this context see, especially, Kerman, *Contemplating Music*, pp. 81–85. For a critique of what Kerman calls the "ideology of organicism," see Joseph Kerman, "How We Got into Analysis, and How to Get Out," *Critical Inquiry* 7 (Winter 1980). And for an apparently unintended rebuttal to the latter, see the discussion of "Aus meiner Thränen fliessen," the second song of Schumann's *Dichterliebe*, in David Neumeyer, "Organic Structure and the Song Cycle: Another Look at Schumann's *Dichterliebe*," *Music Theory Spectrum* 4 (1982). Like Kerman in his discussion of the same song, Neumeyer is alert to the difficulties of applying Schenkerian analysis: the close relationship between the first and second songs, the placement of the first note of the *Urlinie*, the double cadences, and so forth. Unlike Kerman, however, Neumeyer shows, in a stunning analysis of both music and text, just when and how Schenker's ideas are indeed appropriate and revealing. The response to these separate articles, however, has been typical. Among scholars generally, Kerman's critique has fueled the bias against theory and Schenker in particular, while Neumeyer's conclusions have gone largely unnoticed. For another rebuttal to Kerman's discussion of the Schumann song (or, rather, to Kerman's discussion of Schenker's analysis of the song), see Nicholas Cook, "Music Theory and 'Good Comparison': A Viennese Perspective," *Journal of Music Theory* 33, no. 1 (1989).

48. See Kevin Korsyn, "Schenker's Organicism Reexamined," *Intégral* 7 (1993). Korsyn stresses the association of early organicist thought with the instinct and the unconscious ("instinctive necessity"), above all with what was natural rather than artificial, willed, or mechanical. "Organicism must also be seen in re-

Indeed, how better to approach the individuality of a given work than by analogy to the living organism, to the individuality of the single being? How more appropriately to consider the implications of this concern? Here, too, the metaphor can point not only to relations among parts and wholes but to their sensed particularity as well, to the concrete reality of the whole. And such a reality—what may be sensed as truly identifying—can never be reduced to abstracted parts, but involves a transcending sense of the whole that overwhelms all parts in one way or another. To return briefly to the opening four bars of the Adagio theme of the Beethoven Ninth, Example 2 in chapter 1: the neighbor notes and passing tones that embellish the arpeggiation of the tonic triad in this theme are integral to the context at hand, notwithstanding the purposes they fulfill as common tonal phenomena. And while the bass line of these bars is identical to that of the opening bars of the slow movement of the Pathétique Sonata (Example 3), it too can be experienced as entirely consistent with the individual context of the Adagio of the Ninth.

And so it is, it seems to me, with the physical features and qualities of the individual being. The quality of shyness or reservedness may be shared by a great many individuals. Yet its meaning is derived from the single instance, is defined anew by the context that is provided by each individual whole. And it is the latter whole that is valued by the humanist, the whole that is prized, cherished, and loved accordingly; parts take on meaning or "expressive content" only as they define and are defined by that whole. Homilies of this kind are familiar enough to Gestalt psychology; their association with Schenkerian theory and analysis should not prove hostile to the concerns of the humanist scholar. On the contrary, and as understood here, they underlie those concerns.

---

lation to mechanistic and materialistic trends, as a response to everything that threatened to reduce human beings to mere mechanisms. Thus organicist discourse establishes a polar opposition between organicism and mechanism, in which organicism is the valorized term" (p. 91).

5

The Ninth and Beyond

I

The suggestion has been that, far from being "technically" alienating, many of the traditional practices of theory and analysis can assist in drawing us closer to the musical context. Indeed, we have argued that many of today's complaints have less to do with the practices themselves than with the manner in which they are processed, the outside uses to which they are put, the social, institutional, and professional ends they have come to serve. They have, it seems to me, much to do with manifestations of power, whether institutional, professional, cultural, or defined in terms of gender. For, with the mind's ear properly engaged, the practices themselves can heighten an awareness of the detail of music. And that awareness can become a part of experience, of that which attracts. By such means, music can be made more fully a part of ourselves.

We shall return to the variation theme of Beethoven's Ninth Symphony, examining its content not from the standpoint of Schenkerian theory and analysis, as we did in chapter 1, but from that of the motive and its manipulation. Schenker dealt with motives too, of course, but Schoenberg will be our point of departure here, the tradition of motivic analysis as it has evolved over the past century or so. In particular, we are interested in the close identification of the motive with the individual context, the role of the motive in the building of a context. Individual parts are of concern, in other words, the motivation of those parts as motives, that of the whole by its parts. For although motives can be relatively nondescript in and of themselves, all the various aspects of a context can play a role in their definition, including melody, harmony, rhythm, and instrumentation. They are thus the result of an interaction of those aspects and can reflect the whole as well as the sum, the transcending context itself. And it is their nondescriptness that allows them both to define and to be defined in this way, to become so entirely both an instrument and a reflection of the context. They serve in such a capacity by virtue of the comprehensive nature of the transformation, their transition from abject commonality to contextuality. And the idea, once again, is that an investigation of these matters can enhance not only a sense of intimacy with the materials of music but an appreciation as well.

We shall also be manipulating the motive as a set of interval classes, theorizing by way of the pitch-class set, a practice that must surely rank as the epitome of all that today's New Musicologists most strenuously oppose in theory and analysis. (Pitch-class set analysis would seem to exemplify most conspicuously the formalism, "technical" expertise, and insularity discussed in this connection in earlier chapters.) This is a matter to which we shall be returning in the Epilogue. For the moment, many of the terms and concepts of set theory should be of use, even if we bypass some of the systematic methodology with which those terms are often associated.

We shall want to test the limits of the motive as a means of comparison, a way of moving from one context to another. Transforming motives into pitch-class sets, moving from tonality to atonality (relating as well as separating the two), we shall be examining a number of cases of symmetrical construction in the music of Glinka, Rimsky-Korsakov, and Bartók. From there, our original set will be examined as the referential hexachord of Schoenberg's Suite, Op. 29, a realization that will invoke yet another set of practices, those having to do with the theory and analysis of twelve-tone music.

So, too, aesthetic issues of immediacy and reflection will continue to be of concern in chapter 6. There they will be discussed in

EXAMPLES 10–12. Beethoven, Symphony No. 9, III.

terms of the public-relations wars of Stravinsky's neoclassicism of the 1920s and 1930s. The motive will concern us there as well, as it relates to the alleged dual structures of neoclassical works, the separation of tonal residues from atonal structures. Chapter 7 will examine a number of wider contexts for Stravinsky's music from the standpoint of both pitch and rhythmic structure. Throughout, the octatonicism of Debussy's piano preludes will prove useful as a foil. Nonetheless, our attention will turn from the individuality of separate works to that of the oeuvre and beyond.

2

Shown in Examples 10, 11, and 12 are three separate motivic readings of the opening variation theme (first phrase only) of the Adagio movement of Beethoven's Ninth. In the first of these (Example 10), the four-note motive D–A–Bb–F and its imitation in the bass

EXAMPLE 13.   Beethoven, Symphony No. 9, I.

are bracketed. Here, the motive itself is halved by imitation, halved by its "falling fourths," in effect, the imitation of D–A by B♭–F. And much could be made of the pairing of just these fourths, of the relationship of this pairing to the Adagio as a whole, to this movement's separate variation worlds of B♭ major and D major. Indeed, the origin of those worlds could be traced back to the exposition of the first movement, to the second-theme group in B♭ major (VI), and to the paired statements of the principal theme as well (see Example 13).

At the same time, the four-note motive circumvents structure in the Schenkerian sense of an underlying framework that is elaborated at the surface.[1] For, as shown in Example 11, the opening three and one-half measures of the variation theme arpeggiate the tonic triad (B♭ D F), an arpeggiation that extends from the primary tone D5 to D4 and then back to D5. (See the earlier discussion of this arpeggiation in connection with Example 2 in chapter 1). In re-

1. For Schenker's early views of the motive, see Heinrich Schenker, *Harmony* (1906), ed. Oswald Jonas, trans. Elisabeth Mann Borgese (Chicago: Chicago University Press, 1954), pp. 4–21. For his later views, see Heinrich Schenker, *Free Composition*, trans. Ernst Oster (New York: Longman, 1979), pp. 93–107. See also Charles Burkhart, "Schenker's 'Motivic Parallelisms,'" *Journal of Music Theory* 22, no. 2 (1978); and John Rothgeb, "Thematic Content: A Schenkerian View," in David Beach, ed., *Aspects of Schenkerian Analysis* (New Haven: Yale University Press, 1983), pp. 39–60. The issue of the motive in Schenkerian theory and analysis—that of deciding when the repetition of a segment is indeed a repetition and therefore motivic according to Schenker's later notions of structure, consistent with the integrity of the structural levels—can be a difficult one. Schenker was by no means consistent in his approach, even in his later analyses in *Free Composition*. The issue is given its most comprehensive treatment in Richard Cohn, "The Autonomy of Motives in Schenkerian Accounts of Tonal Music," *Music Theory Spectrum* 14, no. 2 (1992). Here, of course, the four-note motive of "falling fourths," D–A and its imitation in terms of B♭–F, represents a different *grouping* (and hence *structure*) of the four pitches in question from that defined by the arpeggiation of the tonic triad (B♭ D F) and the neighbor note A.

lation to this arpeggiation, the A of the D–A–B♭–F motive functions as an embellishment, an incomplete neighbor note to the B♭.

Consequently, the structure of the four-note motive, the manner of its segmentation, its division into parts and the interrelation of those parts, is far from clear-cut. The motive consists of its falling fourths D–A and the transposition of D–A down a major third to B♭–F, or it consists of an arpeggiation of (B♭ D F) in relation to which the A, grouped with the B♭, is a lower neighbor note. And the larger context fails to resolve this issue. When viewed from different perspectives, each interpretation can seem meaningful.

Critical at this point, then, is the integrity of D–A–B♭–F as a motive. In what sense is it a segment, a part of the thematic whole? If motivic, how is it distinguished as such? Beyond recurrence, what are the conditions of that distinction?

The third reading ignores the falling fourths altogether and opts at least in part for the neighbor-note inflection. Bracketed in Example 12, it consists of the first three notes of the four-note motive, D–A–B♭. And with the motive reduced in size, the motivic plot thickens considerably. Indeed, the imitation in the bass is remarkable at this point. Beginning with the retrograde form G♭–F–B♭, primes, inversions, and retrogrades are linked by one or two notes. And the effect of these transpositions and transformations is one of modification. Each variant singles out aspects of the parent motive D–A–B♭, causing those aspects to be heard and understood in a different light. Traces of D–A–B♭ appear in the surrounding parts, in other words, parts which are made motivic as a result. In turn, the singular identity of D–A–B♭ is gradually undermined. With the distribution of a number of its components, its identity is made more dependent on an evolving context. Indeed, it too could be made a variant. With the process pressed to the limit, D–A–B♭ could lose itself in the context of its surrounding parts, becoming one with those parts, indistinguishable in this respect. And by allowing its segments to be disseminated in this fashion, the theme itself is made contextual. It too is drawn into a "developing variation," is made a part of a larger whole in this respect, dependent on that whole for its meaning and expressive effect. In this way, D–A–B♭ and its variants are made determining factors in the building of

EXAMPLE 14. Bach, "Ach Gott und Herr," *Orgelbüchlein.*

EXAMPLE 15. Stravinsky, *In Memoriam Dylan Thomas*, Prelude.

a context, even if their role in this determination is secondary, subject to the constraints of the tonal process.

All of which is not to suggest that the process in question, context-building by way of the motive and its variants, is unique to the Ninth, the music of the nineteenth century, or beyond. Its dynamics are felt in contexts as diverse (and as extreme) as Bach's chorale prelude "Ach Gott und Herr" (Example 14)[2] and the Prelude to Stravinsky's *In Memoriam Dylan Thomas* (Example 15). Notwith-

2. See the motivic analysis of this prelude in Alexander R. Brinkman, "The Melodic Process in Johann Sebastian Bach's *Orgelbüchlein*," *Music Theory Spectrum* 2 (1980): 47.

standing the discrepancies in pitch structure and general orientation, each of these examples underscores the same process, by these
means relates both to the other and to the variation theme of the
Ninth. And it is by way of such a relationship that the most revealing distinctions concerning these varying contexts are brought to
the fore. (The analytical annotations in Example 15 are Stravinsky's
and were made a part of the published score.)

At this point the motivic plot of the variation theme could be
thickened still more by relaxing the standards of relatedness. We
could ignore tonal structure altogether, the function of A as a
neighbor note to B♭, for example, or that of G♭ as an upper neighbor-
bor to F in the retrograde of the motive, G♭–F–B♭. Indeed, moving
up the ladder of abstraction from a most to a least determinate stage
(with the lower stages subsuming the upper ones), we could disregard order and convert intervals into classes of intervals. Eventually, we would reach the pitch-class set, set-class 3–4—or (0 1 5), to
adopt Allen Forte's nomenclature[3]—according to which D–A–B♭
would be defined by its interval-class content, its vector [100110].
And a willingness to accept the implications of this step, relatedness
or equivalence apropos of D–A–B♭ and its variants at this rather
high level of abstraction, would depend on the context, the sorts of
questions that an engagement might pose.

Accordingly, in Examples 16 and 17, D–A–B♭ is identified by its
interval classes, the motive and its variants by the unordered set of
those classes, (0 1 5). What counts is interval-class content, not
pitch, rhythm, contour, order, or, indeed, distinctions affecting
the linear and harmonic dimensions. And, as the circles demon-

---

3. See Allen Forte, *The Structure of Atonal Music* (New Haven: Yale University
Press, 1973). For a condensed version of Forte's methods, see Allen Forte, *The
Harmonic Organization of "The Rite of Spring"* (New Haven: Yale University Press,
1979), pp. 1–17. As this method is commonly understood, unordered sets of
pitch-classes are reduced to set types by means of transposition or by inversion
followed by transposition; the set types are then compacted into "best normal or-
ders" and finally into "prime forms," to ensure easy comparison. It seems advan-
tageous here to regard the prime forms as defined primarily by interval-class content, notwithstanding the Z-related pairs, pairs of sets that are equivalent in
interval-class content but not in (abstract) pitch-class content. See, in this connection, Christopher F. Hasty, "An Intervallic Definition of Set Class," *Journal of Music Theory* 31, no. 2 (1987): 183–204.

EXAMPLE 16.   Beethoven, Symphony No. 9, III.

EXAMPLE 17.   Beethoven, Symphony No. 9, III.

strate in Example 16, the number of variants increases considerably, in a manner that can bring to mind the pitch-class set analysis of atonal music. Indeed, taking the bracketed variants of Example 12 into account as well, a point of "motivic saturation" would seem to have been reached, one cited often enough in the analysis of atonal music as symptomatic of the atonal idiom itself, indeed, of atonal "coherence."[4] Finally, Example 17 points to five corresponding samples, but without specific reference to the Adagio of the Ninth.

We should note, of course, that many of the variants in Examples 16 and 17 are related in ways more determinate than those defined by the pitch-class set. And it is often the case in the analysis of atonal music as well that Forte's labels are applied irrespective of the ways in which the designated segments relate more determinately. In Examples 16 and 17, all variants are confined to the diatonic set of B♭ major; all are subsets of that set and of that particular trans-

4. See, for example, Joseph N. Straus, *Remaking the Past: Musical Modernism and the Influence of the Tonal Tradition* (Cambridge: Harvard University Press, 1990), p. 27: "Motivic saturation is an organizational principle most closely associated with Schoenberg, Webern, and Berg, yet an overwhelming preoccupation with motivic coherence characterizes a whole range of early twentieth-century music, including much of the work of Stravinsky and Bartók." Straus's analysis of the first of Schoenberg's Three Pieces for Piano, Op. 11, underscores the "motivic orientation" of this music, its "motivic density," "motivic riches," and "extraordinary motivic saturation"—indeed, the "dense web of motivic associations [that] defines the pitch structure of 'freely atonal' music" (pp. 24–26).

position of that set. G♭ is the flatted sixth degree, a species of modal mixture that can be shown to anticipate flat-side "key areas" in the variation sections that lie ahead. The G♭ also relates to the B♭ as B♭ relates to the D, a symmetrical configuration to which we shall be turning in due course. For the moment, however, what is of concern is the local motivic significance of G♭—G♭'s role as a member of G♭–F–B♭ and of the unordered sets (F G♭ B♭) and, by extension, (0 1 5).

Yet the problems that can beset an application of these more abstract forms of relatedness are also apparent in Example 16. Chief among these is the segmentation, which in Example 16 bears little or no relationship to tonal structure. Indeed, the encircled notes and intervals are grouped independently of tonal structure, and often in contradiction to it. (A similar objection could be raised against many of Rudolph Reti's analyses of thematic similarity. With Reti, too, notes may be grouped without regard to their varying contrapuntal functions.)[5] And with few, if any, ties to the tonal process, a process capable of providing this passage with a far more determinate model than that from which a model of the motive and its variants is derivable, the segments in Example 16 are likely to seem arbitrary and beside the point. Crucially, motives and their variants imply no rationale with respect to temporal order.[6] Independently of tonal structure, that is, there can be no implication of succession, no conception of how, for example, one variant might follow another.

And with the analysis of atonal music, where, as a rule, no structure of a determinacy comparable to that of the tonal may be inferred, the segmentation is apt to become that much more problematic.[7] There is no fundamental unit of vocabulary that could be

5. See Rudolph Reti, *The Thematic Process in Music* (London: Faber and Faber, 1961). The same objection could also be raised against Schoenberg's motivic analyses of tonal works. See the discussion of this in Straus, *Remaking the Past*, pp. 29–37. Or see John Rothgeb's review of Walter Frisch's *Brahms and the Principle of Developing Variation* in *Music Theory Spectrum* 9 (1987).

6. See the discussion of the motive and of motivic analysis in general in Leonard B. Meyer, "A Pride of Prejudices; Or, Delight in Diversity," *Music Theory Spectrum* 13, no. 2 (1991): 244–247.

7. I have discussed problems of segmentation at greater length in Pieter C. van

compared to the triad, for example, so that, to an extent far greater than in tonal music, individual structures are indeed individuals; each structure begins anew, as it were, creating its own vocabulary and syntax. So, too, in confronting such a vocabulary even within individual structures, the analyst is forced to retreat to greater abstraction; seeking first to identify and then to relate the segments of a segmentation as sets, he or she must focus on interval classes and abstract pitch-class sets. And the problem here is that, in focusing abstractly in this manner, he or she must remain dependent on an initial segmentation all the same, a process that is apt to depend on those more specific levels of structure from which he or she has been forced to retreat. (Segmentation or grouping implies a more comprehensive process than set-identification and may involve, however unconsciously, a consideration of rhythm, meter, and instrumentation as well as pitch.) Moreover, in keeping with this analytic-theoretical retreat, segments are apt to become identified with abstract sets (and vice versa), recurring sets with motives. And this can be problematic as well, the extent to which such relationships are indeed favorably described as motivic, the extent to which motivic relations can be made to absorb all other functions. Such a one-dimensional approach to musical structure, more specifically to the atonal or post-tonal works of Schoenberg, Berg, and Webern, can seem implausible.

Yet it cannot be denied, it seems to me, that it was by way of the motive and its potential for generalization, the motive pursued from the standpoint of its shape, rhythm, and ordering as well as its pitches, its intervals, and their classes, that Schoenberg was led from the "extended tonality" of such works as *Verklärte Nacht* (1899) and *Pelleas und Melisande* (1903) to the atonal period and beyond. Recalling his discovery of the twelve-tone method circa

---

den Toorn, "What Price Analysis?" *Journal of Music Theory* 33, no. 1 (1989). See also, in this connection, William Benjamin, "Ideas of Order in Motivic Music," *Music Theory Spectrum* 1 (1979); and Richard Taruskin, "Reply to van den Toorn," *In Theory Only* 10, no. 3 (October 1987). For a more detailed account of the sorts of criteria that might apply in the grouping process ("proximity," "dynamics," "registral spacing," etc.), see Christopher F. Hasty, "Segmentation and Process in Post-Tonal Music," *Music Theory Spectrum* 3 (1981).

1921, he noted that his earlier, atonal method had consisted of "working with tones of the motive."[8] And it seems to have been in that light, in fact, that features of that earlier method were regarded as traditional, the process itself as a continuation of the "technique of developing variation."[9] Schoenberg had cited the latter as a "progressive" element in the music of Brahms, in an analysis of Brahms's String Quartet in A Minor, Op. 51/2, that—tellingly here—omitted all mention of tonal voice-leading and harmony.[10]

And so a history of Schoenberg's atonality could no doubt be sketched from the standpoint of the motive and the issue of its abstraction. Such a history could feature the motive as a frontier, relate how the logic of the motive had taken hold, how it had asserted itself independently of tonal constraints, of the framework from which it arose. Moving from "extended tonality" to atonality, it could cite to advantage a number of Schoenberg's recollections:

In my *Verklärte Nacht* the thematic construction is based on Wagnerian "model and sequence" above a roving harmony on the one hand, and on Brahms's technique of developing variation—as I call it—on the other.[11]

The . . . symphonic poem *Pelleas und Melisande* suggests a more rapid advance in the direction of extended tonality. . . . Many of the melodies contain extratonal intervals that demand extravagant movement of the harmony.[12]

The Second String Quartet (1908) . . . marks the transition to my second period. In this period I renounced a tonal center—a procedure incorrectly called "atonality." In the first and second movements there are many sections in which the individual parts proceed regardless of whether or not their meeting results in codified harmonies.[13]

---

8. Arnold Schoenberg, *Style and Idea*, trans. Leo Black, ed. Leonard Stein (Berkeley: University of California Press, 1975), p. 248; "Composition with Twelve Tones (2)" (ca. 1948).

9. Schoenberg, *Style and Idea*, p. 80; "My Evolution" (1947).

10. Schoenberg, *Style and Idea*, pp. 429–431; "Brahms the Progressive" (1947).

11. Schoenberg, *Style and Idea*, p. 80; "My Evolution" (1947).

12. Schoenberg, *Style and Idea*, p. 82; "My Evolution" (1947).

13. Schoenberg, *Style and Idea*, p. 86; "My Evolution" (1947).

Indeed, the escape from what Schoenberg termed the "shackles of tonality" could be described in terms of the motive and its "emancipation."[14] The music could be dubbed—has been dubbed—"motivic,"[15] rather than atonal or "contextual" (Milton Babbitt's term),[16] and for reasons that are compositional and historical as well as analytic-theoretical. Benjamin Boretz's account of these developments runs as follows:

> One might consider that a "motivic" musical language had "grown up" independently "inside" the tonal superstructure in Mahler and Schoenberg, and that the "atonality" of [Schoenberg's Three Pieces for Piano, Op. 11] just realizes the independent-structural implications of this "inner" language, without the tonal superstructure that had actually become a "dichotomous" rather than a "concomitant" aspect. Surely the sound of Op. 11—the surface of simultaneity, register, and duration- and pitch-contour configurations—is virtually that of the "interstices" of [the Chamber Symphony, Op. 9].[17]

My suggestion that "motivic" is a conceptually preferable term for this [atonal] literature derives from a notion that the basis of the compositional approach involved is to be found in the interstitial, non-triadic counterpoint in "extended-tonal" music, where the elaborations between asserted triadic references are so extensive that an "inner" referential basis is essential if one is to account for the structures with a degree of specificity. . . . Thus the triadic sonority model for all linear expansion even in such maximized tonality as is observable in Brahms . . . crosses a threshold in some works of Mahler and Schoenberg, where the maximally extended triadicity is further expanded through a non-triadically referential contrapuntal elaboration. . . . In creating such *internal* phraseological articulations, this counterpoint obviously requires a contextually defined basis for constructing coherent small- and large-scale successions. These are no longer adequately conceivable . . . as simple triadic neighbor-note relations.[18]

---

14. Schoenberg, *Style and Idea*, p. 88; "My Evolution" (1947).

15. See, for example, Benjamin A. Boretz, "Meta-Variations Part IV: Analytic Fall-out (II)," *Perspectives of New Music* 11, no. 2 (1973): 176; and Benjamin, "Ideas of Order in Motivic Music."

16. Milton Babbitt, *Words About Music*, ed. Stephen Dembski and Joseph N. Straus (Madison: University of Wisconsin Press, 1987), p. 9.

17. Boretz, "Meta-Variations, Part IV," p. 177.

18. Boretz, "Meta-Variations, Part IV," p. 176.

Of course, the lure of the motive was felt contextually. And in
this respect it was perhaps not so much a question of a frontier, of
breaking through an atonal sound-barrier, as it was of the individual context and its motivation. The motive was a means toward
that end, toward the context; it served as a way of motivating the
context. And this can be sensed and felt in the variation theme of
the Ninth, it seems to me, even if the tonality of this music lacks
the "extended" features commonly associated with more deliberate
forms of "motivicism." There, too, as is illustrated in Examples 10,
11, and 12, motives and their variants, detached as segments of the
theme, assist in the development of a context. (To explain "developing variation," Schoenberg had relied on the music of several
composers, of course, including that of Beethoven. And his rather
extensive analysis of the first movement of the Beethoven Fifth in
this regard refers to both small-scale motives and larger profiles.[19]
My sense of much of this, in fact, is that an account of what
Schoenberg might have meant by "developing variation," or what
that term can now revealingly be made to represent in tonal music
can bear scrutiny only when tied to Schenkerian notions of harmonic and contrapuntal structure. And this would remain true
even if the motivic path overreached Schenker's structural categories at times and if Schenker's own views of the motive were less
than consistent.)[20]

But according to a history that has grown familiar enough, there
came a point at which the harmonic vocabulary of the Ninth, the
tonal system in general, could no longer be sustained against the
demands of the individual context. Pressed by those demands, the
system could no longer motivate or be motivated. In actual experience, it began to pull too insistently toward its own established
use, one which, in the interests of the context, could no longer be
made transparent. Hence the way of the motive and its "variation,"
a process suggestive of a logic of its own, one that could be pursued
relatively free of the tonal constraints from which it emerged.

19. Schoenberg, *Style and Idea*, pp. 164–165; "Folkloristic Symphonies"
(1947).
20. See Cohn, "The Autonomy of Motives," and cf. footnote 1, above.

For it is not as if the individuality of a context could be confined to a mere part, even a motivic part, segment, configuration, or character trait of one kind or another (shyness, for example). It is not as if, sensed and felt, the individual context could be judged here but not there, a part of this but not of that. Rather, with varying degrees of intensity, a sense of the whole can overwhelm all parts. All parts can partake of the quality of the whole, including arpeggiations, three-note motives, and neighbor-note inflections. All can resonate accordingly, be cast anew by such means, made contextual, individual. And this is consistent with the interests of the observer, it seems to me, which would seem to be to experience each part as integral to the context (as organic in this respect), and for the purpose of experiencing that much more of the context, that much more of that which attracts, in other words.

And the motive and its variants are both carriers and makers of the whole, a circumstance that may well have given rise to Schoenberg's idea of the "basic shape" or *Grundgestalt*. In the long run, everything could be related in one way or another. Relatedness was a matter of kind and degree:

What happens in a piece of music is nothing but the endless reshaping of a basic shape. Or, in other words, there is nothing in a piece of music but what comes from the theme, springs from it and can be traced back to it; to put it more severely, nothing but the theme itself. Or, all the shapes appearing in a piece of music are *foreseen* in the "theme."[21]

So, too, the process is reciprocal. Since the whole both defines and is defined by its parts, the impression it leaves can be that of a whole motivated from within. And it is here that the motive and its contextuality become linked to the notion of an organic whole, one whose parts, being entirely of the whole, are natural rather than artificial or forced from without. Here, too, Schenker's idea of a spontaneously induced whole can take effect, the connection made between naturalness and musical intuition, that which is conceived,

21. Schoenberg, *Style and Idea*, p. 290; "Linear Counterpoint" (1931).

EXAMPLES 18–22. Beethoven, Symphony No. 9, III.

as Schenker put it, with the "sweep of improvisation."[22] And the central issue of music criticism can become relevant as well, insofar as this issue concerns the determination of what might or might not be *true* (natural) to a given context, that is, the nature of a context and its support.

To illustrate these points, and above all that which concerns the context and its making, Examples 18–22 focus on yet another motivic segment of the variation theme of the Ninth, that of the descending third-progression F–Eb–D. This progression is introduced as a preface to the theme (Example 18), where it attaches itself to the fundamental tone D. It then appears in the second and third phrases of the theme (Example 19). Finally, it serves to link the two sets of variations in this movement, the separate worlds of Bb major and D major (Examples 20–22).

Thus, in the final bars of the theme's fourth and final phrase (Example 20), F–Eb–D reappears with its D harmonized in terms of (F♯ A D). The immediate effect of this chord is that of an applied dominant, an application realized in the subsequent repeat of this material at mm. 65–82; there, (F♯ A D) does proceed to (G B D). In Example 20, however, (D F♯ A) is tonicized for the length of the second variation theme. (Recall the "point of recapitulation" in the first movement, where (F♯ A D) is introduced with applied dominant implications, implications that are left unrealized for some twenty-five bars.)

Then, at the end of this second variation theme (Example 21), F–Eb–D reappears with its initial F harmonized in terms of (Bb D F), the chord of the flatted sixth degree in D major. Hence, the shift back to the tonic Bb occurs by means of a deceptive cadence. And of consequence here is the bass line, where the cadence materializes by way of the four-note motive D–A–Bb–F. Hence, in what might appear as a mere incident in the part-writing, the bass line of a deceptive cadence becomes an instrument of the context, one of several whereby the transition is given a contextual bearing.

---

22. Heinrich Schenker, "Organic Structure in Sonata Form," trans. Orin Grossman, in Maury Yeston, ed., *Readings in Schenker Analysis* (New Haven: Yale University Press, 1977), p. 39.

EXAMPLE 23.   Beethoven, Symphony No. 9, III.

Observe, too, that there is a *continuation* of the theme at this point: A–D–B♭–F in the bassoons and lower strings becomes linked to the third-progression F–E♭–D in the clarinet, a linkage that yields the larger thematic segment A–D–B♭–F–E♭–D. And, as is shown by the reduction of this passage in Example 22, a further continuation of the theme in the clarinet straddles the double bar, allowing for a stretto with the entrance of the first violins at m. 43. In these ways a sense of the "presentness" of this music is sustained and enhanced. At stake is the context itself, its integrity, the common tonal functions that are realized accordingly. Sought above all is an image ever more specific, one that can invoke a sense of immediacy, sustain and nourish an aesthetic presence.

In effect, the return to the tonic and the initial variation theme comes by way of a cadential cliché, the deceptive cadence to the flatted sixth degree in D major. And in terms of the context, the cadence is motivated not only by the key relationship, B♭ as ♭VI in D major, but also by the ability of the four-note motive D–A–B♭–F to be redefined in these terms. Thus, too, both keys, B♭ major and D major (III), are approached abruptly and deceptively; as is reproduced in Example 23, each of the two tonics is approached by way of the dominant of the other, and then by way of a dominant seventh in root position with its seventh on top. In each case, too, the cadence is attached to the third progression F–E♭–D.

There are other correspondences as well. Encircled in Example 24 is the F–G♭ unit in m. 2, a neighbor-note motion that anticipates enharmonically the deceptive F–F♯ shift to D major (III) in m. 23. And D–A of the four-note motive in m. 3 is likewise linked to the

EXAMPLE 24.   Beethoven, Symphony No. 9, III.

deceptive shift to (F♯ A D) at m. 23. Hence, as Schoenberg would no doubt have insisted, the transition to and from D major is "foreseen" in the theme; the details of these passages stem from, are of consequence by virtue of, the theme. Once again, the theme and its disengaged motives carry the context, act as a principal means by which the context makes itself felt.

And there can be no better way of representing this music, it seems to me, of drawing the listener into the web of its detail. For it is precisely by "noticing" that detail, the detail of an individualization, that the experience is given greater depth. Indeed, for those mindful of the context, the objective likely to surpass all others is that of experiencing more of that context. And the greater the depth, the more intense the experience; the greater the potential for intimacy. As one astute observer put it:

The experience of hearing one melodic line as an inversion of another while being aware only of a vague similarity between them differs from the experience of *noticing* that the one melody is the inversion of the other. (To notice something is, approximately, to perceive it while acknowledging one's perceiving of it.) So an analysis which, by specifying what I hear in a piece, helps me to acknowledge what I hear in it, changes my experience at the same time that it enhances my understanding of it.[23]

So analyses are probably, more often than one might have thought, specifications of what we hear. The possibility is open that even the Schenkerian deep structure of a piece, or the fact that the foreground and middleground are elaborations of the deep structure, is in fact an unacknowledged part of the content of musical experiences even of ordinary listeners. Listeners' inability to specify the tone row of a twelve tone piece is not sufficient to establish that they do not hear it. An analysis of a piece may amount to a speculation about what might be in the unacknowledged content of the analyst's or other listeners' experiences.[24]

So, too, detailed analyses of the kind offered here of the motive and its context need not supersede or conflict with more general forms of comment, including sociopolitical comment. As was exemplified by the variation movement of the Ninth, third relations or common-tone modulations have been viewed as a large-scale alternative to the "heroic" style of Beethoven's middle period. Included more specifically from that movement have been the third-related worlds of D major and B♭ major, the abrupt shifts between those worlds, their calm, lyrical quality, and their ramifications in thematic character and form. (The Ninth's twin worlds are "foreseen" not only in the variation theme, the four-note motive and its falling fourths, but in the first and second theme groups of the first movement as well. They are anticipated by the paired thematic statements in the exposition of that movement, as was shown in Example 13.) And the character of this alternative could no doubt be described as "sensually gratifying," "pleasurable," even "casual"

23. Kendall L. Walton, "Understanding Humor and Understanding Music," *Journal of Musicology* 11, no. 1 (1993): 43.
24. Walton, "Understanding Humor," p. 42.

or "self-indulgent,"[25] that of the contrasting "heroic" style as "driven," "developmental," "demonic," "patriarchal," and so forth. The problem here derives, not from the descriptions themselves, but from their pursuit. In the present case, the two styles of Beethoven's music, late and "heroic" (or middle-period), have been tied to conflicts of gender and sexual orientation. With the music of Schubert, for example, third relations of a kind similar to those encountered in the Beethoven Ninth have been linked to Schubert's sexuality, to details of his supposed sexual indulgence, "hedonism," or homosexuality.[26] But the relations in question are equally characteristic of the Beethoven Ninth and other late works of this presumably heterosexual composer.[27] Against the demonstration of a sexual particularity, then, the music cannot respond in kind. Greater detail on one side of the equation cannot be matched on the other, so that, as was seen in earlier chapters, the connection itself is placed in doubt. Beyond the suggestion itself, the initial point of contact, the premise cannot be sustained. And my own view is that a detailed account of Schubert's sexual life would contribute very little to an understanding of his music, to, above all, his instrumental music. And this would apply generally as well. For we cannot assume that, consciously or unconsciously, the homosexual composer (if this is what Schubert was) would be any more inclined toward an imagined musical acknowledgment of his sexual identity and its sociopolitical ramifications than of his intersecting or transcending ties, of an imagined celebration of that which separates rather than which binds, of, that is, idiosyncrasy rather than commonality and convention.[28]

25. See Susan McClary, "Constructions of Subjectivity in Schubert's Music," in *Queering the Pitch: The New Gay and Lesbian Musicology,* ed. Philip Brett et al. (New York: Routledge, 1994). See also Maynard Solomon, "Franz Schubert and the Peacocks of Benvenuto Cellini," *19th-Century Music* 12, no. 1 (1989): 193–206.
26. See McClary, "Constructions of Subjectivity."
27. Of the many works that apply in this respect, see, for its many third relations, the Adagio of Beethoven's String Quartet in E♭ Major, Op. 127; or the famed Cavatina from the String Quartet in B♭ Major, Op. 130, whose contrasting middle section moves directly from E♭ to C♭, the key of the flatted sixth degree, and by way of E♭ as the sustained "common tone." Subsequently, C♭ major moves to A♭ minor.
28. See, in this connection, Susan McClary's analysis of the first movement of

Moreover, while innumerable composers can no doubt be cred-
ited with the idiosyncrasies of a distinctive voice, the medium of
music, in contrast to that of art or literature, is too indirect to be
able to reflect the kinds of specifics alluded to here. So precarious
are some of these identifications, in fact, that, for this observer at
least, their motivation continues to appear entirely sociopolitical.[29]

Tchaikovsky's Fourth Symphony, in Susan McClary, *Feminine Endings: Music,
Gender, and Sexuality* (Minneapolis: University of Minnesota Press, 1991), pp. 69–
79. In what appears to be an obvious reference to the composer's homosexuality
(and to McClary's evident sympathy with that biography), McClary alleges that
the "patriarchal grid" of the sonata form has undergone a number of modifications: Tchaikovsky is alleged to have replaced the expected "masculine" or "heroic" first theme with a "limping" one that is "vulnerable and indecisive" in character and to have succeeded to the latter with a "sluttish" second theme that is
marked by "chromatic slippage," and that is "seductive and slinky" as a result (p.
71). At the same time, the sympathetic protagonist (first theme) is victimized both
by "patriarchal expectations" and by "sensual feminine entrapment" (p. 76); the
narrative may "operate off of the stereotypical late nineteenth-century characterizations and narratives of misogyny," but it is "not standard misogyny" (p. 79).
The expectations for this music are astonishing, in my view—the specific circumstances it is expected to reflect, the services it is to render. Spurred evidently by
sociopolitical sympathy as well as by the politics of the issue, McClary's description of the music is bluntly stereotypical, tied explicitly to stereotypical images of
homosexuality and sociopolitical struggle in this regard. But to the extent that her
aim was in fact the sympathetic appreciation of Tchaikovsky rather more than
Tchaikovsky's music, that aim too may be open to question. For her approach in
this latter respect is trite, sentimental, and ultimately self-serving; that to homosexuality in general, very nearly conventionally homophobic in its implications.
One suspects that Tchaikovsky himself would have been more pleased had the focus remained on his music rather than on McClary's sympathies, her somewhat
tarnished views of homosexuality and its wider implications. Indeed, in a final
about-face, she advises that the first movement need not be heard and understood
along these lines at all, that it can be heard "as portraying a more 'universal' oedi-
pal pattern, or as a nonspecific struggle with both power and sensual enticements,
or in any number of ways" (p. 77).
    29. A similar conclusion is reached in James Webster, "Music, Pathology, Sex-
uality, Beethoven, Schubert," *19th-Century Music* 17, no. 1 (1993): 92–93. But see,
nonetheless, that issue of *19th-Century Music*, edited, with a preface, by Lawrence
Kramer, devoted in its entirety to the matter of Schubert's sexuality, and with con-
tributions by Rita Steblin, Maynard Solomon, Kristina Muxfeldt, David Gramit,
V. Kofi Agawu, Susan McClary, James Webster, and Robert Winter. Most curious
in this collection (apart from its complete lack of musical illustrations) is the opening exchange between Steblin and Solomon, one as positivist in tone as anything
imaginable from the more expected sources, including applications of set theory.
(For the New Musicologists, evidently, "correctness" involves subject matter as

Laudably, no doubt, they can sometimes promote the sociopolitical interests of groups with a record of suppression and illtreatment—of homosexuals, in this instance. But the interests of music and its appreciation are made marginal as a result.

Of continuing concern here, then, is the four-note motive, and specifically its transformation from the tonal environment of the Ninth to one that is symmetrical. With the additional link of a fourth, in fact, it can be made a part of various recurring cycles and, in the process, can exude a musical logic different in kind from that of tonality. Still, its history can be traced from the standpoint of its context, of the tonal constraints that were gradually subverted and set aside. Here, however, it will be its symmetrical implications that will be examined in light of that gradual subversion.

3

Indeed, a sense of intimacy can pervade relations of considerable abstraction. Even the properties of an abstract set, especially when symmetrical or when exhibiting what Richard Cohn has termed "Transpositional Combination,"[30] can assume a tangible character, be identifiable from one context to the next. They can serve as points of intersection, in other words, as a framework from which

---

well as attitude; only "correct" subjects such as sex and sexuality could have been treated so "incorrectly," in my view, in a way so wearily painstaking and eloquently detached.) Also curious here is Solomon's disclaimer of the musical significance of his disclosures, to the effect that "[i]t ought to go without saying that neither Schubert nor his music is definable by his sexuality" (p. 45). In other words, following the most elaborate inquiry into Schubert's sexual proclivities, there is at the end little more than the beating of a hasty retreat; on the crucial matter of the effect of these proclivities not only on the composer himself and his composing but on the reception of his music, the effect of knowledge of them on our ability to hear, understand, and appreciate that music, Solomon begs off. One could legitimately question the point of Solomon's publication, above all in a journal of music.

30. Richard Cohn, "Inversional Symmetry and Transpositional Combination in Bartók," *Music Theory Spectrum* 10 (1988). "Any pitch set or pitch-class set has the [Transpositional Combination] property if it may be disunited into two or more transpositionally related subsets" (p. 23).

	mm. 40–41		m. 41	
	(A)	G	F	E♭
cl. 4-note motive (descending)	D	A	B♭	F
		V7		V7
	D major		B♭ major	

Figure 1.

to gauge greater detail. They can partake of the quality of a whole, be made to resonate with such a quality.

In the variation movement of the Ninth, consider the symmetrical implications of the key relationship between B♭ major and D major. D is III in B♭, of course, and B♭ is ♭VI in D. Yet there is a separateness to the relationship, a separation between the two keys and the material presented, that can be understood irrespective of these tonal degrees and functions, of two major scales (or triads) relating to each other by a major third. And the separation is underscored not only by the contrasting material but also by the abruptness of many of the shifts from one area to the other. The two worlds relate, in other words, yet are separate, and in a way that need not be hierarchical.

Consider, too, the four-note motive and its falling fourths, D–A and B♭–F. In the first movement of the Ninth (Example 13), the two fourths are represented by the two third-related keys, harmonized in terms of (D F A) and (B♭ D F), respectively. In the Adagio, however, they are paired under one key, that of B♭, and in the principal variation theme. Yet the separation is evident here as well, above all in the deceptive cadence at m. 41 (Example 23), where D major is cut off abruptly by the return to (B♭ D F). No doubt, (B♭ D F) at m. 41 is colored by D, just as D is colored retrospectively by the deceptive return to B♭. Locally, however, the two worlds are split, cut off from each other by the falling fourths: D–A relates to D, B♭–F to B♭. The passage can be conceptualized as shown in Figure 1.

The symmetrical implications of the four-note motive may be completed by an additional transposition to B♭, down a major

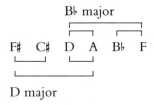

Figure 2.

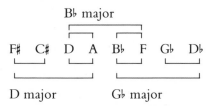

Figure 3.

third. The result is a cycle of intervals, defined by alternating intervals of 1 and 5 (alternating half-steps and fourths). With D–A as a common link, the conception is as shown in Figure 2. B♭–F could also function as such a link, in which case the spelling of the graph would reflect B♭ major as much as D major, with G♭ as one of two flatted sixth degrees. An overlapping of one link would be required, namely, F♯–C♯ or G♭–D♭ (Fig. 3).[31]

Observe, however, that Figure 3 is also a compound cycle, a combination of two interval-4 cycles, two augmented triads. And the earlier clarinet segment (A)–G–F–E♭ has been omitted. Along with the falling fourths of the four-note motive, it too could be extended a notch, for the purpose of completing a cycle, an interval-2 cycle, a whole-tone scale (Fig. 4). (Recall the role of (A)–G–F–E♭ in the deceptive cadence at m. 41, the third-progression F–E♭–D in moving to and from D major. See Examples 23 and 24.)

No doubt the tonal interpretation is problematic at this point, especially given the bluntness of the formulation, the vertical line separating B♭ major from D major. As was suggested in connection with the flatted sixth degree, F♯ (G♭) on the right side can relate

31. Overlapping three-note motives could also have been featured in these graphs, the parent motive D–A–B♭ and its transpositions B♭–F–G♭ and G♭–D♭–D.

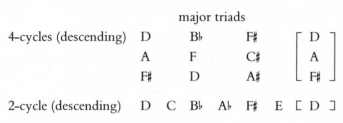

2-cycle (cl.)	A	G	F	E♭	C♯	B	A	G
4-cycles (descending)	D		B♭		F♯		D	
		A		F		C♯		A
	B♭ major				D major			

Figure 4.

		major triads						
4-cycles (descending)	D	B♭	F♯	⌈ D ⌉				
	A	F	C♯	A				
	F♯	D	A♯	⌊ F♯ ⌋				
2-cycle (descending)	D	C	B♭	A♭	F♯	E	⌈ D ⌉	

Figure 5.

EXAMPLE 25.   Glinka, *Russlan and Ludmilla*, Overture.

to B♭ major on the left, just as B♭ on the left can relate to D major on the right. Indeed, the entire cycle is interpretable in terms of one of the three third-related keys, D, B♭, or G♭.

Indeed, it is likely to be at this point that the musical logic of the cycle takes hold. Founded on symmetry and an equal division of the octave, its pulls and attractions may be felt independently of tonal functions. This is true of the passage quoted in Example 25, a passage drawn from the overture to Glinka's *Russlan and Ludmilla* (1842). There, a sense of the symmetrical confinement of the interval-4 cycle, of the three triads rooted on D, B♭, and F♯, is unmistakable. And as the cycle descends, the fourths of the triadic succession are exposed as well. In addition, the bass outlines an interval-2 cycle, a descending scale stretching to and from the tonic D (Fig. 5).

EXAMPLE 26.   Glinka, *Russlan and Ludmilla*, Overture.

EXAMPLE 27.   Rimsky-Korsakov, *Antar Symphony*, Introduction.

Yet it would be difficult to isolate this passage from the overture as a whole, separating it from its tonal surroundings. Significantly in this respect, both cycles descend; B♭ can relate to the flatted sixth degree in D (it can resonate accordingly, in my view), while the 2-cycle in the bass can relate to the descending D-major scale, one that is chromatically altered. (See, in this connection, Example 26.) In other words, pitches along both cycles *intersect* with tonal degrees (D as the tonic and B♭ as the flatted sixth degree, for example), an intersection that can cause the functional behavior of both cycles and of the D-major tonality to become blurred, the structure itself to become ambiguous. And the ambiguity of structure, of a symmetrical construction tied as yet to tonal degrees and functions, is typical of much of the chromatic music of the latter part of the nineteenth century, as it is indeed of much of the music of Bartók and Stravinsky.

Indeed, it is exemplified again in the introduction to Rimsky-Korsakov's *Antar Symphony* (1876), the opening measures of which are shown in Example 27. The triads rooted on F♯, D, and B♭ are

minor triads

C♯	D	A	B♭	F	F♯	(C♯)
F♯	F	D	D♭	B♭	A	(F♯)

4-cycle   A   F   D♭   (A)

Figure 6.

minor instead of major, yet the cycles of alternating intervals of 1 and 5 and of 1 and 3 lie fully exposed. So, too, the falling fourths are exposed, above all by the triplet motives C♯–D–A and A–B♭–F that spring from the initial progression. At the same time, the symmetrical implications eventually interact with diatonic material. The symmetry may be designed as shown in Figure 6.

For the moment, however, we might focus our attention on what has figured centrally in this discussion, namely, the hexachord comprising the three falling fourths D–A, B♭–F, and F♯–C♯. Three representations have surfaced thus far: falling fourths (a hybrid cycle of alternating 1s and 5s), two augmented triads (two interval-4 cycles), and three major or minor triads rooted along one of the latter augmented triads. Given the common pitch-class content, a common designation would seem to be in order, one capable of referring to all three representations. Here, Forte's "normal order" would seem an appropriate choice; it would place the six pitch-classes in ascending order and compress them to within the smallest interval.[32] The result is (A B♭ C♯ D F F♯) in the present case, although, given the symmetrical implications, the same intervallic ordering could have been obtained at C♯ and F. Notice that the ordering is a hybrid cycle, one of alternating 1s and 3s.

And were we to include transposition in the equation, a neutral medium would be appropriate, a numbering by semi-tonal count, for example, with the results transposed to zero (0 = C) as a point of reference: (9 10 1 2 5 6) transposed to (0 1 4 5 8 9). We would then have arrived at the pitch-class set once again, but to a symmetrical set, one that inverts into itself. The set (0 1 4 5 8 9) is the "prime

---

32. Forte, *The Structure of Atonal Music*, pp. 3–5.

form" of Forte's set-class 6–20.[33] It is also Ernö Lendvai's "1:3 Model" scale, one of many scales with which Lendvai has scanned the systematic imprint of Bartók's music.[34] And it is one of Babbitt's "source sets" as well, one of six all-combinatorial hexachords.[35] In generalized form, 6–20 has a history, in other words, one that can be heard and understood to straddle different idioms and compositional methods.[36] In a referential capacity of one kind or another, it figures heavily in the music of Bartók, and to some extent in that of Scriabin as well.[37] It is the hexachord of Webern's Concerto (1934), Op. 24, and of both Schoenberg's Suite (1926), Op. 29, and his *Ode to Napoleon* (1942), Op. 41. It figures in Babbitt's music, above all in the *Composition for Four Instruments* (1948), third and fourth movements, and the *Composition for Twelve Instruments* (1948). Yet it plays virtually no role in the music of Stravinsky.

And its properties are worth noting. Lacking 2s and 6s (whole tones and tritones), its encompassed symmetry is of a high degree, one of 6, in fact, according to John Rahn's calculations: 6–20 maps into itself three times under transposition and three times under inversion.[38] Thus, the prime form (0 1 4 5 8 9) duplicates itself under transposition at 0, 4, and 8; under inversion, at 1, 4, and 9. So, too, in pitch-class content, there are but *four* distinct forms of 6–20: apart from complete invariance, a given form may intersect with two others by way of an augmented triad, and with one other—its twelve-tone complement—not at all. (Only the whole-tone hexachord, 6–35, is more redundant in this respect. Under transposition or inversion it yields sets that are either completely identical or

33. Forte, *The Structure of Atonal Music*, p. 180.
34. Ernö Lendvai, *The Workshop of Bartók and Kodaly* (Budapest: Editio Musica, 1983).
35. Milton Babbitt, "Some Aspects of Twelve-Tone Composition," *The Score and I.M.A. Magazine* 12 (1955): 57.
36. See the discussion of the hexachord 6–20 and its application in Rzewski's music in Robert W. Wason, "Tonality and Atonality in Frederic Rzewski's *Variations on 'The People United Will Never Be Defeated,'*" *Perspectives of New Music* 26, no. 1 (1988).
37. See the discussion of Scriabin's Tenth Sonata in James M. Baker, *The Music of Alexander Scriabin* (New Haven: Yale University Press, 1986), p. 214.
38. John Rahn, *Basic Atonal Theory* (New York: Longman, 1980), p. 91.

EXAMPLE 28.   Bartók, *Concerto for Orchestra*, III.

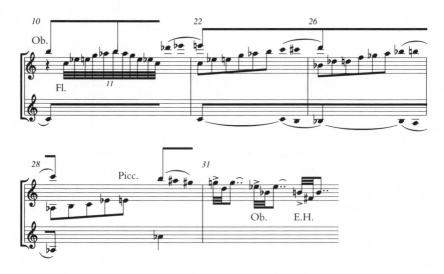

nonidentical.) Although limited, the subset structure of 6–20 is exotic: two augmented triads exhaust the set, as do six minor and major triads rooted along one of the two augmented triads. Its other
two trichordal subsets are (0 1 4) and (0 1 5).

Shown in Example 28 is a passage from the third movement
("Eligia") of Bartók's *Concerto for Orchestra* (1944). Here, the set appears motivically as a cycle, Lendvai's "1:3 Model" scale of alternating 1s and 3s. It is introduced as an arpeggio, C–E♭–E–G–A♭–B,
and is repeated as such for some nine measures in an exchange between the clarinet and flute. The high B is isolated from the configuration and repeated in the oboe and piccolo as a separate layer. The
cycle returns at m. 22 and is subjected to a series of transpositions
by whole step. When, at m. 28, A♭ is reached, the original content
is retrieved, allowing for a return of the high B in the piccolo. A
final transposition exposes the now familiar falling fourths, at m.
31 along the G–E♭–B interval-4 cycle.

Of course, the twelve-tone system imposes conditions that are
new and different. Situated on each side of a hexachordal bar, 6–20
is ordered twice, with each ordering representing, in pitch-class
content, the twelve-tone complement of the other. And while, at

EXAMPLE 29.   Schoenberg, *Suite*, Op. 29, Gigue.

various levels of structure, each of the 6–20 hexachords may be treated independently of the other, the row imposes an ordering on all twelve pitch-classes: operations of transposition and inversion permute that which is given as a premise. At its most fundamental level, then, the system is driven by considerations of order.

Thus, in the Gigue of Schoenberg's *Suite* (Example 29), many of the characteristics of the older form are preserved: the 12/8 signature along with a fugal texture that is introduced with a series of fugal entries. Yet the theme itself is a twelve-tone row, P_3 in the clarinet, a form that is answered by its inversion (a contour-inversion, in fact), I_8 in the bass clarinet.[39] More significantly, the answer is accompanied in the piano and clarinet by a second statement of the prime form, P_3. And the relationship defined by these simultaneously imposed row forms is combinatorial: the corresponding hexachords of these forms combine to produce two aggregates, totalities of the twelve pitch-classes that are ordered only

39. The numbering of the transpositions begins with $0 = C$; the pitch-class numbering is fixed accordingly.

P₃: E♭ G F♯ B♭ D B   C A A♭ E F D♭

I₈: G♯ E F D♭ A C   B D E♭ G F♯ B♭

Figure 7.

with respect to the individual hexachords, not with respect to their combination. The P_3 and I_8 forms are as shown in Figure 7.

Moreover, the transposition that occasions this relationship is defined by the interval of 5. And here, too, a detail in the serial apparatus of the *Suite* would ultimately become an integral part of Schoenberg's method: as is well known, his rows are constructed in such a way that, between the first hexachord of a prime form and its inversion at the interval of 5, no pitch-classes are held in common. Schoenberg never explained the significance of the interval of transposition or of the aggregate-forming potential of the combinatorial relationship.[40] He spoke more generally of a theme in need of an accompaniment, and of an accompaniment in need of a hexachord, one that could avoid octave doublings:

Personally, I endeavor to keep the series such that the inversion of the first six tones a fifth lower gives the remaining six tones. The consequent, the seventh to twelfth tones, is a different sequence of these second six tones. This has the advantage that one can accompany melodic phrases made

40. For a discussion of closely related issues, however, see David Lewin, "Inversional Balance as an Organizing Force in Schoenberg's Music and Thought," *Perspectives of New Music* 6, no. 2 (1968). Discussion by others of the combinatorial relationship has been extensive. See, for instance, Babbitt, "Some Aspects of Twelve-Tone Composition," pp. 53–61; Milton Babbitt, "Set Structure as a Compositional Determinant," *Journal of Music Theory* 5, no. 1 (1961); Donald Martino, "The Source Set and Its Aggregate Formations," *Journal of Music Theory* 5, no. 2 (1961); Daniel Starr and Robert Morris, "A General Theory of Combinatoriality and the Aggregate (I)," *Perspectives of New Music* 16, no. 1 (1977); Daniel Starr and Robert Morris, "A General Theory of Combinatoriality and the Aggregate (II)," *Perspectives of New Music* 16, no. 2 (1977); Bruce Samet, *Hearing Aggregates* (Philadelphia: Pennsylvania State University Press, 1989). The general idea can be gained from a number of surveys and textbooks: see especially Charles Wuorinen, *Simple Composition* (New York: Longman, 1979), pp. 121–127; and Joel Lester, *Analytic Approaches to Twentieth-Century Music* (New York: W. W. Norton, 1989), pp. 175–218.

I₃	7	6	10	2	11	0	9	8	4	5	1	
P₃	Eb	G	F#	Bb	D	B	C	A	Ab	E	F	Db	**R₃**
11	B	Eb	D	F#	Bb	G	Ab	F	E	C	Db	A	
0	C	E	Eb	G	B	Ab	A	F#	F	Db	D	Bb	
8	Ab	C	B	Eb	G	E	F	D	Db	A	Bb	F#	
4	E	Ab	G	B	Eb	C	Db	Bb	A	F	F#	D	
7	G	B	Bb	D	F#	Eb	E	Db	C	Ab	A	F	
6	F#	Bb	A	Db	F	D	Eb	C	B	G	Ab	E	
9	A	Db	C	E	Ab	F	F#	Eb	D	Bb	B	G	
10	Bb	D	Db	F	A	F#	G	E	Eb	B	C	Ab	
2	D	F#	F	A	Db	Bb	B	Ab	G	Eb	E	C	
1	Db	F	E	Ab	C	A	Bb	G	F#	D	Eb	B	
5	F	A	Ab	C	E	Db	D	B	Bb	F#	G	Eb	

RI₃

Figure 8.

from the first six tones with harmonies made from the second six tones, without getting doublings.[41]

It remains curious nonetheless that a fixed interval of transposition should have been applied to 6–20, a hexachord with such an extraordinary capability along these lines. Twelve row forms reproduce the combinatorial relationship described above. More specifically, it is reproduced at three transpositional levels of the standard permutations, and an additional set of twelve forms reproduces the relationship in reverse, from the standpoint of its retrograde. The matrix is as shown in Figure 8.

All of which is not to suggest that Schoenberg was unaware of this potential. Several sketches reproduced in Martha Hyde's study list the first twelve combinatorially related forms, and there are others that suggest an awareness of the second set of twelve as

41. Letter from Schoenberg to Josef Rufer, 8 April 1950, quoted in Martha Hyde, *Schoenberg's Twelve-Tone Harmony: The Suite Op. 29 and the Compositional Sketches* (Ann Arbor: UMI Research Press, 1982), p. 99.

well.[42] Hyde herself examines a great many sketches that group tri-chords and tetrachords, segments of row forms that are not invari-ably combinatorial in these specific respects. And some of these are exquisite, pointing to the variety of combinations that were evi-dently tried and tested in one way or another. Indeed, Schoen-berg seems to have started very nearly from scratch, with a great deal of trial and error. And while some of this activity—"pre-compositional," in effect—can be traced to the lack of a systematic focus (as Babbitt has suggested),[43] much of it is symptomatic of twelve-tone composition in general, a method that builds from the ground up, with very little in the way of shared assumptions. This is reflected in the high degree to which twelve-tone structures are contextual or "self-referential," the degree to which, beginning with the ordering of the row, they refer only to themselves.[44] They

42. Hyde, *Schoenberg's Twelve-Tone Harmony*, pp. 48–49.

43. See Babbitt, *Words About Music*, p. 14: "Schoenberg never understood the generality of the principles involved. . . . Toward the end of his life, he wrote the *Modern Psalms*, a set of little pieces for which he wrote the text. He never realized that the series he used there—a third-order all-combinatorial series—he had al-ready used in the *Ode to Napoleon* and in the Opus 29 *Suite*. He never thought of these hexachords except in a particular ordering, and he never saw the generality of the unordered form."

44. This is Babbitt's view again, namely, that the communal aspects of twelve-tone works are limited to "principles of formation and transposition" (Babbitt, *Words About Music*, p. 17). Babbitt has always insisted on "a completely autono-mous conception of the twelve-tone system . . . in which all components, in all dimensions, would be determined by the relations and operations of the system" (Babbitt, "Some Aspects of Twelve-Tone Composition," p. 55). Ignored, there-fore, is the "transference to twelve-tone composition of criteria belonging to triadic music" (Babbitt, "Some Aspects of Twelve-Tone Composition," p. 55). Yet it was precisely that "transference" to Schoenberg's twelve-tone music of the forms of tonal music ("rondo," "gigue," "sonata," and the like), as well as the "transference" of processes of thematic construction and motivic development, that led Boulez to dismiss that music as "dead" (in Pierre Boulez, *Notes of an Ap-prenticeship*, trans. Herbert Weinstock [New York: Knopf, 1968], pp. 268–276); that has led many present-day commentators to regard it as essentially neoclassical (Scott Messing, *Neoclassicism in Music from the Genesis of the Concept Through the Schoenberg/Stravinsky Polemic* [Ann Arbor: UMI Research Press, 1988], and Straus, *Remaking the Past*); and that led Leonard Meyer to equate it with the need to remain musically intelligible. According to Meyer, the "transference" of such forms and processes was not meekly "nostalgic" (as Boulez had insisted), but arose out of a practical need to be understood: "Contemporary composers have employed 'borrowed' forms and procedures not solely (or even primarily) because

EXAMPLE 30.   Schoenberg, *Suite*, Op. 29, Overture.

share operations more readily than structures. In the case of the *Suite*, the residue is marked by a wealth of charts, tables, and scribblings, much of it without direct reference to the music.

Shown in Example 30 are the opening two measures of the *Suite*. As is indicated, a separate row form is assigned to each dotted-

they considered themselves to be heirs to the great tradition of European art music . . . but because they had virtually no alternative. They could not do without some way of deciding how the motivic variants they invented should be combined with or succeed one another" (Meyer, "A Pride of Prejudices," p. 247).

	P₃			I₈			I₁₀			I₃		
winds	B	D♯	F♯	C♯	E	G♯	E♭	G♭	B♭	E♭	G	B
strings	B	D	F♯	A	C♯	E	B	D♯	F♯	E	G	B
	G	B	D	F	A	C	G	B	D	E	G♯	B
cello, b. cl.*	(E♭)	G	B♭	F	(A♭)	C	G	(B♭)	D	A♭	C	(E♭)
piano	A	C	E	G	B	D	A	C♯	E	F♯	A	B♭
	D♭	F	A♭	E♭	G♭	B♭	F	A♭	C	D	D♭	F

*encircled pcs

Figure 9.

quarter-note beat: P₃, I₈, I₁₀, and I₃. And the segmentation of these forms is clearly hexachordal. The chords in the wind and string sections state the first hexachord of each form while the piano states the second. And the articulation of the first hexachord is chordal, whereas that of the second is linear. A more incisive delineation of the hexachordal bar would be difficult to imagine.

At the same time, totalities of the twelve pitch-classes extend not only vertically to the individual row forms but horizontally across the bar line as well. Aggregates (or secondary sets) are formed by the first two chords of the wind and string sections, the first hexachords of P₃ and I₈, and by the second and third chords as well, the first hexachords of I₈ and I₁₀. Here again, of course, the same formula applies to the complementary hexachords in the piano. Figure 9 gives a summary of the scheme, with brackets indicating the four overlapping aggregates.

But this, too, could be condensed. Since each of the four distinct forms of 6–20 is a combination of two augmented triads, each could be identified in these terms. The four augmented triads are as follows:

$$A = \text{E♭} \quad G \quad B \qquad\qquad C = \text{D♭} \quad F \quad A$$
$$B = D \quad \text{F♯} \quad \text{B♭} \qquad\qquad D = C \quad E \quad \text{G♯}$$

	P_3	I_8	I_{10}	I_3
winds, strings	AB	CD	AB	AD
piano	CD	AB	CD	BC

Figure 10.

And by applying these labels to the hexachords themselves, the scheme shown in Figure 10 results. Notice that hexachords AB and CD to the left of the vertical line share the augmented triads A and C with their corresponding hexachords to the right; no aggregates are formed with these corresponding hexachords, therefore, and row forms I_{10} and I_3 are not hexachordally combinatorial. The articulation of the final chord in the wind section is altered, with the substitution of an augmented triad for the triad.

Most astonishing, however, is the triadic segmentation of the hexachords. As has been noted, 6–20 contains six triads, three minor and three major triads rooted along one of two augmented triads. Four triads are assigned to each of the first three chords in the wind and string sections, three to the fourth and final chord. Additional triads, representing the complementary hexachords, are separated by the left and right hands of the piano part. In all, *fifteen* triads are sounded within the first two measures of the *Suite*, a period spanning five or so seconds. The problem is that the sound of these triads is obscured by the density of the configurations. And it is obscured by the complementation as well, by the frequency with which the total chromatic is sounded. Yet the segmentation and its notation are scrupulously triadic. (The one exception is the bass clarinet part, which doubles the cello line.)

And the distance separating these measures from the passage examined from *Russlan and Ludmilla*, Example 26, can seem formidable. In the earlier example, a single form of 6–20 prevailed for a considerable duration. (This was true as well, of course, of the passage from Bartók's *Concerto for Orchestra* shown in Example 28.) And not only did the triads of the passage succeed one another, but two of the triads, (D F♯ A) and (B♭ D F), related handily to the D-major tonality of the overture as a whole. But in the opening measures of the *Suite*, all four forms of 6–20 are represented. And the first hexachord of each of the first three row forms is a superimposition of four triads; the first hexachord of the fourth and final chord, a superimposition of three. And each of these hexachords is followed by its twelve-tone complement. Indeed, four row forms, together with four aggregates in overlapping sets of two, are completed within the given period. And so the triad remains at issue, not only from the standpoint of its audition but conceptually as well. Is the effect of its superimposition, a clashing of triads separated by major thirds, lost to a hearing and understanding of this material, an appreciation of its detail? If so, how is the triad to be assessed? What is the significance of its instrumental and notational definition?

Analytically, of course, it can be temporarily severed from its immediate context. From such a position it can be encouraged to rejoin that context, and by resonating with the hexachord of which it is a part, the remaining triads of that hexachord, and the larger hexachordal framework of which that hexachord is in turn a part. Such are the means of analysis, the means by which a sense of the context is gained, an image constructed of its terms.

So, too, from the same severed position the triad can resonate with a sense of its past as well, not in the form of tonal degrees or functions, to be sure, but as a familiar piece of vocabulary. For the notion of a superimposition of triads implies just that, namely, that an entity of some familiarity is being superimposed, but confined to a new and unfamiliar set of relations.

Other considerations arise in this regard. The spelling of the bass clarinet and cello parts is E♭–A♭–B♭–E♭, a bass line whose tonal implications are, of course, I–IV–V–I. The latter can resonate accordingly, in my view, and a good deal more convincingly than, given a possible tonal interpretation, the triadic superimpositions of the wind and string sections can. Indeed, a point of contention could be imagined, one pitting the I–IV–V–I line in the bass against the successive crunches of the four triadic configurations. Although articulated individually in a conventional manner, the triads are hopelessly uncooperative in their combined response of superimposed groups of four and three. From such a perspective, the opening measures come to seem comical.

Undeniably, then, the triad is an aspect of the opening measures of the *Suite*, of the hexachord 6–20 and of the twelve-tone framework of which that hexachord is a part. At the same time, however, exposed to the mind's ear, the triad is no mere subset, one like any other. Schoenberg could hardly have regarded it in that light. "In twelve-tone composition," he advised in 1923, "major and minor triads . . . almost everything that used to make up the ebb and flow of harmony, are, as far as possible, avoided."[45] He expressed a similar view some twenty years later:

> Even a slight reminiscence of the former tonal harmony would be disturbing, because it would create false expectations of consequences and continuations. The use of a tonic is deceiving if it is not based on *all* the relationships of tonality.[46]

But such a "reminiscence" is not a factor here. However obvious it is to the eye, the triad is obliterated in sound. And so its notation and instrumental definition remain open to question: to what extent is the sense of this music conveyed by that definition, indeed, by the triad's concealment? Here, the underlying rationale of Schoenberg's twelve-tone structures could be assessed, to the extent that that rationale has already been assessed in relation to tonality, in terms of a "negation" of tonality.[47] From such a perspective, another mini-drama could be fashioned, this time from the standpoint of the twelve-tone apparatus of the *Suite* and its battle with the triad and the triad's tonal past. Articulated with triple stops and exacting by those means the fullest in sound from each stringed instrument, each triad responds in full—indeed, as if oblivious to its twelve-tone transformation.

And therein lies the contradiction underlying much of Schoen-

---

45. Schoenberg, *Style and Idea*, p. 207; "Twelve-Tone Composition" (1923).

46. Schoenberg, *Style and Idea*, p. 219; "Composition with Twelve Tones (1)" (1941).

47. See, for example, Theodor W. Adorno, "Zu den Georgeliedern," in Arnold Schoenberg, *Fünfzehn Gedichte aus "Das Buch der Hängenden Garten" vom Stefan George* (Wiesbaden: Insel-Verlag, 1959), p. 78.

berg's twelve-tone music, the frustration of much of it. While the surface apes the motivic, developmental, rhythmic, chordal, and dynamic gestures of the tonal past, a past defined above all by late German Romantic music, pitch structure remains essentially static. For it consists in the main of a constant pumping of the twelve pitch-classes in rows and aggregates, one in which tendency is constantly denied, cut off. And what may therefore have struck some observers as a symptom of self-reference has struck others as a symptom of the very opposite, namely, sameness; with the constant churning of the twelve pitch-classes, the notes lose their capacity to be differentiated, to acquire different functions under reasonable standards of perceptual discrimination; they lose their capacity to "speak."

Of course, the triad may have remained a symbol of the tonal past, a past whose forms, motivic developments, and phrase structures remained an option, and to whose tradition Schoenberg felt himself as yet allied. On the other hand, making the case for an "anxiety of influence" in the concealed triadic opening of the *Suite*, one with terms subterranean and ferocious, would serve little purpose here.[48] Without an explicit model the advantage of a musically particularizing motivation is lost; the effect is too general and obvious. At the same time, the strife-ridden terms could both belabor the character of the music and trivialize the underlying struggle with the tonal tradition, one whose symptoms in the *Suite*, and indeed in Schoenberg's twelve-tone music generally, are neither here nor there specifically but everywhere generally.

As has been suggested already, the triads that open the *Suite* are incidental to the piece as a whole. Playful rather than vengeful in this respect, they are at most the residue of a battle either long past or fought at a considerable distance. On the other hand, their obliteration could have represented a form of defiance on Schoenberg's part, a thumbing of the nose at the composer's hecklers. "You want triads?" he might have been asking. "Here, then, are fifteen. How-

48. See the application of Harold Bloom's theories of poetic influence in Straus, *Remaking the Past*, pp. 12–20. Cf. the analysis of Brahms's *Romanze*, Op. 118, No. 5, in Kevin Korsyn, "Towards a New Poetics of Musical Influence," *Music Analysis* 10, nos. 1–2 (1991): 3–72.

ever, they are the creation of my method of twelve-tone composition and of the hexachord of this particular row, not of the tonality with which you are familiar. I'm giving them to you—but you won't hear them."

So, too, in the three passages examined in this brief survey from the music of Glinka, Rimsky-Korsakov, Bartók, and Schoenberg, obvious features underscore a separation by period, idiom, structure, and compositional method. Informed of the idioms in question, a more deliberate analysis might have stressed the dissimilarity rather than the connections. Here, the four passages are joined on the basis of a shared interval-class content, the fact that all four refer to the hexachord 6–20. That notion of an interval-class content is undeniably abstract, even in relation to a hexachord that inverts into itself, lacks whole tones and tritones, and exhibits by these means a remarkable degree of symmetry. In a history of the materials of Western music, one with the foregoing featured perhaps as a small segment, little could be accomplished by way of such an account.

When realized more concretely, however—in the form of a subset structure of triads separated by major thirds, for example, and in pitch- and pitch-class-specific terms with transpositions on the side—abstractions of this kind can be engaged in substantial ways. The set itself can take on a tangible character, can begin to resonate with the memory of its wide and varied use. Helpful above all is an ability to improvise on the materials abstracted from that use, both at and away from the keyboard. Access is gained not only to the wider pitch-universe to which the initial abstraction makes reference, but, as has been suggested, to the implications of that abstraction in pitch-class-specific terms.

It is from such a perspective that analysis enters. It proceeds by means of a foil, an abstract conceptual arrangement that sets the details of a given context in relief. In the foregoing, the idea for such a foil arose from the material itself, and with the understanding that such a derivation, a manipulation of the materials at various levels of abstraction, offered the most effective means of entry. For the purpose of a theoretical foil is never one of confirmation alone but of engagement, of allowing the materials to be heard and understood in a different light, one capable of renewing and sustaining a sense of intimacy. As Boretz puts it:

A theory applied to the data of a musical experiment is supported by the richness of identity it thereby confers on the data. . . . No one is interested in creating musical entities that merely duplicate entities already created; and to learn to hear a unique thing as a categorical thing is a net loss for musical experience. The qualification, hence, of the individual is the devolution point of all musical thought, for whose sake alone the class generality—all the way out to the term "music" itself—is reified.[49]

49. Benjamin Boretz, "Musical Cosmology," *Perspectives of New Music* 15, no. 2 (1977): 130.

6

Neoclassicism Revised

I

Whether a musical object be Baroque, Classical, or, as in the cases under consideration here, neoclassical, the issue of its appreciation remains unchanged. That issue concerns, on the one hand, the immediacy of aesthetic contemplation, that which is sensed and felt, and, on the other, the musical traditions (or social conditions, possibly) that are alleged to enter into that immediacy. For while we would like to think of the experience itself as the final arbiter on the question of mediation, we tend to believe that the greater the intensity of the experience, the greater our fidelity to its source, to what a musical object is for its own sake, not for what it can be made to represent historically or sociopolitically.

And so our interests have been divided, and no doubt irremediably. As heard and understood, music clearly cannot be a thing unto itself, unreflective of the world at large, of the beliefs and sensibilities within which it is conceived and nurtured. No less evident, however, is our capacity to love essentially, to love an object for what that object is in and of itself, what it is wholly, not for what it could or might possibly represent, and represent only in part. Such a capacity—one that can connect with music in such a way that, sensed and felt, a musical object is whole and not the sum of its parts, irreducible in this respect and therefore unique, unique and capable of being appreciated for what it is rather than for the outside uses to which it could be put or for the sociopolitical views it could serve ("art for art's sake," to use the cliché of formalism)—such a capacity corresponds to romantic love, love that is felt irrespective of tradition or social circumstance, independently of religious or sociopolitical claims. Within such a framework, formalism can manifest itself as an outgrowth of nineteenth-century Romanticism.[1] And appreciation can seem less a matter of education and formal training than of an innate sensitivity, one capable of ignition by a variety of stimuli processed as "personal knowledge."[2]

More traditionally, of course, the divide separating immediacy from reflection has been defined in terms of subjects and objects, inner and outer worlds, spirit and matter. Underlying all such definitions, however, is the fact that immediacy "knows nothing of itself."[3] Unable to hold fast, it yields to reflection, which constructs an image of that which is felt in immediacy. The two move back and forth, often in rapid succession, and with each affecting the other. They move in search of such an image, one of "presentness," the immediate sense of a particular object.[4] Reflection follows in an effort to secure that sense and to deepen aesthetic pleasure. Its role is practical in this respect.

And so we are left with reflection and analysis, with attempts to capture and sustain the felt aesthetic presence of a given object. And the issue turns on generosity, which is how I interpret the following remarks of Milton Babbitt on the early neoclassical works of Stravinsky:

For Stravinsky, "Back to Bach" was just that, an alliteratively catchy slogan, which had no pertinence to professional activity or professional discourse. It was there, permitted to be concocted like "neo-classicism," to be talked about by those who could not and should not talk about music,

---

1. See Leonard B. Meyer, "A Pride of Prejudices; Or, Delight in Diversity," *Music Theory Spectrum* 13, no. 2 (1991): 248–249.

2. See Michael Polanyi, *Personal Knowledge* (New York: Harper, 1962).

3. Carl Dahlhaus, *Esthetics of Music*, trans. William W. Austin (Cambridge: Cambridge University Press, 1982), p. 85.

4. Leo Treitler, *Music and the Historical Imagination* (Cambridge: Harvard University Press, 1989), pp. 37, 40.

who didn't even bother to hear the music, but who, when they bandied about the catch words, were "talking about Stravinsky."[5]

To suggest that serious "talk about music" be pertinent to "professional activity and professional discourse" is to leave oneself open to charges of elitism.[6] Yet the context of the suggestion is generous all the same: generous in its approach to the divide, which is unequivocal; generous in the transcending perspective by which it views the interests of music and its appreciation. For it assumes that those interests are separable from those of the persuasive voice.[7]

5. Milton Babbitt, untitled memoir, *Perspectives of New Music* 9, no. 2, and 10, no. 1 (1971): 106. Cited in Martha Hyde, "Neoclassic and Anachronistic Impulses in 20th-Century Music," paper read at the joint meeting of the Arnold Schoenberg Institute and the Music Theory Society of New York State, 4 October 1991, Columbia University, New York. The Stravinsky for whom Babbitt claimed to be speaking was the serial Stravinsky, of course, one whose attitudes may have been very different from those of the early neoclassicist.

6. Richard Taruskin, "Back to Whom? Neoclassicism as Ideology," *19th-Century Music* 16, no. 3 (1993): 288. "To equate music," Taruskin writes, "with the techniques of manufacturing music . . . and to sanction only such locutions as may describe or analogically represent that manufacture, is of course merely to practice another politics of exclusion." But Taruskin's politics are no less exclusionary in this regard. While condemning "professional discourse" as "by nature conservative" and one of "entrenched power," he praises "public discourse" for its "enormous illocutionary force" and its ability "to make things happen" (p. 289)—without realizing that the opposite is just as easily the case. "Public discourse" in the *New York Times* can be as elitist and abusive of the wares of music—indeed, of the listener of music—as anything in, say, *Perspectives of New Music*. And the "entrenched power" of the former is, in its own way, no less than that of the latter. Moreover, there can be little reason why professional composers and musicians, leery of public indifference to or abuse of their wares, yet cognizant of the impossibility of formulating a discourse that would in fact be fully transparent or neutral, should not seek a more relevant, specialist form of communication, one that could address the issues of music and its making with a greater sense of focus and detail. Indeed, Taruskin's appeal to the "illocutionary force" of public discourse and opinion can seem demagogic. As an example of the "force" of that discourse, we might cite the Schoenberg-Stravinsky wars of the 1920s, a dialogue in which, as Babbitt has suggested and Scott Messing has demonstrated, few seem to have bothered with the music at all but to have focused, rather, on the sociopolitical or personal-political issues raised and promoted by only a few. See the descriptions of various concerts of contemporary music and its reception, in Scott Messing, *Neoclassicism in Music from the Genesis of the Concept Through the Schoenberg/Stravinsky Polemic* (Ann Arbor: UMI Research Press, 1988), pp. 140–142.

7. It assumes that the interests of music and its appreciation can be free of opinion, in other words, of the public voice of persuasion, promotion, and propaganda.

What counts, evidently, is the inner, personal connection with music, the insularity of that connection, its built-in protection from the "slogans" and "catch words" of the marketplace, whether academic, journalistic, or commercial. To the fullest extent, it would seek to cultivate such a connection by ensuring listeners a chance to respond on their own. And the emphasis would not be on an elusive autonomy, on essences that are irreducible, but on an ability to focus on a musical object and on the ability of that object to elicit such focus. For it is only by suspending ourselves in this fashion, by allowing ourselves to become immersed in an object for its own sake (giving way temporarily), that we are able to transcend consciousness and its divisions, doing so in a manner that is rapturous.[8] At the same time, such divisions are brought into play by way of the reflection that follows immediacy. Music summons consciousness in its wake, inner life and the possibility—merciful here, however—of an alternative to everyday life. (The divided self need not always be shunned as hapless and dysfunctional, a self without advantage. Moments of rapture, of self-forgetting at-oneness with the world through music, may not be possible without the divisions of which the self rids itself in such moments of attunement.)

From such a perspective, the concerns of the positivist or formalist need not always be placed in opposition to the humanist's concerns for the expressive force of music and its impact not only on the general listener but on scholars and their scholarship as well. Humanists are distinguished in these matters not by the passion of their response, the ecstatic heights of their attunements, but by their desire to give vent to that passion, to "go public," as it were,

---

8. Only a form of squeamishness, a fear of being unsuspecting sociopolitically, unalert or out of step in this respect, prevents the New Humanist from acknowledging fully the passion of immediacy, the suspension of the self in contemplation. That suspension is associated with sexual surrender, I suspect, and specifically with that of the female. But New Humanists are caught in a dilemma all the same: while championing the role of passion, irrationality, and the subjective in music and music appreciation, in opposition to traditional approaches which are dubbed dry, "technical," objective, and formalistic, they undermine that passion by reducing it to trite sexual and sociopolitical rationalizations (or generalizations). In this way, as has been suggested already, they are ungenerous not only to music but to music listeners as well.

to make known the psychology of their experience. What distinguishes them is a reluctance to be left alone with these implications. And what they seek, therefore, is an audience that can respond in kind; more subtly (but comically too), one that can assure them that an individual passion is not sensed and felt in vain, that all is not capable of being reduced to an ulterior motive.

But in whom or in what could such a trust be placed? In seeking an image of that which is indeed sensed and felt, do we direct our attention at the composer or at the composition, at ourselves or at the thing made? The answer to this question can be unequivocal, as it was for Stravinsky:

My mind does not count. I am not mirror-struck by my mental functions. My interest passes immediately to the object, the thing made; and it follows that I am more concerned with the concrete than with the other thing, in which, as you see, I am easily muddled.[9]

A composer's work is the embodiment of his feeling and, of course, it may be considered as expressing or symbolizing them—though consciousness of this step does not concern the composer.

The composer works through a perceptual, not a conceptual, process. He perceives, he selects, he combines, and is not in the least aware at what point meanings of a different sort and significance grow into his work. All he knows or cares about is his apprehension of the contour of the form, for the form is everything. He can say nothing whatever about meanings.[10]

Such a gift may be divine, of course; never to be "mirror-struck" by one's "mental functions," overly preoccupied with the self; that one's attention should be held steadfastly and effortlessly by the object itself; that one's interest should pass "immediately to the object, the thing made."

But does such a focus differ from that which accompanies the rapture of aesthetic contemplation? My sense is that it does not, and that the theory and analysis which also follow immediacy, assisting

9. Igor Stravinsky and Robert Craft, *Retrospectives and Conclusions* (New York: Knopf, 1969), p. 48.
10. Igor Stravinsky and Robert Craft, *Expositions and Developments* (New York: Doubleday, 1962), p. 115.

in keeping our attention fastened on "the thing made," are no less tied to such a form of concentration. They follow as extensions of the reflection that follows immediacy, and with the purpose of sustaining immediacy.

The special irony here is that, irrespective of Babbitt's comments on Stravinsky's neoclassical works (his attempt, as it were, to rescue this music from the distractions of its critics), Stravinsky himself seems not to have been innocent of the many "slogans" that were "bandied about" in support of his music and its imagined aesthetic during the 1920s and 1930s. On the contrary, Stravinsky seems to have taken a hand in their cultivation. "I go back to Bach," was his reply to a question about his Piano Concerto (1924) in 1925, "not Bach as we know him today, but Bach as he really is."[11] And there can be no doubt about the connection itself in neoclassical works such as the Octet (1923), the Piano Concerto, and the Piano Sonata (1924). Only the significance of that connection in an appreciation of these varying contexts may be open to debate, not its fact or circumstance.

And Stravinsky was not alone in this inclination. An allegiance to Bach in the form of a *retour*, coming by way of a reaction to modernism, above all to Schoenberg and the atonal idiom, was shared by a great many musicians and critics in the years following World War I. Indeed, much of the polemic that accompanied performances of the above-noted works originated not with Stravinsky, strictly speaking, but with Stravinsky's adoption of an existent aesthetic formula. It developed as the "culmination," as Richard Taruskin has noted, "of a process by which the composer was co-opted to a longstanding French aesthetic program."[12] Featured as

---

11. Henrietta Malkiel, "Modernists Have Ruined Modern Music, Stravinsky Says," *Musical America* (10 January 1925): 9, quoted in Messing, *Neoclassicism in Music*, p. 142.

12. Taruskin, "Back to Whom?" p. 291. The "French aesthetic program" to which Taruskin refers was conservative and nationalistic in spirit, consisting in the main of the Société Nationale de Musique, founded in the wake of the Franco-Prussian War, and *La Nouvelle Revue française*, a journal of criticism founded in 1909 by Jacques Rivière. But "coopted" can seem a bit strong nonetheless, implying, for neoclassicism, the absence of any distance between the composer's immediate aesthetic impulses and the "program" itself, as if those impulses were the

"catch words" of this program were terms such as "objective," "pure music," "simplicity," "impersonal," "counterpoint," and "precision," many of which were to prove applicable to Stravinsky's music generally. And the negatives were even more revealing: the program was anti-Impressionist, anti-modernist, anti-German, anti-Wagner, and anti-Schoenberg. (Musically, Stravinsky's neoclassical change-of-heart began with *Pulcinella* in 1919, which is for the most part an orchestration and recomposition of various arias and trio sonatas by Pergolesi, and a work to which the composer later referred as "the epiphany through which the whole of my later work became possible.")[13]

So, too, as Stravinsky's reputation grew, so did the momentum and circulation of his polemic. His anti-modernist views, as expressed at various interviews at the time of his first American tour in 1925, were translated and published widely throughout Europe, prompting reactions from a number of composers. One interview made explicit reference to Schoenberg and the twelve-tone method: in it, Stravinsky complained of "modernists" who worked with "formulas instead of ideas."[14]

---

creation of various right-leaning literary and sociopolitical trends in France. "There is no better illustration of the influence of public discourse, and its embodiment in music," Taruskin writes, "than the story of the neoclassical Stravinsky. What Messing calls . . . the 'aesthetics which attempted to define his style' in fact virtually shaped that style" (p. 289). Here again, however, Taruskin exaggerates the role of "public discourse" in the making, shaping, and appreciation of Stravinsky's neoclassical style. Ignored is the farcical nature of many of Stravinsky's own press interviews (see footnote 16, below), the extent to which the composer aimed for promotional effect, rattled his prejudices (he associated Schoenberg's music, which he did not know, with "modernism," "modernism" in turn with Bolshivikism and the communist regime in Russia), and used the press to his own advantage. Nor is the musical excitement of neoclassicism given its due, the degree to which Stravinsky was led by the refashioning of his own musical habits and predilections: "I looked, and I fell in love," was his recollection of his initial response to the Pergolesi texts in 1919, and there is little reason to doubt the excitement of that moment, his first recognition of the promise that it held; or to doubt, for that matter, the impression gained of an immensely tough and determined composer in pursuit of a musical appetite (Stravinsky and Craft, *Expositions and Developments*, p. 127).

13. Stravinsky and Craft, *Expositions and Developments*, p. 129.
14. Quoted in Messing, *Neoclassicism in Music*, p. 141.

In turn, Schoenberg, interrupting work on the *Suite*, Op. 29, composed the *Drei Satiren*, Op. 28, with its venomous Foreword aimed at the "half-measures" of "quasi-tonalists" and "folklorists."[15] Here, however, the politics of the matter seem to have soared above both music and aesthetics, to a point at which Babbitt's injunction against the sloganizers "who didn't even bother to hear the music" could just as easily have been directed at the composers themselves. Scott Messing summarized the situation:

> Schoenberg's judgement was scarcely based on his acquaintance with Stravinsky's scores. Like that of Stravinsky, Schoenberg's assessment of his contemporary was gleaned from what he read, not from what he heard: contemporary reviews and essays of their music made up the evidence upon which the composers made their aesthetic conclusions.[16]

Integral to this history were Stravinsky's attempts to revise his folkloristic past to suit his neoclassical "fealty to the values of 'pure music.'"[17] To this end, he falsified the conception of many of his earlier Russian-period works, including, most remarkably, that of *The Rite of Spring*.[18]

Ordinarily, the sloganizing residue of an activity of this kind ("verbal sparring" is Messing's description of the Stravinsky-Schoenberg duel),[19] would be met with a certain skepticism, given not only the immediate purpose of that activity (promotional, in large part), but the complex nature of the aesthetic experience itself and the comparative ease with which it can be made a form of representation. (In Stravinsky's case, the reactionary, anti-modernist

---

15. Schoenberg's Foreword to the *Drei Satiren* is translated and quoted in full in Messing, *Neoclassicism in Music*, p. 144.

16. Messing, *Neoclassicism in Music*, p. 145. A German reporter remarked upon the carnival atmosphere of Stravinsky's interviews, referring to one session as a "two-act farce" ("Herr Stravelinski verabscheut die moderne Musik oder die enttäuschten Reporter," *Der Auftakt* 5, no. 2 [1925], quoted in Messing, *Neoclassicism in Music*, p. 142).

17. Richard Taruskin, "Russian Folk Melodies in *The Rite of Spring*," *Journal of the American Musicological Society* 33, no. 3 (1980): 502.

18. For a summary of these revisions, see Pieter C. van den Toorn, *Stravinsky and "The Rite of Spring"* (Berkeley: University of California Press, 1987), pp. 1–15.

19. Messing, *Neoclassicism in Music*, p. 142.

polemic was kindled in part by his hatred of "Lenine" and the Bol-shivik Revolution, the exile into which he was forced after World War I.) Here, however, a certain musical, or at least aesthetic, sig-nificance has attached itself to the residue, and not without an inner logic of its own, a dialectic indicative of its own particular time and place. For the opportunistic nature of much of Stravinsky's early commentary stands in contrast to the icy integrity with which he seems to have cloaked himself in later years, above all during the years of his "conversations" with Robert Craft, from about 1957 to Stravinsky's death in April 1971.

Still, were aspects of the residue to be deemed seriously relevant to pressing musical issues, it could be countered that yesterday's aesthetics (or "catch words"), even if judged to have been present at the creation, are in no way privileged. At the time of the Di-aghilev revival of *The Rite* in 1920, Stravinsky had disassociated himself from much of the pagan symbolism that had lain behind the original conception of this music; in an interview at the time, he described the score as a "objective construction," claiming that its conception had proceeded as "a work of pure musical construc-tion."[20] Yet the aesthetics of "pure instrumental music" that lay be-hind this particular fabrication were felt no less keenly by the com-poser—and no less relevantly, to judge by the subsequent success of *The Rite* in the concert hall. Both sides of the coin—pagan symbol-ism and "pure musical construction"—need to be taken into ac-count in any history of this work.

But it is the music itself that deserves to be taken seriously enough to be given a chance to create a focus of its own. And if such an argument can be made by today's humanists and postmodernists at the expense of theory and analysis, and with the suggestion that the latter refrain from interrupting the listening experience with preconceived notions of structure and analytical procedure, then it can be made at the expense of the new humanism as well, of those

---

20. Igor Stravinsky, "Les Deux *Sacres du Printemps,*" *Comoedia* (11 December 1920), reprinted in François Lesure, ed., *Le Sacre du Printemps: Dossier de Presse* (Geneva: Editions Minkoff, 1980), p. 13. An English translation, "Interpretation by Massine," may be found in Minna Lederman, ed., *Stravinsky in the Theatre* (New York: Pellegrini and Cudahy, 1949), pp. 24–26.

fields that would predicate their pursuits on the reduction of music to a "product of culture," the reduction of its study to a branch of sociology, and the reduction of its appreciation to a form of personal politics.

2

Yet the inner, personal connection with music, that which would seem to underlie Babbitt's claims of indifference to the "slogans" of Stravinsky's early neoclassicism, has less to do with music as such than with the individual musical context. And to the extent that our interests do in fact rest primarily with the "presentness" of such a context, analysis is likely to treat it not as a "sample from a musical population"—to quote from Babbitt again—but as a "singular, individuated accomplishment."[21] It is likely to concern itself not with the confirmation of general terms and concepts but with the integrity of the context, its particular motivation. And while such an approach can seem to place itself in opposition to history—pitting aesthetic effect against history, the sensed here and now of an individual context against the historian's conscious concern for the larger perspective—this need not be the case at all. At issue is not the separation of immediacy from historical reasoning—the subject-object debate, in other words—but historical reasoning as a form of analysis, a way of invoking and sustaining the aesthetic presence of a given context.

Of concern, then, are forms that can respond to an individuality, can allow a context to suggest the means of its analysis even if those means entailed established analytic-theoretical procedures. Such forms could move sideways and to the front as well as to the back, remaining relatively unaffected by considerations of origin, chronology, and precedence. As Dalhaus explains:

The process of "isolation" that typifies structuralist aesthetics does not mean that the analyst no longer makes connections; it merely means that historical and chronological connections are not the only valid and fun-

21. Milton Babbitt, *Words About Music*, ed. Stephen Dembski and Joseph N. Straus (Madison: University of Wisconsin Press, 1987), p. 4.

damental ones, and that our interest has been rechanneled from the connections themselves to the works they connect.[22]

But the contextual approach to the study of music need not be confined to matters of immediacy and aesthetic effect, to that which is merely sensed and felt. It can claim its own version of history, one which, extending through the tonal era and into the twentieth century, traces how musical structures did in fact become increasingly individual or "self-referential."[23] As was suggested in the preceding chapter, it can claim the motive as one of its frontiers, examining the extent to which the logic of the motive asserted itself independently of the tonal framework from which it emerged. And it can avail itself of the history of its aesthetic, to the extent that that history has been sketched in considerable detail in the writings of Carl Dahlhaus.[24] For to argue for the context (as Babbitt has argued), is to argue for its "autonomy," the autonomy of the individual structure, "self-contained work" or "self-sustaining entity" (Dahlhaus's terms).[25] It is to argue for placing the "intrinsic quality" of a musical context over features of inheritance, genre, form, and historical position.[26] And it is to equate that "intrinsic quality" with aesthetic effect, with the immediacy or "presentness" of a context. (According to the aesthetics of the contextual, inherited features are in reality—as part of an experienced reality, that is—contextualized to a point of irrelevance. Only in analysis, and in an analysis undertaken in a deliberately anachronistic vein, would such features be brought to light. Here, then, the contextual is associated with uniqueness and individuality, with what is essential and therefore irreducible, with what is sensed and felt, given immediately in experience. By contrast, the general is identified with the analytical, with what remains open to analysis.)

22. Carl Dahlhaus, *Foundations of Music History*, trans. J. B. Robinson (Cambridge: Cambridge University Press, 1983) p. 25.
23. See Babbitt, *Words About Music*, p. 9.
24. See, especially, Dahlhaus, *Foundations of Music History*, pp. 19–33.
25. Babbitt, *Words About Music*, pp. 3–4, 9, 146–151, 167–171; Dahlhaus, *Foundations of Music History*, pp. 27–28.
26. Dahlhaus, *Esthetics of Music*, p. 15.

In this way, Babbitt's idea of "self-reference,"[27] of the growing individuality of music during the nineteenth and twentieth centuries—that is, the increasing degree to which the musical structures of this period referred only to themselves—coincides with the process traced by Dahlhaus in terms of an "autonomy principle" or "cult of originality." Self-reference is discussed by Babbitt not only in relation to Schoenberg, atonality, and the twelve-tone method, but in relation to the music of Brahms and of Wagner's *Tristan* as well.[28] And to the extent that that discussion finds its counterpart in Dahlhaus's discussion of autonomy and the self-contained work,[29] no more extreme illustration could be found of this coincidence than in the beliefs attributed by Babbitt to himself, in Babbitt's approach to composition, theory, and appreciation.

On the other side of this divide is tradition, of course, that which is shared or held in common, "communality" (another Babbitt term),[30] features that comprise the language, grammar, or practice of which the single context is an instance. And the greater the emphasis laid on the communal, the less on the contextual. For no structure can stand alone in this respect, be an island unto itself, a wholly contextual, self-contained entity. Terms of this kind tend to

27. Babbitt, *Words About Music*, p. 9.
28. Babbitt, *Words About Music*, pp. 146–152. Other contextual analyses of the *Tristan* Prelude, analyses that are nontonally functional, are Benjamin A. Boretz, "Meta-Variations, Part IV: Analytic Fall-out (II)," *Perspectives of New Music* 11, no. 2 (1973); John Rahn, *Basic Atonal Theory* (New York: Longman, 1980), pp. 78–79; and Allen Forte, "New Approaches to the Linear Analysis of Music," *Journal of the American Musicological Society* 61, no. 3 (1988). It may seem curious that an approach emphasizing the contextual should do so by way of the unordered pitch-class set, an entity of such considerable abstraction. But the connection is between the contextual and the motive, the motive generalized as a pitch-class set, reduced in the main to a set of interval classes. On the other hand, many of the motivic relations traced by Babbitt, Boretz, Rahn, and Forte in *Tristan* are not incompatible with tonally derived interpretations, at least not on a local level. Forte has published several motivic analyses of nineteenth-century works. See, especially, Allen Forte, "Motivic Design and Structural Levels in the First Movement of Brahms's String Quartet in C Minor," *Musical Quarterly* 69, no. 4 (1983); "Middleground Motives in the Adagietto of Mahler's Fifth Symphony," *19th-Century Music* 8, no. 2 (1984); and "Liszt's Experimental Idiom and Music of the Early Twentieth Century," *19th-Century Music* 10, no. 3 (1986).
29. Dahlhaus, *Foundations of Music History*, pp. 19–33.
30. Babbitt, *Words About Music*, p. 10.

be applied relatively. To some extent, pieces are expressive in relation to other pieces, and then by way of their external relations as well, their historical and sociological contexts. Traditionally, scholarship has confronted this larger picture, the perspective from which, it is claimed, a sense of the individual arises.

Thus, too, no one could judge the contextual independently of the communal or vice versa or contend that the issue was not ultimately one of kind and degree. In a larger sense, the communal is a part of every analytically abstracted segment. And the contextuality of a piece is its sensed particularity, the quality of its whole, a matter that could likewise hardly be confined to a segment, judged a part of this but not of that. In pieces of considerable effect, pieces in which the context is likely to matter a great deal, a sense of the individual is likely to overrun all else. And these dynamics are reciprocal. In classic organic fashion—the aesthetic ideal to which reference is made here—the whole not only defines but is defined by its parts; the impression it leaves is that of a whole motivated from within. Parts are thus sensed as contextual, specific to the whole of which they are a part, never forced or artificial in this respect, never untrue or false to the context. And they are chronologically dependent as well, dependent on the *particular* successions of rhythms or spans of which they are a part.

Is it here, then, in confronting the idea of an organic whole, that neoclassicism poses special problems? In its resurrection in overt and substantial ways of features of a familiar yet nonimmediate past, are there gulfs that are unbridgeable? Are there special problems of assimilation, problems with the whole and its integrity? Or does a sense of dislocation manage a quality of its own, something capable of standing on its own in this respect?

In a recent study of "anachronistic impulses" in neoclassical music, Martha Hyde has argued both ways: for dislocation on the one hand, assimilation on the other.[31] Seeking to replace the tarnished image of neoclassicism with a new theory of imitation, she identifies a number of concrete relationships to the past. With much subtle overlapping, these relationships are graded on a scale from most

31. Hyde, "Neoclassic and Anachronistic Impulses."

to least overt, from most overtly neoclassical to what is termed "a deeper, more dramatic . . . engagement with the past."[32]

For the moment, however, I am drawn to the most severely tarnished of these relationships, the most decadent from the standpoint of the neoclassical tinge, and by way of *Pulcinella* (1919), a bar-by-bar recomposition of remote, distant texts. Here, it seems to me, the notion of the contextual is put to the test. And at issue is the context itself, the integrity of a context of this kind; more specifically, whether the notion of the contextual can be applied analytically as well as aesthetically, as a category having to do with the nuts and bolts of analysis, with tangible means of separating the contextual from the communal, as well as with aesthetic effect, with what is sensed and felt. Analytically, the means need not be crude: features of a given configuration can be identified from both perspectives, as tending to imply the contextual in certain respects, the communal in certain other respects.

But this assumes that the division is indeed open to analytic-theoretical scrutiny. When the contextual is accepted as an aesthetic category, then the greater the effect of a context, the greater becomes the sense of its integrity, of what that context is in and of itself rather than by way of its communal ties (which, as has been suggested, would surface only after the fact, by way of an analysis). In this respect it can matter very little whether, in the recomposed sections of *Pulcinella*, the number of notes retained from the original eighteenth-century sources comprises 10 or 90 percent of the total. What matters is neither the old nor the new, strictly speaking, the eighteenth century or Stravinsky's "added notes," but the newly constructed context, the extent to which the "added notes" are made to connect with the old. For it is assumed that the two components are heard and understood not in isolation but as they relate to one another, as they form relations, and in a way that is suggestive of a whole, something integral and capable of being appreciated as such. Historically, *Pulcinella* may be of interest because of its source materials and the manner in which, for Stravinsky, their recomposition opened up the possibility of a neoclassical ac-

32. Hyde, "Neoclassic and Anachronistic Impulses."

commodation. Aesthetically or musically, however, the piece must work as a context, for what it is here and now.

And my impression, in fact, is that a few "added notes" do change the complexion of several of the dance numbers in *Pulcinella*, do create new identities (wholes, and presumably organic wholes) that are aesthetically convincing in their own right. And so the problem turns into one of overcoming what has thus far figured as the proverbial first step in discussions of this piece, namely, that of assigning the "added notes" to Stravinsky and the remainder of the music to Pergolesi, Gallo, or whomever.[33] What very often happens, in fact, is that two separate and independent structures are inferred on behalf of these initial assignments, each on its own analytic-theoretical terms: segments attributable to Stravinsky, linear or vertical, are treated in a contemporary light, characterized as motivic and identified as unordered pitch-class sets; groupings attributable to earlier composers are judged tonally functional. A weakly determined structure consisting of interval-class groupings and labeled "post-tonal" or "atonal" is thus placed in opposition to something determinately tonal, and antiquely so. And the problem is that the conception of a dual structure, what the analysis asserts about our apprehension of this music, is in no way supported by these separate analytical terms. For it can be shown that the embedded source texts are as motivic as Stravinsky's additions and that those texts are no less riddled with pitch-class sets. What we end up with is a bipartite piece, but a piece whose duality is merely the *intent* of the analysis, not its actual doing.

In this way, too, the dual approach underscores the vulnerability of this music to the unsympathetic questions posed just above, and to Schoenberg's polemic during the 1920s, which argued that Stravinsky's neoclassicism was a fraud, its relationship to the past superficial, and its treatment of dissonance a half-hearted "nibbling"

---

33. See Barry S. Brook, "Stravinsky's *Pulcinella*: The 'Pergolesi' Sources," in *Musiques, Signes, Images: Liber Amicorum François Lesure* (Geneva: Minkoff, 1988), pp. 41–66. It now appears that only ten of the twenty-one arias and instrumental sections of *Pulcinella* were composed by Pergolesi. The remaining eleven selections are evidently the work of a variety of eighteenth-century composers, most of whom remain unknown.

without consequence, a cleverness without substance or "idea."[34]
And it underscores that vulnerability notwithstanding the fact that
it is from the standpoint of the motive and its identification with
the context that it takes its cue, ideas about the context and its making that are fundamentally Schoenbergian. What this music lacks
from such a perspective, evidently, is organic structure, a sense of
integrity. Parts are not sufficiently motivated, while the context itself is not adequately developed. Parts point too overtly to an outside use, one not truly communal in the sense of an "unconscious
theory" (something immediately felt and sensed);[35] owing to its
historical nonimmediacy, it is alien and artificial.

And it is from such a perspective that many of the issues underlying Joseph Straus's *Remaking the Past* are drawn, a remarkable
study of contemporary relationships to the past, but one riddled
with contradictions nonetheless.[36] Below is a summary of Straus's
version of the dual approach, as it applies not only to *Pulcinella* but
to other neoclassical recompositions as well, including Stravinsky's
The Fairy's Kiss (1928):

Recompositions are riven by tension. The source piece tries to speak in its
customary way, through its tonal harmony and voice leading, while the
added material tries to put new words in its mouth. This struggle for
priority between post-tonal and tonal, and between twentieth-century
composers and their eighteenth-century models, is waged continuously
in these recompositions.

The struggle produces a composition with two layers of structure, one
based on traditional tonal relations and one based on recurring motivic
structures or pitch–class sets. The tonal layer influences the motivic layer
by providing material for it. At the same time, the presence of the motivic
layer forces a reinterpretation of the tonal layer, and traditional formations come to be heard in a novel way.[37]

34. Schoenberg, Foreword to *Drei Satiren*, Op. 28, cited in Messing, *Neoclassicism in Music*, p. 144.
35. William E. Benjamin, "Schenker's Theory and the Future of Music," *Journal of Music Theory* 25, no. 1 (1981): 170.
36. Joseph N. Straus, *Remaking the Past: Musical Modernism and the Influence of
the Tonal Tradition* (Cambridge: Harvard University Press, 1990).
37. Straus, *Remaking the Past*, p. 64.

Each recomposition is stratified into two distinct layers—one governed by traditional tonal relations and one by the logic of recurring motives (or pitch-class sets)—without any larger resolution or synthesis. In each piece the contrasting styles and structures are locked in a continuous conflict. The power of these pieces resides not so much in their integration of competing elements into an organic whole as in the very intensity of the conflict they embody.

These recompositions are thus the scene of a struggle between styles and between types of pitch organization.[38]

There is a clear delineation of new and old elements. The older elements are recognizable but placed in a new context that confers upon them a new meaning. Works containing this clash of elements may be coherent, although not in an organic sense. . . . Old and new are not reconciled or synthesized but locked together in conflict. The coherence of these works is won through struggle.[39]

With considerable dislocation, then, Straus argues both ways. There is an overwhelming sense of "tension," "struggle," and "conflict" on the one hand, a sense of "reinterpretation" on the other. At odds are two simultaneous and distinct "layers of structure," two "fully developed conceptions of musical structure" that represent the old and the new, the tonal and the post-tonal.[40] The first of these is based on "traditional tonal relations," the second on "the logic of recurring motives," motives which, transposed and/or inverted, are generalized as pitch-class sets. And the result is a "clash" in which the two sides are "not reconciled or synthesized but locked together in conflict." Recompositions such as *Pulcinella* are thus "coherent" but not "organic"; the two sides admit to a degree of "reinterpretation" but are "distinct" nonetheless, clearly delineated, and "locked together in conflict."

However, Straus's descriptive terms betray considerable contradiction. A certain ambiguity may be allowed in conceptions of this kind, to be sure. Yet the two "contrasting styles and structures" cannot remain "locked in a continuous conflict," at odds without "any larger resolution or synthesis," while at the same time admit-

---

38. Straus, *Remaking the Past*, p. 72.
39. Straus, *Remaking the Past*, p. 16.
40. Straus, *Remaking the Past*, p. 59.

ting to a form of transformation, a "new meaning" in which "traditional formations [are] heard in a novel way." The anxiety and conflict that underlie the author's understanding of the role of the tonal tradition in post-tonal music, perspectives that are derived from Harold Bloom's theories of poetic influence,[41] may have forced the author's hand on this matter of the severity of the duality. Straus invokes the aesthetic experience itself in this connection, that is, the general impression left by pieces such as *Pulcinella* and *The Fairy's Kiss.*

Shown in Example 31 is a sequential passage from the Andantino section of *Pulcinella*. The sequence occurs toward the end of the Andantino, with material borrowed from Gallo rather than Pergolesi. In the original version by Gallo, the figuration in the flutes was supported by a bass of descending fifths (see Example 32), an arrangement applied earlier in the Andantino, in fact. Here, however, Stravinsky substitutes a single four-note chord, (F D G C), sustained in the string orchestra and punctuated pizzicato by the soloists. Although conceivable as a form of appoggiatura in tonal music, the chord is sustained independently of tonal function, without resolution, and hence without a sense of harmonic progression. Although diatonic, it is nontriadic. It is the new rather than the old, in other words, a Stravinsky addition that is post-tonal.

Straus brackets the chord and gives it the name and prime-form numbering of its pitch-class set, 4–23 and (0 2 5 7), respectively. The chord is then shown to be related to the first four notes of the canonic imitation in the flutes, C–D and F–G; "taken together," Straus concludes, these notes "form the same set class."[42]

In point of fact, of course, the two groupings in question, those representing the opening of Gallo's sequence and Stravinsky's sustained chord, are related in ways far less abstract than those defined by the pitch-class set. For there are no transpositions or inversions.

---

41. See, especially, Straus, *Remaking the Past*, pp. 12–20. Straus's principal sources are Harold Bloom, *The Anxiety of Influence* (Oxford: Oxford University Press, 1973), and Harold Bloom, *A Map of Misreading* (Oxford: Oxford University Press, 1975).

42. Straus, *Remaking the Past*, p. 60.

EXAMPLE 31. Stravinsky, *Pulcinella*, Andantino.

EXAMPLE 31—*continued*

EXAMPLE 32.   Stravinsky, *Pulcinella*, Andantino.

What they share is a pitch-class content, not just an interval-class content (with the former subsuming the latter, obviously). Indeed, in the measures directly following the prefacing notes C–D and F–G, the motive of a falling fourth, G–D in the first flute and C–G in the second, is confined to the same content, (0 2 5 7) in terms of (C D F G). More significantly still, the spacing of the two falling fourths is reflected in the disposition of Stravinsky's chord, with (D G C) superimposed over F in the viola. And while Straus labels the pizzicato punctuation of Stravinsky's chord an "ostinato," identifying it with the Stravinskian idiom, the sustained version of the chord in the string orchestra, coming at the end of the Andantino, could just as easily be heard and understood as a convention—a pedal, in fact.

Indeed, there are still other ways of relating the chord and its particular disposition to the eighteenth-century source. For the chord is related to the last four notes of the omitted bass line, those of the descending fifth sequence in terms of D–G–C–F (see Example 32). It could be heard and understood as a verticalization of the latter, in other words, the roots of a cadential function in F major: VI–II–V–I.

In sum, the delineation of the old and the new in this passage, the "struggle for priority" between "two layers of structure," two "types of pitch organization," is far less marked than Straus would have us believe, the degree of assimilation far more extensive. And this is true not only for the remaining recomposed sections of *Pulcinella,* but for *The Fairy's Kiss* as well. Here, too, the post-tonal is said to involve "generalizing the motive into a pitch-class set."[43]

43. Straus, *Remaking the Past*, p. 55.

And at No. 4 in *The Fairy's Kiss* Straus infers the motive C–F–E from Stravinsky's arrangement of a Tchaikovsky melody in F minor;[44] following this, C–F–E is reduced to 3–4 or (0 1 5) and cited in terms of C–G–A♭ and (E♭ G A♭). And while the latter are transpositionally or inversionally related to the initial form C–F–E, of far greater determinacy from the standpoint of both the motive and its "developing variation" is the key of F minor and its transposition (or modulation) to the relative major. Far more readily, it is within such an orientation that C–F–E (in F minor) is heard and understood to relate to (E♭ G A♭) (in A♭ major).

The problem, of course, is that the post-tonal cannot be distinguished from the tonal in this manner, by way of the motive as such or of the motive conceived as a pitch-class set. In the sequential passage at No. 49 in the Andantino of *Pulcinella* (Example 32), the pairs of 2s that preface Gallo's sequence, or the falling fourths G–D and C–G that follow in succession, are no less motivic in character, no less pitch-class sets in this respect, representatives of the prime-form numbering (0 2 5 7), than Stravinsky's sustained chord that verticalizes the successive fourths. And the latter verticalization is post-tonal not by virtue of its motivicism, its status as a variant of (0 2 5 7), or even its verticalization of a nontriadic sonority (which, as was suggested, is at least conceivable in F major), but by virtue of its treatment, the manner in which it is handled in this particular context.

Nor, for that matter, by these means of the motive and its development can the Andantino section of *Pulcinella* be distinguished from, say, the variation theme of the Beethoven Ninth (as was discussed in connection with Examples 10–12, 16, and 17 in chapter 5).[45] Straus's "logic of recurring motives" is not greater in the former than in the latter, in the post-tonal than in the tonal, in the music of Stravinsky (or Schoenberg) than in that of Bach, Haydn, or Beethoven. Rather, the distinction rests on a negative, it seems to me, on the absence of tonally functional relations in the post-tonal.

44. Straus, *Remaking the Past*, pp. 55–57.
45. Observe that the Beethoven theme is expressive and lyrical rather than developmental in style; it is ultimately motivic, but not overtly so. And its tonality is far from "extended."

EXAMPLE 33.   Stravinsky, *Pulcinella*, Andantino.

The question may be one of a heavier reliance in the absence of such relations, a greater consciousness on the part of the composer, a more immediate preoccupation, not one of actual content.

Thus, as encountered in the Andantino of *Pulcinella*, Stravinsky's chord is not an isolated event. The significance of the vertical joining of F, D, G, and C cannot be weighed independently of the eighteenth-century sequence from which, presumably, the pitches were drawn; and the sequence cannot be weighed without reference to the vertical joining, the singling out of those four pitches for emphasis, their segmentation in this manner. Indeed, with the exception of E and A, two nonharmonic neighbor notes, the pitch-class content of the first four measures of the passage is given entirely to the set (0 2 5 7) in terms of (C D F G). The boxed-in area in Example 33 illustrates this confinement, along with the exclusion of E and A as neighbor notes. The latter are encircled accordingly.

At the same time, both Gallo's sequence of descending fifths and Stravinsky's sustained chord can suggest an arrangement of (0 2 5 7) as a four-note segment of the circle of fifths, the interval-5/7 cycle, one that can point to a cyclic arrangement of the F-major collection as well:

F–B♭–E–A–[D–G–C–F]

(C D F G)

(0 2 5 7)

Such an arrangement serves the interests of assimilation, it seems to me, of the combined effect of the sequence and its accompanying chord, of the eighteenth century and Stravinsky's post-tonal addi-

EXAMPLE 34.   Stravinsky, (0 2 5 7) fragments: *Petrushka*, I.

EXAMPLE 35.   Stravinsky, (0 2 5 7) fragments: *The Rite of Spring*: Introduction; Introduction; "Ritual of Abduction"; Introduction (Part II).

tion. For it represents a more abstract conception of the diatonic set, one that can straddle the two components by retreating somewhat from the side of tonality and the eighteenth century, specifically, from the greater determinacy of the F-major scale.

Moreover, it is precisely by way of such a retreat, by movement in the direction of greater abstraction (treating the chord as a pitch-class set, in fact, an unordered set of interval classes), that the configuration can be shown to relate closely to the diatonicism of Stravinsky's earlier Russian-period works. It relates to many of the ostinatos and repetitive, folkish fragments of those works. Thus, in Example 34 from the opening of *Petrushka,* the flute melody and its accompanying tremolos reduce to (0 2 5 7) in terms of (D E G A); Example 35 lists four (0 2 5 7) fragments from *The Rite of Spring*; and Example 36 reproduces the opening melodic fragment of *Renard*, which reduces to (0 2 5 7) in terms of (F G B♭ C). Further, the ostinatos in Examples 37 and 38, from *The Soldier's Tale* and *Les*

EXAMPLE 36.   Stravinsky, (0 2 5 7) fragments: *Renard.*

EXAMPLE 37.   Stravinsky, (0 2 5 7) fragments: *The Soldier's Tale,*
March.

EXAMPLE 38.   Stravinsky, (0 2 5 7) fragments: *Les Noces,* III.

Noces, reduce to (D E G A) and (G A C D), while that from the final
movement of the *Symphony of Psalms* (Example 39, and a neoclassical example at that) reduces to (E♭ F A♭ B♭). Observe that the ostinato in Example 37 lacks a fourth pitch-class, which is supplied
by the reiterated A of the clarinet fragment; and that the ostinato of
Example 39 is similar in this respect, with its fourth pitch-class
being supplied by the sustained A♭ in the oboe and altos.

The reduction of these diverse configurations to a single pitch-
class set can serve a useful purpose, for it can underscore both the
general and the specific, the notion of a Stravinskian idiom as well
as that of a particular manifestation of that idiom; it can point to
different kinds and degrees of communality and individuality. And

EXAMPLE 39.   Stravinsky, (0 2 5 7) fragments: *Symphony of Psalms*, III.

although the intersection itself (defined by shared interval classes, for the most part) is relatively abstract, it is tangible enough to allow for meaningful comparisons. In effect, the set (0 2 5 7) can be read into each of the given contexts, in this way becoming a means of comparison, a way of distinguishing one context from another and of testing the behavior of each. Relations surrounding the treatment of (0 2 5 7) as an ostinato in the third tableau of *Les Noces* (Example 38) may be compared to those surrounding the similar treatment of (0 2 5 7) in the final movement of *Psalms* (Example 39). Through such a point of intersection, in other words, each of the contexts can serve as a foil for the other, a way of sensing and feeling the quality of the other. And the particular attributes of the pitch-class set are marked clearly in this analysis. The covering uniformity it confers is not confused with relations of greater determinacy; rather, it is employed as a way of highlighting that greater determinacy.

But the usefulness of analytic-theoretical endeavors of this kind is not owing entirely to the sorts of comparisons illustrated by Examples 34–39. Here, it is owing at least in part to the special properties of set class 4–23, to the fact that 4–23, lacking two intervals, semitones and tritones, can exhibit a high degree of symmetry. In this way, it is made more tangible, more readily identifiable from one context to the next.

On the other hand, as is demonstrated in Examples 34–39, (0 2 5 7) identifies with the diatonicism of Stravinsky's Russian-period works, the folk-like, modal inflections of that diatonicism. And it is not surprising, therefore, that Stravinsky's additions to *Pulcinella* should reflect that emphasis. Composed for the most part in 1919 following *The Soldier's Tale* and the piano version of *Les Noces*, they are more reflective of the Russian period than of the neoclassical, and can be heard and understood in that light, notwithstanding their wider implications, their role in precipitating the accommodation that was to follow.

3

In truth, however, the issue of this chapter has differed little from that with which Dahlhaus has dealt in terms of the writing of history: the question as to whether history can be reconciled with aesthetic autonomy, with the idea of the self-contained work, without necessarily slighting the aesthetic qualities of such a conception.[46] For the underlying rationale had to remain consistent with current aesthetic assumptions. Here, too, the concern has been for the individual qualities of given works, for the extent to which an application of necessarily general terms and concepts could work to the advantage of such qualities. In this connection, however, a special plea was made for the terminologies of theory and analysis, and on the basis of their ability to penetrate the detail of individual works and to allow for a "close reading" of the materials. It has been felt that a sense of intimacy is encouraged by such contact.

But to answer Straus's analysis, it must be said that a history of the motive in the nineteenth and twentieth centuries could no doubt be sketched retrospectively from the standpoint of Schoenberg, atonality, and serialism. It could cover the generalization of the motive, its identification with the context, and its contribution to the individuality of the context. But the transfer of such an understanding to the whole of the twentieth century, its characterization (by Straus) as a "common practice" or "norm of post-tonal usage,"[47] seems unjustified. Generalized as pitch-class sets, motives

46. See Dahlhaus, *Foundations of Music History*, pp. 3–33.
47. Straus, *Remaking the Past*, p. 17.

can be found everywhere, of course, not least in the music of the four post-tonal composers cited by Straus: Schoenberg, Stravinsky, Berg, and Bartók. But they are everywhere far too different in their application, too varying in their separate idioms and contexts. And the process itself, that of a manipulation of motives, is too often overshadowed by other compositional, historical, and aesthetic issues. In the case of Stravinsky's music, for example, techniques of accentual displacement come readily to mind.

Above all, the notion of the pitch-class set is too abstract to serve as the basis of a "common practice." Its current use in theory and analysis reflects the pluralistic mold of post-tonal music, the analyst's difficulty in inferring tangible commonalities from that music, his or her retreat to terms and concepts of greater abstraction. Simply put, we cannot claim for the music of this century's (assumed) leading composers, or for the music of many of these composers taken individually, a syntax or "practice" (and hence a theory or analysis) comparable in determinacy to that of past tonal eras or past tonal composers; we cannot claim that the musical idioms of the post-tonal era are similar in kind to those of familiar bygone eras and that, with the passage of time, a bridging commonality will assert itself along the familiar lines of what a future generation will deem relevant to itself. My sense, indeed, is that the motive and its manipulation have pulled too significantly in the direction opposite to the one pursued by Straus, namely, in the direction of the individual context and its autonomy.[48] For while the process itself is necessarily communal, it is so in a way too indeterminate to be judged the defining characteristic or "practice" of a single period, idiom, composer, or group of composers. (Recall its inability to imply order, functions of temporal succession, suggestions as to why one motivic event would succeed another.) And it is by this indeterminacy that it serves the individual context, twists and turns conspicuously on its behalf.

We should note, however, that the context of a neoclassical work

48. See Babbitt, *Words About Music*, p. 171. "A motive is something defined within a piece," Babbitt writes, and "composing with the tones of a motive [is] the ultimate contextual idea with regard to musical structure." The reference is to Schoenberg's middle, atonal period.

EXAMPLE 40. Stravinsky, *Octet*, II.

EXAMPLE 41. Stravinsky, *Octet*, II.

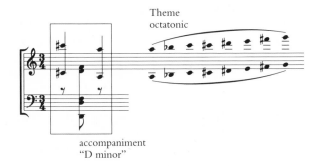

need not be pursued without reference to the old and the new—Straus's version of a duality in this respect. Thus, in the variation movement of the *Octet* (Examples 40 and 41), the split is defined by an octatonic theme standing in opposition to a pseudo–D-minor reference in the accompaniment. The theme asserts A as a pitch-class of priority, A as a point of departure and return. At the same time, A attaches itself segmentally to the (0 1 3 4) tetrachord as (A B♭ C C♯), which is transposed to (C C♯ D♯ E) at No. 25. In turn, these octatonic implications are superimposed over a "tonic" D and (D F) unit in the accompaniment, factors that are not accountable to the octatonic theme above. Hence, among other tonally derived ambiguities, a bond is sealed between the theme and its accompaniment in the form of a dominant-tonic relation, a superimposition of the theme over its accompaniment. And the latter is consummated in the final measures by a "tonic resolution" on D in which

EXAMPLE 42.   Stravinsky, *Octet*, II.

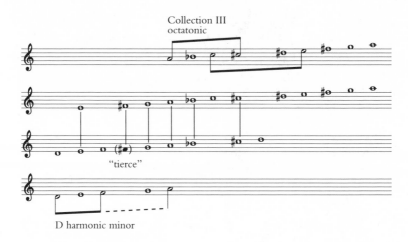

the theme's terminal F♯ unites the octatonic set with the D-minor reference in a *tierce de Picardie*.[49]

Such an interpretation can move in the direction of an integration, it seems to me, by describing one component (the octatonic) in terms of the other (the D-minor reference of the accompaniment). The peculiarity of Stravinsky's dominant rests with its duplicity: although a member of the octatonic theme, it is heard and understood as a dominant in relation to the accompaniment. Indeed, as is shown in Example 42, other significant points of intersection (the B♭, for example) could be drawn between the octatonic scale and the harmonic minor scale on D.

Moving still further in the direction of an integration, the combined effect of the two components could be assessed from the standpoint of pitch, register, and chordal disposition. The opening sonority could be judged in this manner and the implications weighed against the variation movement as a whole and beyond.

Two segmentations are cited briefly in Examples 41, 43, and 44. Example 41 considers the C♯ and A of the theme in combination with the punctuating (D F) of the accompaniment; the opening two

49. See Pieter C. van den Toorn, *The Music of Igor Stravinsky* (New Haven: Yale University Press, 1983), p. 335.

EXAMPLE 43. Stravinsky, *Octet*, II.

EXAMPLE 44. Stravinsky, *Octet*, II.

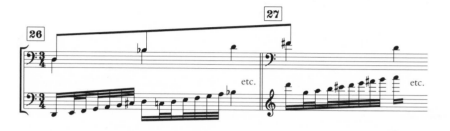

pitches of the theme, octatonic with respect to the theme as a
whole, are rendered nonoctatonic. And while the resultant sonority, (D F A C♯), is not featured in the variation movement as a
whole (in the transposition of the theme at No. 25, the relationship
of the theme to its accompaniment is very different from that in the
opening measures), it is featured in the outer movements, in the articulation of Theme II in the sonata form of the first movement, for
example. Hence, in place of a segmentation that separates the octatonic theme from its accompaniment, one that underscores in this
way the neoclassical split between the old and the new, Example 41
focuses on the vertical combination, one in which, at least initially,
the C♯ and A of the octatonic theme are grouped with the (D F) of

EXAMPLE 45. Stravinsky, "Basel" Concerto in D, I.

the accompaniment. Here, too, greater emphasis is placed on the registral disposition of the configuration.

The second segmentation, in Example 43, focuses on the middle register and the (0 1 3 4) tetrachord. The combined effect of the theme's C♯ and the (D F) of the accompaniment is identified as a subset of that tetrachord. More determinately, and with C♯ as an axis, two such tetrachords are inferred from the first four pitches of the octatonic theme (A B♭ C C♯) and its accompaniment (C♯ D E F). Of particular note is the embedded augmented triad of the resultant configuration, (A C♯ F) here, which does in fact play a role in subsequent variations A and D (Example 44).

The foregoing can seem slight, no doubt, even given that it is intended to serve the interests of assimilation. There is no reference to dislocation, to the old and the new, and hence no acknowledgment of neoclassicism, the analytical means being relatively neutral in this respect. And while those means can straddle the two sides of the accommodation, they cannot transcend a form of segmentation, the division of the context into parts of one kind or another. A conclusion might be, therefore, that each approach can offer something of an illumination in relation to the other. For whatever the merits of the undivided context, of the identity of such a context, what is sensed and felt as unique and therefore irreducible, reflection must deal with what is known and what is knowable, with parts that can relate accordingly. And the context of this particular piece may not be served all that well by ignoring the issues of neoclassicism (as introduced by Taruskin, Hyde, and Straus), ignoring the most obvious of all segmentations, those having to do with the conventions of a nonimmediate past and their reinterpretation in a contemporary light.

Indeed, even with contexts that are wholly octatonic, a neoclassical form of accommodation can suggest itself. In the introductory passage of the "Basel" Concerto in D for strings (1946; Example 45), the total pitch-class content is octatonic in terms of (D F F♯ A B). And notwithstanding the symmetrical implications of that content, the major-minor third "clashes" involving (D F F♯) and (F F♯ A), tonal conventions are unmistakable: in the theme itself, the assertion of (F/E♯) as a chromatic neighbor to F♯, the third of a (D F♯

EXAMPLE 46. Stravinsky, "Basel" Concerto in D, I.

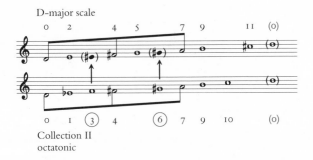

EXAMPLE 47. Stravinsky, *Danses concertantes.*

A) "tonic" triad, and, at m. 11, the assertion of B as an appoggia-tura, an incomplete neighbor to A, the fifth of the same triad. Here too, then, a duality of function can manifest itself, one that is un-derscored by various points of intersection (see Example 46).

Indeed, useful commonalities can often be pursued in twentieth-century music, if not on the basis of an entire oeuvre, then on that of a select portion thereof. The opening of Stravinsky's Concerto

EXAMPLE 48. Stravinsky, *Symphony in 3 Movements*, II.

in D can bring to mind the passage at No. 30 in his *Danses concertantes* (1942; Example 47); and the latter can point to passages at Nos. 112 and 117 in the slow movement of the *Symphony in Three Movements* (1945; Example 48). Each of these passages affirms neoclassical practices that are distinguishable from the music of Stravinsky's earlier Russian period.

So, too, each passage can point to a "stutter" motive that is characteristic of Stravinsky's melodic invention more generally. Acknowledged by the composer,[50] the motive is one to which we shall

---

50. Igor Stravinsky and Robert Craft, *Themes and Episodes* (New York: Knopf, 1969), p. 58.

be directing our attention briefly in the chapter that follows. For it is one that is articulated differently from one period to the next, from the Russian to the neoclassical, and hence in ways that can point to those larger commonalities, ones quite capable of lending themselves to analytic-theoretical definition.

7

A Case in Point:
Context and Analytical
Method in Stravinsky

I

An appropriate framework for Stravinsky's music, one that can
transcend pluralism and address that sense of a distinctive musical
presence on which there has always been such insistence, is elusive.
A pluralistic view of "Stravinsky and the traditions" will no doubt
always be possible. Such an approach can compare the composer's
jazz adaptations to authentic, improvised versions, the *Symphony in
C*, first movement, to a sonata-allegro drawn from Haydn, or the
serial mechanisms of the late works to those of Webern or Schoenberg. And to the extent that our immediate aesthetic concerns are
tied to specific works rather than to the further abstraction of an
oeuvre, such studies can point the way to an understanding of a
transcending musical identity. Getting beyond their locality, however, pinning down the more comprehensive framework of a musical tradition, is a different matter. In the end, we may be left with
impressions of Stravinsky and the music of this century that are as
sharply divided as those with which we began—scattered connections of one kind or another, networks that point in many different
directions, directions largely unaffected by considerations of precedence, origin, and chronology.

Model B (Russian)

	i	ii	iii	iv	v	vi	vii	viii	(i)
Collection I:	E	d	C♯	b	B♭	a♭	G	f	(E)
Collection II:	F	e♭	D	c	B	a	G♯	f♯	(F)
Collection III:	F♯	e	E♭	d♭	C	b♭	A	g	(F♯)
pitch numbers:	0	2	3	5	6	8	9	11	(0)
intervals:		2	1	2	1	2	1	2	(1)

	(0	2	3	5)	6	8	9	11
Diatonic D-scale:	(0	2	3	5)	7	9	10	0
Diatonic C-scale:	0	2	4	5	7	9	11	0
	(0	1	3	4)	6	7	9	10

	i	ii	iii	iv	v	vi	vii	viii	(i)
Collection I:	E	f	G	a♭	B♭	b	D♭	d	(E)
Collection II:	F	f♯	A♭	a	B	c	F	e♭	(F)
Collection III:	F♯	g	A	b♭	C	d♭	E♭	e	(F♯)
pitch numbers:	0	1	3	4	6	7	9	10	(0)
intervals:		1	2	1	2	1	2	1	(2)

Model A (Neoclassical)

Figure 11.

Consider the octatonic pitch-structures that figure significantly in the music of a great many twentieth-century composers, including Debussy. Several of Debussy's piano preludes feature an octatonic vocabulary that can hook up to Models A and B (see Fig. 11), the two models of octatonic partitioning that may be inferred from Stravinsky's music when considered as a whole.[1] And cross-references of this kind are useful in that they can force the analyst into greater specificity: if Stravinsky's harmonic vocabulary is characterized by a tendency to superimpose octatonic subsets

---

1. The two models are discussed at length in Pieter C. van den Toorn, *The Music of Igor Stravinsky* (New Haven: Yale University Press, 1983), pp. 48–61. They will be reviewed briefly here.

(triads, for example), such a tendency is in little evidence in Debussy's preludes. At the same time, superimposition brings the matter of superimposed rhythmic pedals in its wake, a matter linked to the patterns of metric irregularity and displacements of accent that are a part of the Stravinskian idiom generally, regardless of its Russian, neoclassical, or serial orientation. Here again, as with superimposition, such practices are of no special significance in the octatonicism of Debussy's preludes.

But nor are they of much concern in the music of Stravinsky's immediate predecessors. Accentual displacement in Stravinsky's music may have originated in the flexible stresses that accompany Russian popular verse, yet the musical realization of this flexibility was peculiarly Stravinsky's own; there are few, if any, precedents in the music of his immediate Russian predecessors. And the same is true of the method of superimposing rhythmic pedals. Indeed, to the extent that Stravinsky's rhythmic practices harbor assumptions of steady metric periodicity, those practices relate to the role of meter and rhythm in Western tonal music generally rather than to anything that could be construed as specifically Russian. And what may astonish most about this oeuvre, in fact, is not the ties that bind it to its immediate past but the distance that separates it from that past, the distance that separates even relatively early works such as *Petrushka* (1911), *Zvezdoliki* (1912), and *The Rite of Spring* (1913) from the music of Stravinsky's Russian predecessors.

Why, then, assume a special advantage in the relationship of this oeuvre to its immediate past? More specifically, why should Rimsky-Korsakov's octatonic uses be any more compelling as a framework or foil than those of Debussy or Bartók?[2] Why not accept the context of twentieth-century music, the pivotal role assumed by

2. For a discussion of octatonic relations in Debussy, see Richard S. Parks, "Pitch Organization in Debussy: Unordered Sets in 'Brouillards,'" *Music Theory Spectrum* 2 (1980); and Richard S. Parks, *The Music of Claude Debussy* (New Haven: Yale University Press, 1990). See also Allen Forte, "Debussy and the Octatonic," *Music Analysis* 10, nos. 1–2 (1991). Octatonic relations in Bartók are discussed in Elliott Antokoletz, *The Music of Bela Bartók* (Berkeley: University of California Press, 1984), pp. 204–270; and in Richard Cohn, "Bartók's Octatonic Strategies: A Motivic Approach," *Journal of the American Musicological Society* 44, no. 2 (1991): 262–300.

this oeuvre in the shaping of the pluralism of that context, even if this acceptance leads to abstractions such as the pitch-class (or interval-class) set, abstractions that remain relatively indifferent to the sorts of distinctions that pertain to style, idiom, and oeuvre?

Such questions occupy the bulk of this chapter. Before proceeding, however, we should review the case for Models A and B, discuss the distinctions raised by these models in connection with the Russian and neoclassical "stylistic" periods, and compare this methodology to applications of interval cycles and pitch-class sets. With the foregoing as a frame of reference, we can turn to those larger issues that arise from consideration of Stravinsky's rhythmic practices and of the octatonicism of several of Debussy's preludes.

2

Among the many striking features that distinguish Stravinsky's early Russian-period works are the whole-step reiterations or 2s that litter their articulative surfaces. Many of these reiterations are little more than intonations with neighbor-note inflections, whereas others are fastened more securely to folk-like fragments and ostinatos of one kind or another. Stravinsky himself, when occupied years later with the serial miniature *Elegy for J.F.K.* (1964), acknowledged the predilection:

Two reiterated notes are a rhythmic-melodic stutter characteristic of my speech from *Les Noces* to the ["Basel"] *Concerto in D*, and earlier and later as well—a lifelong affliction, in fact.[3]

Conspicuously, however, the "reiterated notes" that characterize the motivic invention in the neoclassical string Concerto in D (1946) are composed of half-steps, not whole steps as in *Les Noces* (1917–23) and the Russian period generally. My own view of this distinction in reiteration is that it reflects the many critical changes that accompanied the neoclassical "change of life" (as Stravinsky later called neoclassicism),[4] changes that relate to the melodic and

3. Igor Stravinsky and Robert Craft, *Themes and Episodes* (New York: Knopf, 1969), p. 58.
4. Stravinsky and Craft, *Themes and Episodes*, p. 23.

harmonic character of the diatonic and octatonic components. For if, on the diatonic side of octatonic-diatonic interaction, neoclassicism often replaced earlier modal inflections with a vocabulary that implied, in however impure or contaminated a fashion, the major-scale ordering of the diatonic set, the interacting octatonic component could be viewed from a similar perspective, as having undergone a similar transformation and with similar implications in referential ordering.

More specifically, Russian whole-step reiterations and their more determinate groupings imply the 2–1 ordering of the octatonic scale, that ordering in which the scale's second degree lies at the interval of 2 from its first. Neoclassical works such as the Concerto in D imply the reverse, the 1–2 ordering in which the scale's second degree lies at the interval of 1 from its first (see Figure 11). And although these considerations of scalar ordering may seem, in the face of all that is profoundly new and different in this music, quaint and even reactionary, they are in fact hardly so if the representational character of the orderings is kept in view, if contact is maintained with the concrete phenomena—in this case, the reiteration or "rhythmic-melodic stutter," the "lifelong affliction"—which these orderings reflect at a rather high level of abstraction.

The referential implications of the Russian period's whole-step reiterations are traced in Figure 12. The whole step or 2 is attached to the (0 2 5) trichord, a unit that serves not only as the basic cell for much of *Les Noces* and *The Rite of Spring* (1913) but as a kind of motto for the Russian period as a whole. Viewed either as a trichord or as an incomplete or "gapped" (0 2 3 5) Dorian tetrachord, this (0 2 5) unit is a subset of the diatonic and octatonic sets and often serves, by way of that neutrality, as a point of intersection in passages of octatonic-diatonic interpenetration. It may also serve as that unit which is articulatively shared between blocks or sections of material that are referentially distinct in this octatonic-diatonic respect.

On the left side of Figure 12 are the implied diatonic references, the (0 2 3 5 7 9) hexachord and the (0 2 3 5 7 9 10 0) Dorian mode or D-scale; featured on the right is the 2–1 ordering of the octatonic set and its (0 2 3 5 6 8 9 11) numbering. The four—0, 3, 6, 9—sym-

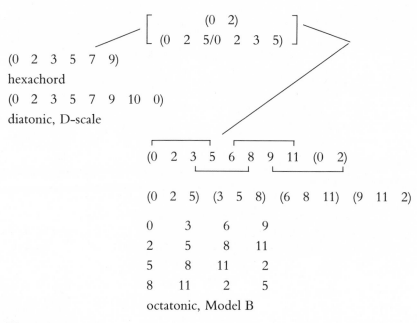

Figure 12.

metrically defined dominant sevenths further down in this display
are an appendage to what is ostensibly an (0 2 3 5) tetrachordal partitioning format. (Conventional terminology is introduced for
purposes of identification, with no intent of invoking tonally functional relations.) And what in turn connects the (0 2 3 5) tetrachord
to the dominant seventh is the embedded (0 2 5) trichord, the basic
cell or motto of the Russian period. Elsewhere I have referred to
this Russian (0 2 3 5) tetrachordal format in Figure 12, primarily
linear in conception, as Model B.[5] In contrast, Model A is made to
encompass the triads, (0 3 4 / 3 4 7 / 3 6 7) major-minor third trichords, and (0 1 3 4) tetrachords that imply the 1–2 ordering of the
octatonic set that identifies more readily with neoclassical works.

In Example 49 and Figure 13, Model B is activated by way of the
opening two blocks of *Les Noces*. According to the activation itself
in Figure 13, the soprano's E assumes priority as the point of departure and return while, at letter A, D is introduced as a neighbor-

5. See van den Toorn, *The Music of Igor Stravinsky*, p. 51.

EXAMPLE 49.   Stravinsky, *Les Noces*, First Tableau.

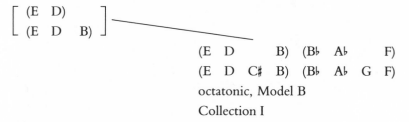

```
┌ (E  D)        ┐ ──────────────
└ (E  D    B) ┘            ──────────────
                    (E   D        B)  (B♭  A♭      F)
                    (E   D   C♯  B)  (B♭  A♭  G  F)
                    octatonic, Model B
                    Collection I
```

Figure 13.

note inflection to this intonation. More determinately, the E–D whole step is grouped with the (E D B) trichord. Then, at letter B, the (E D B B♭ F) pitch content retains (E D B) as the connecting link: B♭ and F, pitch numbers 6 and 11 in relation to Model B's (0 2 3 5) (6 8 9 11) tetrachordal numbering, intrude to signal the intervention of octatonic relations. And while the Collection I content is incomplete, it foreshadows the interacting octatonic-diatonic circumstances that prevail more generally in *Les Noces*. Indeed, inasmuch as the F♯ grace note is nonoctatonic in relation to Collection I, the interaction at letter B qualifies as a form of interpenetration. Observe, also, that the scales, pitch letters, and pitch numbers associated with Model B descend. This is in order to reconcile pitch-class priority and (0 2 3 5) tetrachordal partitioning with pitch-class content. Thus, had we ascended from the E with the 2–1 ordering of the scale as implied by the (0 2 5) trichord, such an arrangement would have yielded Collection III instead of Collection I.

Still another illustration of Model B's tetrachordal format is given in Example 50, from the Introduction to *The Rite of Spring*. Here, the (0 2 3 5) tetrachord in terms of (D C B A) is inferred from the opening diatonic melody in the bassoon. And, as marked off by the dotted line in this example, the C–A–D–A contour of this fragment anticipates the D♭–B♭–E♭–B♭ contour of the succeeding ostinato. Then, at No. 13, the ostinato's (E♭ D♭ B♭) trichord is attached to a dominant seventh on E♭ which is superimposed over an E in the bass (as pitch number 11 in relation to the E♭). In this final transaction, E♭, D♭, and B♭ of the ostinato's (E♭ D♭ B♭) trichord are retained as the root, seventh, and fifth, respectively, of the E♭ seventh chord. Indeed, the disposition of this chord—closed position, first

EXAMPLE 50.   Stravinsky, *The Rite of Spring,* Introduction.

inversion, and in the same register at No. 13—exposes the persistence of E♭, D♭, and B♭ as a tightly articulated (E♭ D♭ B♭) trichordal link. Hence, (0 2 5) functions as a link not only in octatonic-diatonic interaction but also in connecting (0 2 3 5) tetrachords with dominant-seventh formations. Finally, the E♭-seventh is transposed to C, A, and F♯ to complete a 0, 3, 6, 9 partitioning of Collection III at No. 42.

3

The formulations in the above examples are typical of the modeling with which I sought, some years ago, to pin down the regularities governing octatonic-diatonic interaction in Stravinsky's music. The assumption was that the Stravinskian stamp—the characteristics of the relations Stravinsky employed—could often be traced to the specifics of this referential interaction. So, too, in seeking to distinguish Russian from neoclassical idiosyncrasy, it seemed that a theoretical definition of those specifics could be given a sharper, more determinate focus. Not all of Stravinsky's music could be approached advantageously by way of this definition (a problem that proved especially apparent with some of the lengthier works, in which only single movements or sections applied—a condition of localized referentiality hardly unique in the music of this century, however); yet my preference, given the objectives at hand, was determinacy rather than still greater abstraction.

Moreover, the methods employed in this pursuit were circular. Formats similar to those outlined above were inferred from this diverse body of works whose members were then called upon to exemplify the formats. But this should not imply that analysis was pursued as a form of theory confirmation. The preoccupation at the outset may have been to find an underlying regularity, but the intention was that such regularity would serve as a foil, would provide a framework within which to set the details of individual contexts.

Nonetheless, scalar orderings and numberings can raise problematic questions of priority and hierarchical structure. Those questions could have been avoided here by resorting to interval cycles, treating the diatonic set as a seven-note segment of the interval-5/7 cycle and the octatonic as the sum of two interval-3 cycles related by the interval of 1 or 2.[6] And in fact the role of the interval-

6. See the analysis of the opening of *The Rite of Spring* in George Perle, "Berg's Master Array of the Interval Cycles," *Musical Quarterly* 63, no. 1 (1977): 10–12. Cycles and their application are discussed in greater detail in Elliott Antokoletz, "Interval Cycles in Stravinsky's Early Ballets," *Journal of the American Musicological Society* 39, no. 3 (1986).

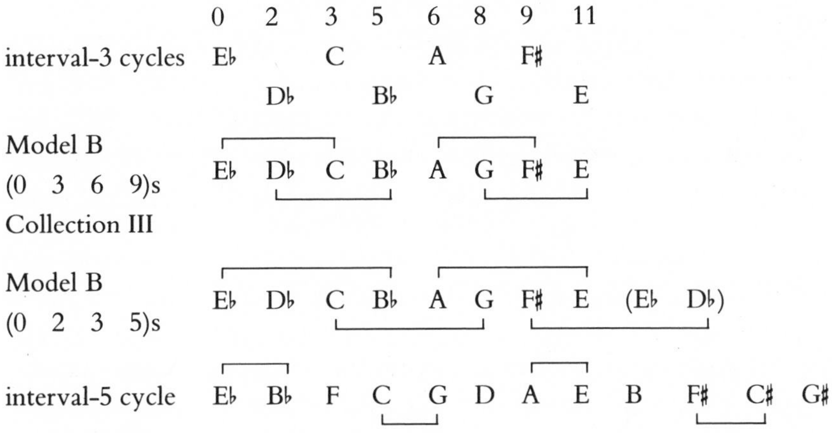

	0	2	3	5	6	8	9	11
interval-3 cycles	E♭		C		A		F♯	
		D♭		B♭		G		E

Model B
(0 3 6 9)s
Collection III

E♭ D♭ C B♭ A G F♯ E

Model B
(0 2 3 5)s

E♭ D♭ C B♭ A G F♯ E (E♭ D♭)

interval-5 cycle   E♭ B♭ F C G D A E B F♯ C♯ G♯

Figure 14.

5/7 cycle in octatonic-diatonic contexts of the Russian period is of-ten quite explicit.

Thus, in Examples 34–39 in chapter 6, each of the melodic frag-ments reduced to set-class 4–23 or (0 2 5 7). Yet the articulation can point just as easily to the interval-5/7 cycle as a referential factor, in relation to which each fragment would figure as a four-note seg-ment. Indeed, in the more extended contexts surrounding these fragments, transpositions are often pursued with unmistakable reference to that cycle, especially the 5-cycle whose fourths hook up to the (0 2 3 5) tetrachords and connecting-link networks of Model B.

The octatonic (Model B) side to this cyclic approach could be represented by two interlocking 3-cycles a whole step apart (read-ing down), the first of which would coincide with the 0, 3, 6, 9 par-titioning elements of the set, the elements of internal transposition. Intersections with the interval-5 cycle, coming by way of the (0 2 3 5) tetrachord and its encircling fourth (as connecting links), could be plotted along the lines indicated in Figure 14.

Yet the issue of priority is less easily dismissed as it extends be-yond interval classes to pitch-classes and pitch-class-specific sets. I would argue that the insistence in many Russian-period contexts on reiterated pitches and (0 2 3 5) tetrachordal links as points of departure and return and as connecting links between blocks of varied referential implications points quite unmistakably to assumptions of priority and hierarchical structure, even if these assumptions, applicable on a sectional basis, are no longer tonally motivated and are without reference to the major-scale ordering of the diatonic set.

Moreover, (0 2 3 5) tetrachordal formations, which are registrally fixed and confined to the interval of 5 in Russian-period contexts, readily suggest scalar orderings as an appropriate means of representation. Octatonically, these formations stand in a fixed, polarized opposition to the lower pitch–number 11, a span that suggests the 2–1 ordering of the set in Model B. Interval cycles are implied in many of these contexts, but they should not, even at deep levels of structure, obscure the essentials of vocabulary and articulation that are of such marked consequence to an octatonic and octatonic-diatonic reading of the Russian period.

In addition, of course, the orderings and numberings of the preceding examples could be reduced to Allen Forte's "prime forms" and submitted to the wider and more general considerations of relatedness made possible by that reduction.[7] Presumably, the advantage of such a reduction would be that of providing Stravinsky's music with the sort of literature-wide coverage that is denied to the more determinate, context-sensitive rulings associated with the models and networks surveyed above. In particular, the octatonic web could be extended by nonliteral complement and subset relations, extensions that could plug many of the gaps left open by an approach focused in large part on pitch-classes and pitch-class-specific sets.

But the term *set* (or *collection*), as it is applied here and indeed more generally as part of the octatonic-diatonic approach to Stravinsky's music, already presupposes this reduction. It presupposes the fact that, without regard to vocabulary or articulation (or composer, for that matter), octatonic contexts can be identified as oc-

7. See Allen Forte, *The Structure of Atonal Music* (New Haven: Yale University Press, 1973). See footnote 3 in chapter 5, above.

tatonic on the basis of their interval-class content alone, that at this higher level of abstraction the three transpositions as well as the two inversionally related interval orderings are equivalent. And an appreciation of the implications of reduction along the lines proposed by Forte and others, an appreciation of the larger, less determinate universe to which access is gained, will always be an essential part of the pitch-structural approach.

The problems that have arisen stem less from the relations themselves than from their application. Underlying the process of segmentation are assumptions that pertain to the grouping of pitches and pitch-classes, assumptions that, given the level of abstraction presumed by the interval-class set, are not easily confronted and assessed. And there are difficulties on the other side of this process as well, difficulties that pertain to the significance of relations which, inferred at this rather high level of abstraction, are brought to the surface without a qualifying syntactical premise.

Yet the larger universe is not open to dispute on perceptual or theoretical grounds. However remote or "oceanic" its deliberations (to quote Richard Taruskin),[8] however vast its assumption may be in the analysis of tonal works, it too is a framework within which discriminations can be set forth. And they can be set forth not by way of an insulated speculative theory but by way of a musical predicament that is as historical in its implications as it is analytic-theoretical. Linked to the problem of segmentation is the problem of pluralism, that of the high degree of self-reference or contextuality that is exhibited on the part of individual atonal or post-tonal works. And this intense self-reference has meant that analysis, in seeking to formulate a wider context, has had to retreat to higher levels of abstraction, more abstract forms of relatedness. Much of the history of contemporary theory and analysis could be sketched along these lines.

The distinction for much of Stravinsky's music and its analysis rests, it seems to me, on the notion of reference, that is, on the de-

8. Richard Taruskin, review of James M. Baker's *The Music of Alexander Scriabin, Music Theory Spectrum* 10 (1988): 156.

gree to which the diatonic and octatonic sets are heard and understood not as local segments defined motivically, chordally, or instrumentally, but as categories of reference that subsume these segments on a literal, pitch-class-specific basis. The relevant contexts are invested with a content determinacy that extends beyond interval classes to pitch-classes; they derive their character from confinement to single transpositional levels for periods of significant duration.

At the same time, operations of transposition and inversion are constrained in narrow and specific ways. Octatonic subsets transposed at 3, 6, and 9 remain confined to a single transposition. The (0 3 5) trichord (reading down), although inversionally related to (0 2 5), never assumes, for the reasons discussed above, the same significance in octatonic-diatonic contexts of the Russian period as (0 2 5) does. And similar qualifications pertain to the half-diminished seventh chord and its inversionally related dominant seventh, and, indeed, to the two inversionally related orderings of the octatonic set that distinguish Model A from Model B and, ultimately, Russian-period idiosyncrasy from neoclassicism. The point is not that interval-class sets and their relations are irrelevant but that they can be subsumed under considerations of greater determinacy.

Two passages from *The Rite of Spring* and the first movement of the Concerto in D are shown in Examples 51 and 52. The two excerpts face each other so that the Russian context is juxtaposed with the neoclassical, Model B in turn with Model A. The octatonic pitch content, incomplete and fragmentary in each case, refers to Collection II. Yet the particulars of vocabulary and articulation are precisely those to which reference has been made, particulars that underscore the distinctions in referential ordering.

In the passage from *The Rite of Spring* the Db-Bb-Eb-Bb ostinato that prefaces the "Augurs of Spring" at No. 13 is transposed down a half-step to C–A–D–A, back to the original level as outlined by the opening bassoon melody (see Example 50). Joined by a complete (D C B A) tetrachordal fragment in the trumpet, the ostinato stands in opposition to a lower Eb in the bassoon, with Eb as pitch number 11. And while the G in the bassoon fragment is nonoctatonic, the (D C B A)–Eb span that may be inferred from within this passage hooks up to Model B and the implied 2–1 ordering of the octatonic set.

The octatonic complexion is markedly different in the Concerto in D. The punctuated F♯ is inflected by its half-step neighbor, the E♯, just as, at No. 55, A is inflected by G♯. On the Classical major-scale side of the bargain, E♯ and G♯ function as chromatic tendency tones to the third and fifth of an implied (D F♯ A) tonic triad. Octatonically, however, the (D F F♯/F F♯ A/ F G♯ A) major-minor third symmetries and clashes point to the interacting, intruding role of Collection II, a role that implies Model A and the 1–2 ordering of the set. These orderings, then, bring to the fore critical distinctions that relate not only to the octatonic-diatonic vocabulary but to the manner of its articulation in early Russian and neoclassical contexts.

4

More to the point here, however, is the question of a wider context for Stravinsky's music, one defined not alone by sets and subsets, vocabularies and their articulations, but by the (presumably) more comprehensive framework of a musical tradition. On several occasions Richard Taruskin has argued in favor of a full-scale study of the composer's early Russian background, one that would encompass not only the specifically musical ingredients of Stravinsky's early years—the lessons with Rimsky-Korsakov, the models pursued in composition, the habits shared by colleagues and immediate predecessors—but the aesthetic and cultural bearings of these years as well.[9] And his own account of this subject is without question a *tour de force*, a brilliantly argued musical biography of the Russian period that includes, in no small detail, an analytic-theoretical perspective that hooks up nicely to the one surveyed here.[10] Indeed, the connection itself, coming on the heels of a spir-

9. See, for example, Richard Taruskin, review of Allen Forte's *The Harmonic Structure of "The Rite of Spring," Current Musicology* 28 (1979): 119.

10. Richard Taruskin, *Stravinsky and the Russian Traditions* (Berkeley: University of California Press, forthcoming). Taruskin has published a set of articles that figure as chapters in the forthcoming book: "The Rite Revisited: The Idea and the

EXAMPLE 51.   Stravinsky, *The Rite of Spring*, Introduction.

ited debate over Stravinsky's musical inheritance, arrives at a most opportune time.[11] Included are detailed readings of various octa-tonic-diatonic practices shared by Rimsky-Korsakov and his circle. And Stravinsky's manifest preoccupation, in the later years of the Russian period, with the sound and substance of Russian popular verse is treated in convincing and imaginative detail. A wealth of data and opinion is processed as history, biography, analysis, and criticism, a blend that stands, at least to my way of thinking, as one of the truly remarkable achievements in music scholarship today.

Yet I am not all that certain that this early Russian heritage is in-

Sources of Its Scenario," in *Music and Civilization: Essays in Honor of Paul Henry Lang*, ed. Edmond Strainchamps and Maria Rika Maniates (New York: W. W. Norton, 1984); "Chernomor to Kastchei: Harmonic Sorcery, or, Stravinsky's 'Angle'," *Journal of the American Musicological Society* 38, no. 1 (1985); "Chez Petroushka: Harmony and Tonality chez Stravinsky," *19th-Century Music* 10, no. 3 (1986); "Stravinsky and the Traditions," *Opus* 3 (1987); "Stravinsky's Rejoicing Discovery and What It Meant: Some Observations on His Russian Text-Setting," in *Stravinsky Retrospectives*, ed. Ethan Haimo and Paul Johnson (Lincoln: University of Nebraska Press, 1987), pp. 162–199.

11. See, for example, Richard Taruskin, "Letter to the Editor," *Music Analysis* 5, nos. 2–3 (1986): 313–320; and Allen Forte's reply, "Letter to the Editor in Reply to Richard Taruskin," *Music Analysis* 5, nos. 2–3 (1986): 321–337.

EXAMPLE 52. Stravinsky, "Basel" Concerto in D, I.

Model A (Neoclassical)

variably the most useful context within which to position the terms of Stravinsky's musical particularity, be they Russian, neoclassical, or serial in imprint. As has been suggested already, what may astonish most about this music is not the ties that bind it to its immediate past but the distance that separates it from that past.[12] This is not to deny the existence of ties, of octatonic patterns, folksong uses, and orchestral practices inherited in one way or another. But it is to question the extent to which considerations of precedence and origin are in any way privileged in securing a musical context for this oeuvre, one that can relate to, among other variables, the sorts of pitch-relational concerns voiced above.[13]

Even if the ties to Stravinsky's immediate past (or to what could be construed as specifically Russian in his music) were as vivid and as marked as Taruskin suggests, this would not in itself guarantee their musical significance. For the question of an engaging context is an aesthetic as well as a historical and analytic-theoretical one. And once individual works begin to prevail for what they are in and of themselves and not for what they represent, then context itself, as a reflection of this transcendence, becomes less dependent on matters of historical placement. A great variety of contexts can suggest themselves as attention is focused on the works, on the nature of both their immediacy and the relationship that is struck with the contemporary listener. "Burrowing for roots," as Carl Dahlhaus once termed the quest for origins,[14] becomes just one of the many ways of deliberately staking a claim, while the idea that musical "essences" are to be found by probing ever more deeply in this direction can become increasingly reductionist. What may be sought in the abstract are specific connections and networks of

12. Stravinsky was well aware of this distance at the time of composing *The Rite of Spring*. In a letter to André Rimsky-Korsakov on 7 March 1912, he wrote that "it is as if twenty and not two years had passed since *The Firebird* had been composed." Vera Stravinsky and Robert Craft, *Stravinsky in Pictures and Documents* (New York: Simon and Schuster, 1978), p. 87.

13. See the argument in Richard Taruskin, "Reply to van den Toorn," *In Theory Only* 10, no. 3 (October 1987).

14. Carl Dahlhaus, *Foundations of Music History*, trans. J. B. Robinson (Cambridge: Cambridge University Press, 1983), p. 120.

relations, connections less comprehensive in scope, perhaps, but aesthetically viable nonetheless, not just—or even necessarily— historically pertinent.

Much of what is characteristic of Stravinsky's music—its Russian, neoclassical, and serial orientations, its rhythmic emphasis and the relationship of this to pitch structure—can be traced only rather tenuously to the musical preoccupations of his immediate predecessors. At an early stage, superimposed rhythmic pedals began to overwhelm the immediate sense of progression, while the harmonic implications of these pedals, methods of superimposition, transformed the octatonic-diatonic patterns inherited from Rimsky-Korsakov and his circle. (Treating superimposed parts as if, in combination, they were harmonies structurally or syntactically on a par with those of past tonal music is a common approach in pitch-class set analysis that eliminates, in my estimation, much of the sense of the technique, especially as it pertains to Russian-period works.)

Debussy, who first met Stravinsky at the time of the early ballets (1910–1913), seems to have been struck almost immediately by these developments. *The Firebird* was noted for its "extremely unusual combinations of rhythm," while in *Petrushka* the directness of Stravinsky's methods seemed "childish and savage," without "precautions or pretensions."[15] Even after *The Rite of Spring*, a piece that drew a more equivocal response, Stravinsky and his music remained "amazing" and "astonishing."[16] All this does not discount the composer's Russian heritage but suggests that, on the matter of an appropriate context, we are not obliged to move only backwards; we can move sideways and forwards as well, and in all three

15. Letter to Jacques Durand, 8 July 1910, in *Debussy Letters*, ed. François Lesure and Roger Nichols, trans. Roger Nichols (Cambridge: Harvard University Press, 1987), p. 221. Letter to Robert Godet, 18 December 1911, in *Debussy Letters*, ed. Lesure and Nichols, p. 250.

16. For an equivocal response, see the letter to André Caplet, 29 May 1913, in *Debussy Letters*, ed. Lesure and Nichols, p. 306. "It's extraordinarily wild," Debussy wrote of *The Rite*, "as you might say, it's primitive music with all the modern conveniences." For the latter quotes, see the letter to Robert Godet, 4 January 1916, in *Debussy Letters*, ed. Lesure and Nichols, p. 312.

EXAMPLE 53.   Stravinsky, *Symphony of Psalms*, III.

directions without necessarily invoking issues of derivation, origin, and precedence.

5

Consider the superimposed rhythmic pedals that are identified with Stravinsky's music. The technique consists of superimposing two or more fragments which, fixed registrally and instrumentally, repeat according to cycles that vary independently of one another. Extensive applications may be found in *The Rite of Spring* and *Les Noces*, but the technique is by no means peculiar to the Russian period and may be found in virtually all phases of Stravinsky's work.

Example 53 is taken from the Allegro in the final movement of the *Symphony of Psalms* (1930). Here, the principal fragment in the

horns and bassoons is superimposed over an F♯–G–A♭ basso ostinato and eventually, in the upper register, a G–B♭–A♭–C fragment
in the trumpet. As is indicated by the brackets, repeats of the principal fragment are unevenly spaced, a spacing that causes them to
become displaced in relation to the steady 4/4 meter. If the half-
note beat is taken as the pulse (or "beat") with a metronome marking of 80, then these displacements will be heard and understood as
onbeat-offbeat contradictions. The initial offbeat alignment at No.
3 is contradicted by an onbeat alignment at No. 3 + 3. In direct opposition to these displacements, however, the articulation of the
principal fragment remains unchanged. Irrespective of its placement in relation to the steady 4/4 meter, the fragment is always
punctuated with a stress which in turn is always followed by *piano*
and staccato.

These cross-purposes lie at the heart of the rhythmic invention.
The double edge consists, on the one hand, of an effort to displace
or contradict the accentual implications of a reiterated fragment
(which presupposes a steady meter, a frame of reference against
which these displacements can be heard and understood) and, on
the other, of an effort to counter displacement by pressing for a
fixed identity in repetition.

Accordingly, listeners are faced with three options at No. 3 + 3:
(1) conservatively, they can hold fast to the 4/4 meter so that the
onbeat displacement of the principal fragment is immediately
heard and understood as such; (2) radically, they can immediately
shift their metrical bearings at this point to comply with the fragment's initial offbeat placement at the beginning of the Allegro; (3)
moderately, they can succumb to a moment of uncertainty as to the
overriding trustworthiness of either the meter or the fixed articulation of the fragment.

The third option would seem to reflect most persuasively the
point of the invention. For the steady 4/4 meter and its half-note
pulse at the beginning of the Allegro are inferred with reference to
the fragment's initial offbeat placement and the relationship of this
placement to the accompanying part in the bass. Internalized, these
metrical bearings are disrupted by the onbeat placement at No.
3 + 3. Forced to the surface of consciousness, these bearings be-

come disconnected from the fragment; in a moment of disorientation, the pulse is challenged as onbeats become indistinguishable from offbeats. And so the listener's attention is likely to be directed toward regaining the security of his or her earlier bearings, a task that consists of regrouping the quarter-note beats in a higher-level alignment that can once again be internalized, taken for granted. This, in a nutshell, is the nature of the displacement and its effect as metrical disruption and readjustment.

Of course, the composer himself could have opted for the radical approach at No. 3 + 3. Instead of pursuing the steady 4/4 meter he could have shifted the barline so as to preserve the initial offbeat placement of the fragment. This is precisely the rationale that underlies the shifting meter in the opening two blocks of *Les Noces*, a passage discussed earlier in connection with Example 49. In *Les Noces* the meter shifts rapidly in order to preserve a single, fixed identity for the principal D–E fragment. This fragment is always barred as an upbeat-downbeat, over-the-barline succession.

True, the structure in *Les Noces* is different. The accompanying parts or fragments move in unvarying synchronization with the stressed, over-the-barline D–E succession; the xylophone punctuates always, and only, that one particular D which, over the barline, is succeeded by E as the point of departure and return. Consequently, there are no superimposed rhythmic pedals that repeat according to periods that vary independently of one another.

Nonetheless, displacements of the sort encountered in the example from *Psalms* are very much in evidence. For, in opposition to the fixed metrical placement of the D–E fragment, a steady 3/8 meter may be inferred from the opening bars, in relation to which subsequent D–E repeats define a patterned cycle of displacement. As shown in the rebarred version of Example 49, D–E is displaced to the second and first beats of the 3/8 measure until, in the completion of its cycle two bars before letter B, it resumes its initial upbeat-downbeat alignment. Observe, too, that the concealed 3/8 meter arrives on target with the foreground irregularity in these final measures, an arrival that intensifies, retroactively, the "feel" of the steady meter.

6

Now it is entirely possible that the forms of displacement discussed above had as their origin the flexible stresses that are a part of the singing of Russian popular verse. Stravinsky later recalled that his own awareness of this trait had come when, exiled in Switzerland during the war years, he turned his attention to the setting of a number of folk tales, a preoccupation that was to emerge as the later Russian period itself. Quite apart from the question as to what might have spawned these rhythmic innovations, the analogy between them and Russian popular verse is striking:

> One important characteristic of Russian popular verse is that the accents of the spoken verse are ignored when the verse is sung. . . . The recognition of the musical possibilities inherent in this fact was one of the most rejoicing discoveries of my life; I was like a man who suddenly finds that his finger can be bent from the second joint as well from the first.[17]

Yet the "musical possibilities" inherent in this feature had been realized by the composer years before this "discovery"—indeed, in works such as *The Firebird*, *Petrushka*, and *The Rite of Spring*. And as far as I can determine, the realization itself was peculiarly Stravinsky's own. There are few, if any, precedents in the music of his immediate St. Petersburg predecessors.

This is not to suggest that these innovations were context-free. In tonal music, irregularity is common enough at levels of metrical structure above those defined by the pulse and the barline. Beats spanning a measure are frequently added to, or deleted from, two- and four-measure modules with the consequence that restatements of themes and motives are displaced relative to hypermeter. In this way, thematic alignments shift from odd- to even-numbered measures and vice versa. The impact of these higher-level realignments tends to be most conspicuous within relatively short spans, but it

---

17. Igor Stravinsky and Robert Craft, *Expositions and Developments* (Berkeley: University of California Press, 1981), p. 121. The implications of the flexible stress in Russian popular verse for Stravinsky's Russian text-setting are discussed in revealing detail in Taruskin, "Stravinsky's Rejoicing Discovery," pp. 162–199.

can be dramatic indeed when it straddles the repeat of a sonata-form exposition.[18]

Stravinsky can thus be imagined as having shifted these processes of displacement, processes of metrical disruption and readjustment, to shorter, more immediate timespans. And the connection is of some consequence because it points once again to underlying assumptions of periodicity.

Of the many tonal contexts that could apply here, the *Dies irae* section in the final movement of Berlioz's *Symphonie fantastique* (1830) seems ideally suited to our purposes. For, as is detailed in Example 54, the repeated C–C–G figure in the bass, scored for pianos and bells, is a rhythmic pedal, in relation to which successive phrases of the *Dies irae* theme take on the character of a superimposition. Indeed, the issues that one can imagine Berlioz to have faced in this music are of the same kind as those that spring to mind in conjunction with the Allegro in the final movement of *Psalms*.

The invention stems initially from a stratification of parts, which, fixed registrally and instrumentally, repeat in varying periods or cycles. More immediately, it has to do with the alignment of these parts in relation to the steady 6/8 meter and with the subsequent displacements in this alignment that trigger, in the mind of the listener, metrical disruption and readjustment. Thus, too, the harmonic implications of this alignment, although constrained in general by the repetition, are of secondary importance at the local level. The modal, A-scale character of the *Dies irae* theme, its proper harmonization, so to speak, is not an issue here. Rather, the invention is defined more immediately by the rhythmic-metric implications of the alignment than by harmonic coincidence or by harmony as such (which, in structures of this kind, tends to emerge as an effect rather than as a determining factor). And, once again, the difference in relation to the *Psalms* example is that displacement

18. See the discussion of the first movement of Beethoven's Piano Sonata in D Major, Op. 10, No. 3, in Andrew Imbrie, "'Extra' Measures and Metrical Ambiguity in Beethoven," in Alan Tyson, ed., *Beethoven Studies* (New York: W. W. Norton, 1973), pp. 45–66. See also Fred Lerdahl and Ray Jackendoff, *A Generative Theory of Tonal Music* (Cambridge: MIT Press, 1983), pp. 22–25.

EXAMPLE 54. Berlioz, *Symphonie fantastique*, V.

and disruption materialize at metrical levels above those defined by the pulse and the barline.

Indeed, rhythmic values in Example 54 have been reduced by half so as to expose these higher levels of metrical structure. The two-measure module of the score is reduced to a single measure, while the dotted-quarter-note beat (with a metronome marking of 104) becomes a dotted-eighth-note beat. And a form of displacement may already be felt with the second entrance of the C–C–G pedal at m. 134. At an uneven spacing of thirteen dotted-quarter-note beats, the upbeat appearance of the pedal at m. 134 contradicts the initial downbeat appearance at m. 121. And this displacement is underscored by the dotted-quarter-note rendition of the initial *Dies irae* phrase just above. The first four bars of this phrase, Eb–D–Eb–C, are likely to be apprehended as a clearly articulated four-measure unit.

Indeed, felt displacement is a function not only of the irregular spacing of the C–C–G pedal but also of the relationship of this spacing to the higher-level groupings that may be inferred from the *Dies irae* phrases. And although two-, four-, and six-measure units may occasionally be inferred from these phrases, they are, in and of themselves, highly ambiguous from a metrical standpoint. Notice, for example, that the downbeat placement of the initial dotted-quarter-note phrase (beginning with Eb–D–Eb–C, the first stave in Example 54) is contradicted by the offbeat placement of the repeat of this phrase in dotted eighth-notes. This duplicity intensifies the instability of the C–C–G pedal below. Indeed, an onbeat-offbeat contradiction materializes with the dotted-quarter-note and dotted-eighth-note repeats of the second *Dies irae* phrase as well, a phrase that begins with G–Bb–Bb–A just prior to m. 165 and m. 178. Here, however, the placement of G on the downbeat just prior to m. 165 is itself unstable, since it is the repeated Bb of this phrase that, by virtue of its relative length or duration, is the preferred accent, the preferred dotted-half-note beat at the level of the barline.[19]

---

19. The rationale underlying this "preference" is formalized in Lerdahl and Jackendoff, *A Generative Theory*, p. 84. The authors equate pitch repetition with length or duration and apply the following "Metrical Preference Rule": "Prefer a

Significantly, too, repeats of the C–C–G pedal are *evenly* spaced by eight dotted-quarter-note beats at this point, a spacing that exposes the instability of the *Dies irae* phrases above. As is evident, the play of these alignments and realignments is infinitely varied and subtle.

Of course, listeners, even conservative listeners, can be expected to adjust their metrical bearings at certain points. The point of departure at m. 121 in Example 54 is unlikely to hold fast through the entirety of this passage. Still, the spacing of the C–C–G pedal remains highly irregular throughout, so that, in turn, metrical readjustments on the part of the listener are likely to be met with renewed challenges of varying degrees of intensity.

Then, too, in seeking out a context that could relate in specific ways to the rhythmic invention in the final movement of *Psalms*, we need not have plunged one hundred years into the past. Moving in the opposite direction, a host of contemporary contexts could have suggested themselves. Of special note in this connection is the music of Elliott Carter, music with which, as it happens, Stravinsky took pains to familiarize himself during the 1960s.[20] The idea of "simultaneous streams of different things going on together," as Carter himself expressed it,[21] is already a part of the invention in Carter's *Holiday Overture* (1944) and *Cello Sonata* (1948). In his First String Quartet (1951) and *Variations for Orchestra* (1955), these "streams" are defined not only by instrument, intonation, and interval but, more decisively, by the assignment of different speeds or tempos to the individual parts. Here, no doubt, the absence of what has been called an "overriding referential time-unit" radically alters the terms of the differentiation.[22] Yet the instinct behind these in-

---

metrical structure in which a relatively strong beat occurs at the inception of . . . a relatively long pitch-event."

20. See Igor Stravinsky and Robert Craft, *Dialogues and a Diary* (London: Faber and Faber, 1968), pp. 99–101. Stravinsky thought the first two of Carter's string quartets turgid, but pronounced the Double Concerto a "masterpiece."

21. Allen Edwards, *Flawed Words and Stubborn Sounds: A Conversation with Elliott Carter* (New York: W. W. Norton, 1971), p. 101, cited in Jonathan Bernard, "The Evolution of Elliott Carter's Rhythmic Practice," *Perspectives of New Music* 26, no. 2 (1988).

22. David Lewin, *Generalized Musical Intervals and Transformations* (New Haven: Yale University Press, 1987), p. 71. The context is Lewin's analysis of mm.

novations seems not far removed from that which propelled Stravinsky's applications. It is noteworthy here, however, that Carter,
when pressed on the matter of Stravinsky's rhythmic pedals, dis-
avowed any direct connection between them and his own simultaneously imposed "streams."[23] Indeed, to the extent that Carter's
rhythmic practices were influenced in specifically musical ways, he
seems to have drawn his inspiration, at least initially, from the music of Ives and Henry Cowell.[24]

7

That the octatonic set may have figured referentially in the music
of many composers earlier in this century is a proposition no longer
in need of any special confirmation here. What seems to have attracted these composers, composers of different backgrounds and
stylistic persuasions, was the manner in which, confined to the octatonic set, a long-established vocabulary of triads and dominant
sevenths could be transformed and, as it must have seemed, revi-
talized. Octatonicism plays a prominent role in Bartók's music, although in Bartók its complexion is less triadic than is the case with
Stravinsky. Olivier Messiaen, whose source seems to have been the
music of Rimsky-Korsakov, Scriabin, and Stravinsky, classified the
set as the second among "modes of limited transposition."[25] And
for several decades in Holland the set became known, as a result of
its frequent employment in the music of the Dutch composer Wil-

---

22–35 in the first movement of Carter's First String Quartet. The simultaneous
speeds in this passage are also discussed in Bernard, "The Evolution of Elliott
Carter's Rhythmic Practice," pp. 174–177.

23. Benjamin Boretz, "Conversation with Elliott Carter," *Perspectives of New
Music* 8, no. 2 (1970): 21.

24. See Bernard, "The Evolution of Elliott's Carter's Rhythmic Practice," pp.
164–166.

25. Apropos of Scriabin's music, see the analysis of the Seventh Piano Sonata
and Five Preludes, Op. 74, in George Perle, "Scriabin's Self-Analysis," *Music
Analysis* 3, no. 2 (1984). See also James M. Baker, *The Music of Alexander Scriabin*
(New Haven: Yale University Press, 1986). Olivier Messiaen, *Technique de mon
langage musical* (Paris: Leduc, 1944).

lem Pijper (1894–1947), as the "Pijper scale."[26] Here, however, we focus our attention on a few passages from Debussy's piano preludes, passages that would seem to bear more than a casual relationship to Stravinsky's early ballets.

Several excerpts from the seventh of these preludes, Book II, "La Terrasse des audiences du clair de lune," are cited in Example 55.[27] The octatonicism, confined in large part to Collection I, is pervasive from the start. Indeed, the vocabulary of (0 2 5) trichords, triads, and dominant sevenths is one that could easily be hooked up to the models and charts compiled earlier for Stravinsky's Russian-period works. Most astonishing in this respect are the specifics of articulation: reading down, the tritone-related (0 2 5)s in m. 2, confined to intervals of 5 in terms of (G F D) and (C♯ B G♯), hook up to Collection I's dominant sevenths by way of that by now familiar arrangement of the seventh, namely, first inversion and closed position.

But if the impression left by these remarkable intersections is that of a Model B stripped to some degree of its initial focus, it can nonetheless be shown that these Stravinsky-Debussy intersections are of a kind specific enough to allow for the disclosure of a number of interesting and fundamental distinctions. For there can be no question as to the startling contrast between Stravinsky's and Debussy's music: above all, the rhythmic character of this prelude, passive and inconspicuous, seems at odds with Stravinskian adaptations.

Indeed, what may seem immediately striking in the prelude is that the technique of superimposition, conceived rhythmically and harmonically, should have left so few traces. In retrospect, the idea of superimposing the triads and dominant sevenths of the octatonic set can seem rather obvious, given the overlapping pitch content

26. Pijper's Second Piano Sonatina (1925) is almost entirely octatonic and exhibits a vocabulary of (0 2 5) trichords and triads that are frequently superimposed. Missing from Pijper's music, however, is the rhythmic definition of this superimposition, the block structures and rhythmic pedals that distinguish Stravinsky's approach.

27. For a recent pitch-class set analysis of this prelude see Allen Forte, "Les Ensembles motiviques comme facteur fondamental d'unité et de contraste," *Analyse Musicale* 16 (1989).

EXAMPLE 55.   Debussy, Preludes, No. VII, Book II.

within the succession itself. (See the succession of dominant sevenths at m. 31, Example 55.) By comparison, Stravinsky's music,
of course, is inconceivable without it. Superimposed triads related
by minor thirds and tritones spurred not only the clashes of neoclassicism but, as if in compensation, the rhythmic pedals and patterns that were thrust quite suddenly to the surface of the invention. Devoid of harmonic or contrapuntal pull, inherently static by

EXAMPLE 56. Debussy, Preludes, No. VII, Book II.

virtue of their symmetrical content (by virtue of tendencies canceled and turned inward, as it were), these chords were manipulated in the percussive accentuation of patterns placed in counterpoint with one another—or, as has been discussed already, in opposition to a metrical grid. (The opposite is equally plausible, of course, namely, that the rhythmic impulse spurred the invention of these chords and, ultimately, the prolonged predilection for the octatonic set.)

To be sure, triads are occasionally sustained in Debussy's prelude to effect, in suspension, compound sonorities. (See the sustained seventh on G at mm. 1–2, Example 55.) But there are no simultaneous-attack durations in this respect, no instances of superimposition that could be compared to the (E♭ C) simultaneity at No. 37 in *The Rite of Spring* (see Example 50) or to any number of similar configurations in Stravinsky's music. In Example 56, compare Debussy's linear delineation of the tritone-related (0 2 5)s to the superimposed versions of this relationship found at no. 64 in *The Rite* (Example 57) and no. 11 in *Les Noces* (Example 58); although (0 2 5) trichords are sometimes expanded to (0 2 3 5) tetrachords, the distinctions revealed are telling.[28] At the same time, instances of superimposition are not to be found in the music of of Rimsky-Korsakov either. Such (0 2 3 5)s, triads, and dominant sevenths are applied octatonically in the opera *Kastchei the Immortal* (1902), but the superimposition of this vocabulary, along with the new and different pitch-relational terms that would have had to follow from this development, are not a part of the octatonic imagination.

28. An exception may be found at mm. 25–30 in Book II's second prelude, "Feuilles mortes," although the context of this passage is nonoctatonic.

EXAMPLE 57.   Stravinsky, *The Rite of Spring*, "Ritual of the Rival
Tribes."

EXAMPLE 58.   Stravinsky, *Les Noces*.

Events in Debussy's prelude move wave-like in twos and threes.
An idea or configuration, usually a measure or two in length, is followed by one or two restatements that feature fuller and more ani-
mated treatments; occasionally, bridges are added at the seams. The
process is telescoped by the repeated scale patterns or "arabesques"
in m. 2. Here, the single pattern, consisting of a "chromatic" embellishment of the tritone-related (0 2 5)s at G and C♯, is contracted
(or expanded) to within three quarter-note beats: G is followed by
F and D to complete (G F D) on the second beat, and then by (C♯ B
G♯) on the third beat.

But the larger pitch-relational issues in the prelude involve, as
they did earlier in Stravinsky's music, the nature of the interaction

that is forged between the octatonic and nonoctatonic components. And while these issues may be defined broadly, their more problematic aspects are felt at more immediate levels. In m. 1, the F♯ in the "alto" of the second chord is nonoctatonic in relation to Collection I. (Indeed, F♯ is the only nonoctatonic pitch in the first three and one-half bars of the piece.) But is it the F♯ alone or is it, more determinately, the (B D F♯ A♯) chord with which F♯ sounds simultaneously that is nonoctatonic? (The remaining factors of this chord are octatonic, referable to Collection I. Irrespective of transpositional level, however, set 4–19, that set to which this chord is ultimately reducible, is not an octatonic subset.) Or is it the entire configuration in m. 1, the principal motive of the piece, that is made essentially nonoctatonic by the F♯?

Once again, of course, difficulties of segmentation, difficulties that relate to the *grouping* of pitches and pitch-classes at various levels of structure, impose themselves. Of concern here is the resonance of F♯ and its chord as nonoctatonic elements in an initial setting that is overwhelmingly octatonic. For, irrespective of their nonoctatonic status in relation to Collection I, F♯ and its chord are not isolated, atomic elements. The presumption is that they relate and coalesce—if only rather tentatively at first, then more persuasively at some later stage of the development. This would hold true, in other words, even if the dominant sevenths on E and G that immediately follow F♯ and its chord in m. 1 were grouped with the octatonicism of mm. 2–3, a grouping that would isolate them on at least one level of structure.

Alternatively, of course, F♯ could be excused as a "chromatic" neighbor to E♯ of the repeated (B D E♯ G♯) diminished-seventh chord that opens the piece. This would mean treating it as an ornament, as subsidiary to the octatonic forces at work. (In contradiction, however, the A♯ that doubles as a neighbor just above is octatonic.) Thus, too, allowing for the shape and character of this "chromatic" neighbor-note inflection would mean that the configuration in m. 1 would be split into overlapping halves, into two intersecting hexachords. The left side of the configuration in Example 59 (m. 1), nonoctatonic by virtue of the F♯, would feature the neighbor-note motion, while the right side (m. 2), fully octatonic,

EXAMPLE 59.   Debussy, Preludes, No. VII, Book II.

would feature the sevenths on E and G that anticipate mm. 2–3. Between these nonoctatonic and octatonic worlds, the shared (B D E♯ G♯) diminished-seventh chord would figure as a pivot, a role that is confirmed later by the appearance, prefacing several sections, of an arpeggiated (E♯ G♯ B D♯) half-diminished seventh chord. (The emergence of this pitch-class-specific "*Tristan* chord" could easily provoke, as the octatonic element does, a resonating history extending beyond these immediate confines.)

In the modified restatement of the opening configuration in m. 7, the two neighbors F♯ and A♯ reappear as part of a nonoctatonic (D♯ F♯ A♯) triad. In seeking to connect these two versions of the theme, it has been noted by Allen Forte that (E♯ G♯)–(F♯ A♯) in the right hand in m. 1 equates with the G–F♯–D–E melodic outline in the top voice in m. 7.[29] (Inversionally related, these two complexes reduce to set 4–11, a nonoctatonic set.) At the same time, the hexachord on the left side of the configuration, the nonoctatonic side that features (B D E♯ G♯) and its neighbors F♯ and A♯, reduces to set 6–Z29, a set which, although nonoctatonic, is the nonliteral complement of 6–Z50. And 6–Z50 is octatonic and may be inferred, if only marginally, elsewhere in the piece. Nonliteral complements are thus invoked as a means of extending the octatonic web.

29. Forte, "Les Ensembles motiviques," p. 25.

Yet the motivic correlation with respect to set 4–11 at mm. 1 and 7 is obscured, and the distance traveled in securing these relations seems inconsistent with the immediacy of the octatonic component. In effect, the burden of proof has shifted from m. 1 to m. 7. To what extent and in what way is the (D♯ F♯ A♯) triad at m. 7 a stable sonority? Do the Collection I triads at E, B♭, and C♯ merely encircle and surround it as a form of embellishment, or do they coalesce in a more fundamental fashion? Indeed, does the explicitness of the octatonic component at mm. 1–8 prompt groupings that are questionable when the particularity of this piece is considered in greater detail? In other words, is the octatonic reading as it relates to this particularity an arbitrary imposition at this point?

My own view is that, true enough, the (D♯ F♯ A♯) triad in m. 7 is not easily severed from the octatonic triads that surround it and that, therefore, the segmentation of the configuration into octatonic and nonoctatonic components (Example 59) is likely to seem contrived. Yet the sectionalization of the prelude—its local pitch hierarchies and motivic cross-referencing—lends itself to the sorts of networks pursued with reference to Model B, even if the links that were traced earlier to a specifically diatonic component have to be revised.

The preludes of Book II were published in 1913. That was the year of *The Rite*, of course, although Debussy's manuscripts appear to have reached his publisher by January of that year, a full three months before the premiere of *The Rite* on 13 May.[30] Yet the possibility of a link need not be discounted altogether. Debussy had familiarized himself with the piano-duet version of *The Rite* on 9 June 1912 (with Stravinsky at his side),[31] and sonorities attached to the ballet could have impressed themselves on his imagination at that time. Louis Laloy, who was present at this early audition, recalled that the performance, with Debussy playing the bass and Stravinsky the treble, had left the participants "dumbfounded, flat-

---

30. See the letter to Jacques Durand, 7 January 1913, in *Debussy Letters*, ed. Lesure and Nichols, p. 266. Debussy promised his publisher "a complete set" of the preludes "by the end of the week." A batch containing all but two had evidently been forwarded at an earlier date.

31. See Stravinsky and Craft, *Stravinsky in Pictures and Documents*, p. 87.

EXAMPLE 60.   Debussy, Preludes, No. VII, Book II.

EXAMPLE 61.   Stravinsky, *The Rite of Spring*, Part II.

tened as though by a hurricane from the roots of time."[32] Debussy
wrote several months later that *The Rite* "haunted" him "like a
beautiful nightmare as I try in vain to recall the terrifying impression it made."[33] Often recalled in this connection is Debussy's description, following the premiere, of the music as "extraordinarily
wild . . . as you might say, primitive music with all the modern
conveniences."[34] My impression, however, is that a somewhat ambiguous response to *The Rite* in 1913 is what might well have been
expected and that, in any case, Debussy's remarks need not be
viewed as entirely negative in implication.

Consider the two passages cited in Examples 60 and 61 from this
present prelude and the Introduction to Part II of *The Rite*. In each
of these passages, the (D♯ F♯ A♯) triad, nonoctatonic in relation to
Collection I, serves as a point of departure and return. And in each
passage (D♯ F♯ A♯) is embellished by Collection I's triads rooted on
E, C♯, and B♭. The motivic profiles are different, but the harmonic
idea in relation to the octatonic set is much the same.

32. Louis Laloy, *La Musique retrouvée (1902–1927)* (Paris: Librairie Plon,
1928), cited in *Debussy Letters*, ed. Lesure and Nichols, p. 265.

33. Letter to Igor Stravinsky, 5 November 1912, in *Debussy Letters*, ed. Lesure
and Nichols, p. 265.

34. Letter to André Caplet, 29 May 1913, in *Debussy Letters*, ed. Lesure and
Nichols, p. 270.

EXAMPLE 62. Debussy, Preludes, No. VII, Book I.

Consider, finally, the overt octatonicism that opens the seventh prelude in Book I (1910), "Ce qu'a vu le vent d'Ouest." As is detailed in Example 62, an arpeggiated dominant seventh on D is joined in m. 5 by the (A♭ G♭ E♭) trichord to produce tritone-related sevenths at D and A♭. The specifics of this articulation feature, once again, the familiar first-inversion disposition of the seventh. Yet, as is sketched in Example 62, several alternative segmentations suggest themselves in relation to what follows—in particular, tritone-related (0 2 5)s and 2s. Transposed to within Collection III at m. 8 (with the sustained F♯ in the bass as the pivot), tritone-related 2s become linked to the whole-tone set that surfaces at mm. 11–12.

All the same, it is in its embedded dominant sevenths at D and A♭ that the configuration at m. 5 of this prelude bears a very special relationship to the bell-ringing sequence in the "Coronation Scene"

EXAMPLE 63.   Mussorgsky, *Boris Gudonov*, Prologue.

EXAMPLE 64.   Debussy, Preludes, No. VII, Book I.

of *Boris Gudonov*. If the documentation concerning Debussy's familiarity with Mussorgsky's opera is taken into account, this link, pitch-class-specific as it is, must surely have been direct and explicit.[35]

But here again, we need not stumble only backwards but can turn, with or without considerations of immediate or explicit borrowing, to the side and to the front as well. For the history of set-class 6–30, that hexachord (and octatonic subset) to which these varied configurations and articulations are reducible, has been a lively one. As is shown in Examples 63–67, a chronicle could begin with the "Coronation Scene" itself, then turn to the opening of Debussy's Prelude No. VII, Book I (1910), Stravinsky's "*Petrushka* chord" (1911), the referential hexachord in the "Tanzscene" of Schoenberg's *Serenade*, Op. 24 (1924), and finally the passage at mm. 180–242 in Bartók's *Music for Strings, Percussion, and Celesta*, II (1937).

35. On Debussy's familiarity with the opera see, for example, Edward Lockspeiser, *Debussy*, 4th ed. (New York: McGraw-Hill, 1972), pp. 49–50.

EXAMPLE 65.   Stravinsky, *Petrushka*, Second Tableau.

EXAMPLE 66.   Schoenberg, *Serenade*, Op. 24, "Tanzscene."

EXAMPLE 67.   Bartók, *Music for Strings, Percussion, and Celesta*, II.

In Schoenberg's "Tanzscene," 6–30 is unordered and partitioned for the most part by its tritone-related (0 2 5)s, facts which I mention in passing (and somewhat speculatively) because of the genuine affection Stravinsky appears to have felt for this music, at least at the time of his first real encounter with Schoenberg's works during the late 1940s and early 1950s.[36] (The overt neoclassicism of the *Serenade* may have played a role here. As Robert Craft recalled at the time, Stravinsky found much to "admire" elsewhere in Schoenberg's music but little with which to identify aesthetically.)[37]

These specific intersections, coming by way of set-class 6–30, and prompting, by virtue of the level of abstraction implied, some unusual juxtapositions, are meant not to erase cherished distinctions but, on the contrary, to invoke and celebrate distinction. At the same time, 6–30 is likely to take on a provocative character of its own. Resonating with context, it too can become a focus of inquiry and speculation. Indeed, 6–30 is one of the oddest sets on record, being the only one that is transpositionally but not inversionally symmetrical.

My own view of these matters is that, distanced somewhat from the tension of context, the glare of its immediacy, reductions of the kind depicted here can have a sobering effect on the musical consciousness. They can serve as a reminder that beneath the profundity of context, composers as well as listeners have had to deal, in ways that need not have been all that distant or remote, with very simple considerations of pitch, of interval, and of classes of pitch and interval.

My sense, too, is that Stravinsky would not have recoiled from such sentiments. "I compose with intervals," he once noted during his later serial years, "and that is to some extent to compose as I always have."[38]

In retrospect, too, it seems inconceivable that his extraordinary range, his travels from *The Rite of Spring* and *Les Noces* to the neoclassical Concerto in D, *Agon* (1957), and the *Requiem Canticles*

36. See Robert Craft, "A Personal Preface," *The Score* 20 (1957): 12–13.
37. Craft, "A Personal Preface," p. 13.
38. Igor Stravinsky and Robert Craft, *Conversations with Stravinsky* (New York: Doubleday, 1959), p. 22.

(1966), could have been managed without a very immediate and playful awareness of these elementary terms of intersection. This applies to the assumptions of metric periodicity that underlie the rhythmic invention as well. Without an immediate awareness of these assumptions and of the potential for linkage and intersection, this invention could never have been realized neoclassically, and the idea of neoclassicism, of an accommodation, a reinterpretation of Baroque and Classical models in the composer's own "accent,"[39] could never have suggested itself.

And the attraction of this nonimmediate past must have lain to some degree in its preconceptions, in what had been assumed and taken largely for granted. For it was against the backdrop of its square metrical dance schemes that Stravinsky exerted the play of his devices. And the history of his rhythmic invention, the larger context from which it derives much of its point, is the history of meter and the phrase in Western tonal music.

39. Stravinsky and Craft, *Expositions and Developments*, p. 128.

Epilogue

Even with the relatively casual treatment of analytic-theoretical method in the preceding three chapters, the often maligned pitch-class set can prove its point. In chapter 5 it was of some use in climbing the ladder of abstraction; we considered the symmetrical implications of set class 6–20 in passages from the music of Glinka, Rimsky-Korsakov, Bartók, and Schoenberg. As a carrier of known attributes, so to speak, of facts and circumstances gathered on behalf of one context and exercised on behalf of another, 6–20 could be read into each of the given passages, igniting each accordingly. It could serve as a means of comparison, a conduit, a way of setting each passage in relief. So, too, in chapter 6 a number of melodic fragments from the works of Stravinsky's Russian period shared an interval-class content, that of set class 4–23, that could be pursued along similar lines. And in chapter 7 the intersection of a number of octatonic subsets in passages of considerable diversity seemed compelling for similar reasons, and from a perspective that was specific as well as general.

In these analyses the problem of segmentation did not materialize appreciably.[1] In the main, units were marked off and identified as sets according to conventional notions of motivic, chordal, accompanimental, and instrumental grouping. We should note, however, that such notions do not invariably apply in music of the post-tonal era. Especially in the atonal and twelve-tone works of Schoenberg and his school, the manner in which pitches cohere as segments of pitches, segments of intervals, and, more abstractly, classes of pitches and intervals becomes increasingly problematic. There are few common links or units of vocabulary in these works, groupings or sets that are held in common, so that the analyst must rely increasingly, especially in the initial stages of a segmentation, on overt discontinuities of one kind or another. And the problematic nature of the segmentation is tied to the high level of abstraction of the pitch-class set. Faced with the greater contextuality of post-tonal works, the absence of a syntax comparable in determinacy to that of the tonal tradition, theory and analysis retreated to the unordered pitch-class set and to relations among such sets, more abstract or less determinate ways of gauging relatedness or coherence.[2] In doing so, they withdrew from those more specific levels of structure upon which a process of segmentation is bound to depend.

Hence the problem and its source, the contextuality of post-tonal works. For the theory of pitch-class sets identifies and relates abstract sets (by similarity relations, for example, or subset structures), not pitches, pitch-classes, or segments thereof; it presupposes a segmentation. And while a process of segmentation need

---

1. Problems of segmentation in atonal music, in particular as they relate to Forte's methodology, are discussed in William Benjamin's review of Allen Forte's *The Structure of Atonal Music*, *Perspectives of New Music* 13, no. 1 (1974); William Benjamin, "Ideas of Order in Motivic Music," *Music Theory Spectrum* 1 (1979); Richard Taruskin, "Reply to van den Toorn, "*In Theory Only* 10, no. 3 (October 1987); and Pieter C. van den Toorn, "What Price Analysis?" *Journal of Music Theory* 33, no. 1 (1989). For a systematic approach to segmentation in atonal music, see Christopher F. Hasty, "Segmentation and Process in Post-Tonal Music," *Music Theory Spectrum* 3 (1981).

2. The pitch-class set retreats to, and is defined by, inversional as well as transpositional equivalence, and Allen Forte's theory of relating sets assigns special significance to abstract as well as literal complementation. See Allen Forte, *The Structure of Atonal Music* (New Haven: Yale University Press, 1973).

not be entirely divorced from an identification of sets, while the latter (especially the recurrence of sets) can indeed spur the former,
the two sides of the equation are obliged to maintain a degree of
independence if the drawing of relations is not to become entirely
self-serving at a high level of abstraction—if, in other words, the
analysis is to avoid undue circularity by maintaining contact with
the actuality of the music, with the pitches, pitch-classes, intervals,
successions, and rhythms that together comprise that more tangible if evidently unprincipled structure from which the theory retreats. Consequently, segmentation and set-identification are best
kept somewhat apart, with segmentation representing the more in-
clusive of these processes. In perception and analytical review, segmentation can involve a consideration not only of pitch and interval but of rhythm, texture, and instrumentation as well.

And it is in wrestling with the details of a segmentation, in fact,
in confronting that more tangible "foreground" which the theory
forsakes but which the segmentation must presume in some form,
that the analyst is forced to exercise his or her musical judgment,
that the mind's ear must come to terms with the full ramifications
of the individual atonal context. Alternatively, it is in the theory that
is apt merely to follow and hence to stand apart from the immediate
engagement of a segmentation, in the detached manner in which
the results of that engagement can often be processed, that the New
Musicologists might have voiced their concerns a bit more specifically about a positivist, formalist, systematic, insular, "technical,"
institutional, and masculinist theory and analysis. For the bulk of
those concerns can seem evident enough: a theory applied relatively free of the "signifying surface" or "foreground"; musical
facts and circumstances gathered and processed without much regard for their historical, stylistic, or sociopolitical implications; a
"technical" vocabulary of numberings and abbreviations likely to
encourage insularity rather than interdisciplinary exchange, specialization rather than "humanist," literary, or expressive discourse;
and a "technical" knowledge that can become an expertise, lending
itself to process and standardization in its instruction.

Indeed, still more could be made of such a case. Taking as its
point of departure the theory and analysis of twelve-tone music,

especially the analysis of hexachordal types (as pitch-class sets), the more general study of sets and of set-relations began in earnest in the 1960s and culminated with the publication of Forte's *Structure of Atonal Music* in 1973. Important work followed on the music of individual composers. Yet Forte's book had the effect of identifying a field of inquiry with a repertory, pitch-class set analysis with—at least at first—the problematic atonal music of Schoenberg, Berg, and Webern.

Confusions followed here as well, however, in the relationship of the theory not only to specific idioms and repertories but also to compositional practice. Given the level of abstraction, there was nothing to prevent the theory from being applied to post-tonal music more generally; Forte himself, although at times leery about the extension of the atonal stamp, made reference to the music of Scriabin, Stravinsky, and Bartók in his original analyses.[3] On the other hand, there can be no denying the unevenness to which that extension was to lead, the fact that the appropriateness of the theory could vary from one composer or context to the next, a variance seemingly hinging on such issues as indeterminacy, levels of contextuality, and tonal residue. In the end, of course, appropriateness could have as much to do with the manner of the application as with the theory, the manner in which questions of relevance and significance were posed.

At the same time, the combination of Forte, Yale, and atonal set theory might have been criticized on sociopolitical grounds, as a target in the war against "technical" expertise, insularity, and academic "priesthoods." The methodology has after all been a part of a larger entanglement, stretching from the classroom to the lecture hall, from the fledgling paper to the wide-ranging coverage of a theoretical apparatus, from the recruitment of graduate students to their eventual placement within the hierarchy. And on all these fronts, in pursuit not only of his own research but of the discipline of theory and analysis, Forte has been indefatigable. Having founded the graduate program in theory at Yale in 1959, he turned

---

3. Examples from the music of Ives and Varèse were also included in *The Structure of Atonal Music*.

his attention to atonal music in the 1960s; the program itself became split between the study of tonal music (by way of Schenker) and that of atonality (by way of Forte). So, too, as the number of (now apparently analyzable) atonal works increased, so did the number of doctoral dissertations. And for non-Yale students, Forte offered summer sessions sponsored by the National Endowment for the Humanities.

The spin-offs from this activity have been imposing. At Yale University Press, Forte became general editor of a series on the music of twentieth-century composers. With others, he encouraged the founding of a separate Society for Music Theory in 1978, a group which elected him its first president. The package has been something of a phenomenon, in other words, the program itself a model serving numerous graduate programs across the United States, Canada, and England. At the very least, it has offered students an alternative not only to musicology but to theory-composition as well, the traditional hybrid that has come to seem less and less satisfactory in recent years. Professional demand for research and publication has undercut the viability of the latter hybrid, as full-time composers have found it increasingly difficult to keep pace with analytic-theoretical developments.[4] A few have continued, yet the hybrid has been a casualty all the same, and still lamented as such by considerable numbers of both the theory and the composing communities.

There were a number of skeptics, no doubt, and from the very start. From the standpoint of the theory, segmentation proved an early worry,[5] as did the various assumed levels of abstraction. To many, the high level of abstraction presumed by Forte's methods seemed a way not only of guaranteeing analytical results (*some* form

---

4. The problem has not only been institutional or professional, however, but has also involved the increasingly contextual or pluralistic nature of contemporary composition, including academic composition. For further comment, see van den Toorn, "What Price Analysis?" pp. 171–174. Cf. Milton Babbitt, *Words About Music*, ed. Stephen Dembski and Joseph N. Straus (Madison: University of Wisconsin Press, 1987), pp. 163–187. Babbitt's context is "The Unlikely Survival of Serious Music."

5. See, especially, Benjamin's review of Forte's *The Structure of Atonal Music*, p. 177.

of relatedness could be guaranteed at the level of the pitch-class set) but of ruling out the possibility of an interpretation as well. Thus Richard Taruskin has argued that the methodology does not permit a weighing of questions of validity and significance, and that such a weighing can come only with the introduction of a larger historical framework.[6] Still others have identified the approach with the mere production of relations, and the latter with that of papers, theses, articles, and the like. Less charitably, in other words, the approach has been linked with data, not with thoughtful inquiry into the relationship of the data to musical experience.[7] (The circularity of this complaint cannot be denied, however. Given the high degree of contextuality of atonal or post-tonal works, analysts have been forced to retreat to terms and concepts of greater abstraction. Having been forced to retreat in this direction, however, they have been accused of timidity, of retreating not only for the sake of a guarantee but also as a way of dodging the obligation of an interpretation, of translating the data into a tangible means of description and explanation.)

But notwithstanding today's preoccupation with sociopolitical matters, its demand that such matters be taken into account, no such consideration of Forte's methods or of pitch-class analysis in general has been forthcoming from humanists, feminists, or postmodernists such as Joseph Kerman, Leo Treitler, Susan McClary, or Lawrence Kramer. On the contrary, the protest has been general and promotional rather than specific and to the point. And it has dealt with political, social, and literary scientists rather than with the politics of its own academic backyard. (Dreary enough, the latter is at least a politics in which the protesters are implicated directly, so that its consideration would have assured the meeting of one of their more insistent demands, namely, the acknowledgment

6. See Richard Taruskin, "Letter to the Editor," *Music Analysis* 5, nos. 2–3 (1986); and Taruskin, "Reply to van den Toorn," pp. 27–46.

7. See Benjamin, "Ideas of Order in Motivic Music," pp. 23–24. The author warns against "hurling" the theory "at the context which it is meant to transform, with the result that the latter is reduced to a densely packed but incoherent rubble-heap of relations." See Taruskin, "Letter to the Editor," p. 318. The approach is judged a means of gathering as many facts as possible about a musical context.

on the part of scholars of the immediately personal and sociopolitical implications of their scholarship.) Treitler has alluded to the "methodologies of formalist analysis being taught and practiced in North America today" but has confined his remarks to Schenker and Schenker's early treatise on Beethoven's Ninth Symphony.[8] He has urged scholars to become less detached in scholarship, more aware of "secular, mundane politics,"[9] but has referred to national political issues alone, not to the sociopolitics of scholarship or the academy.

So, too, McClary has poked fun at the "loops" with which analysts have grouped the segments of atonal music ("pitch-class amoebas," she has called them), at the analysts' attempts to uncover a degree of relatedness in pieces of extraordinary refraction.[10] But she has failed to understand the underlying issues of intelligibility that could be addressed more specifically by way of such tentative segmentations, issues involving the musically rational as well as the irrational (*her* issues, in fact), the communal as well as the contextual, parts as well as wholes. McClary is far too suspicious of such analytical attempts, it seems to me, which are in fact efforts to arrive at a logical explanation of musical structure; she condemns them as specialist, institutional, or masculinist in character—indeed, as rational, as if logic and rationality were necessarily in conflict with musical experience and appreciation, the former incapable of working to the benefit of the latter. At the same time, she exempts her own sociopolitical analyses from such difficulties, although they are rationalizations no less rational, of course, and no less academic or elitist given their point of departure, no less distanced intellectually from the body politic. Indeed, they are far more problematic in their relationship to musical experience, and because of their hugely generalizing terms, the irremediable character of the generalization.

Among historians or "historical musicologists," only Taruskin

---

8. Leo Treitler, *Music and the Historical Imagination* (Cambridge: Harvard University Press, 1989), p. 66.

9. Treitler, *Music and the Historical Imagination*, p. 8.

10. Susan McClary, *Feminine Endings: Music, Gender, and Sexuality* (Minneapolis: University of Minnesota Press, 1991), p. 109.

has familiarized himself with the mechanics of pitch-class set analysis to an extent permitting a substantial critique of Forte's methods.[11] George Perle has launched his own evaluation along compositional as well as analytic-theoretical lines.[12] But the new humanists have shied away from the specifics of their argument in this case, those relating to atonal set theory and its methodologies. And it may be that the "technical" aspects of the case have had their inhibiting effect, which at this point is likely to have come as a self-fulfilling prophecy.

But intervals and classes of intervals are a part of music, of course, of what we hear in music, whether we acknowledge them as such (become conscious of them) or not. And classes of pitches and intervals grouped as sets, properties and relations heard and understood accordingly, can be immensely useful in analysis, adding another dimension to our understanding of tonality as well as atonality. As has been suggested, however, the tendency has been to dismiss such concerns as "technically" distant, an imposition on the listener and his or her appreciation of the music. Among the new humanists, they have been decried as specialist and insular; elitist, because supposedly available only to trained and accredited professionals; masculinist, because supposedly irrelevant to sensibility, expression, and meaning, variables traditionally identified as "feminine."[13]

In fact, however, it has been the new humanists, feminists, and

---

11. See Taruskin, "Letter to the Editor," pp. 313–320; and Taruskin, "Reply to van den Toorn," pp. 27–46. On the other hand, Taruskin is so overwhelmed by the pitfalls of Forte's approach, it seems to me, above all by the sociopolitical (or colonial) associations referred to here, that he cannot recognize the usefulness of many of Forte's terms, including those having to do with classes of intervals and abstract sets. He associates those terms with a concern solely for musical generality, not for the particularity that it is their purpose to highlight. Issues similar to these were discussed in connection with Schenkerian theory and analysis in chapter 4.

12. George Perle, "Pitch-Class Set Analysis: An Evaluation," *Journal of Musicology* 8, no. 2 (1990).

13. See, for example, Susan McClary, "Terminal Prestige: The Case of Avant-Garde Music Composition," *Cultural Critique* 12 (1989). "Hardcore" analysis and "difficult" academic music are also characterized as misogynist; they reflect the male attempt to exclude women (or the concerns of "expression, pleasure, and community" associated with women) from the academy.

postmodernists who, positivistically as well as meritocratically, have in the underlying assumptions of their arguments stressed the role of institutions and of institutional learning—in effect, of their own priestly guidance—in the acquisition of an appreciation or taste for music. And they have done so to a point at which they seem to deny the ability of "ordinary people," who lack that guidance, to inform themselves about music.[14] Such trust in academia is misguided, in my view, and imposes too heavy a burden. It encourages an over-reliance on the institutions and their functions, and a concomitant misunderstanding about the nature of the engagement with music.

The other side of specialization is sophistication, of course, greater refinement in the making of distinctions. And the need to distinguish is at least as great as that to accommodate. Indeed, the two are often employed jointly in theory and analysis, with accommodation serving as a means of arriving at distinctions. Finer distinctions, moreover, need not supersede rougher approximations, but can come in the form of a supplement, a new addition to both sides of the approach.

But why should talk about sex, gender, politics, and society bring us closer to music and its appreciation, a sense of its immediacy, than talk—even "technical" or systematic talk—about its polyphony, motives, dissonance, and twelve-tone aggregates? Why should the former be judged sympathetically humanist, democratically nonspecialist and correctly interdisciplinary, the latter distant and distancing, as if the materials of music were by nature offputting, a nitty-gritty bound to inhibit appreciation and to alienate those truly in touch? Surely it is one of the businesses of music education to assure that the materials of music are in fact made close, immediate, and tangible. Too often, present-day discussions of

14. See the critique of traditional practices of theory and analysis in Susan McClary, "The Politics of Silence and Sound," Afterword to Jacques Attali, *Noise: The Political Economy of Music*, trans. Brian Massumi (Minneapolis: University of Minnesota Press, 1985), pp. 150–153. McClary exaggerates the influence of academic training, it seems to me, and not only traditional approaches but, by implication, her own sociopolitical and feminist interpretations as well. See footnote 3 in chapter 2, above.

gender and sexuality evade music, the notion of a distinguishable object "out there." And what is offered in its place is a kind of socio-political amplification of the self; or, if not of the self, then of groups whose interests it claims as its own. Either way, however, the self is left as elusive as ever, and notwithstanding the optimistic views of the new humanists and feminists in this regard. It remains confined to something between the lines, a suggestive content which, upon closer scrutiny, slips through the fingers like water.

No doubt theorists and analysts will continue to draw on closely related fields such as history, compositional practice, cognitive and other branches of psychology, aesthetics, and theories of poetic influence. And there is perhaps little reason why ideas about sex, gender, and society should not also be points of reference. (We may grant that the context of music is potentially limitless.) Yet the strength of the discipline will continue to reside, it seems to me, in its focus, its concern for the materials of music, its search, often rigorous and systematic, for music's "organizing principles."[15] And what is of value to closely related fields will continue to be that focus, the sense it can convey of the materials themselves.

Narrowly, our purpose has been the rebuttal of some of today's criticisms of the practices of music theory and analysis. More to the point, however, it has been the demonstration of a number of those practices as a way of laying bare often forgotten, less tangible uses. But this should not suggest that current practices are invariably the most appropriate, that new questions cannot spur newer methods while modifying older ones. Here again, however, the discipline is best served by maintaining its emphasis, one that entails the workings of music, questions about its fit, hold, and perception. It entails examining structure, in other words, investigating how music is structured and how we structure music. So, too, with its object in view, the discipline need not lose sight of the beholder, he or she who listens, perceives, apprehends. Nor need it forget its point of departure, which is the individual context, what is sensed and felt in that light.

15. Kofi Agawu, "Does Music Theory Need Musicology?" *Current Musicology* 53 (1993): 89.

Index

Aesthetics, 18; absolutist, 70–71, 87, 89, 91, 92; contextuality and, 156–157, 196; history and, 152, 153; immediacy and, 4, 7, 49, 50; immersion in music and, 12–14, 66–67; positivism as against, 67; reductionism in, 39; subjectivity and, 53; subject-object dichotomy and, 66; transcendental experience and, 22–23. *See also* Immediacy; Presentness; Reflection

Analysis, 6, 16; as abstract, 191; aesthetic, 18, 77n8; circularity of, 188; close reading, 7; as against criticism, 76; as foil, 55, 77, 141–142, 188; as formalist, 49; general versus individual in, 36, 153; history and, 114, 151, 169; immersion in music and, 14; as insular, 95–96, 97, 223, 227; intimacy and, 102, 120; literary, 89; as masculinist, 227; misrepresentation of, 19–20, 80–81, 88; narrative, 87, 88; nineteenth-century, 87; as process, 19, 80–81, 95; role of, 6; sociopolitical concerns, 58, 120–121, 225–226; tension and, 24–26, 29, 31–33, 37, 55, 158; use of models in, 36. *See also* Detail; Schenkerian analysis; "Technical" analysis

Antar Symphony (Rimsky-Korsakov), 127–128

L'Après-midi d'un faune (Debussy), 26

Atonality: analysis of, 110–111; individuality and, 114–115; motive and, 113; segmentation and, 110–111; triadicity in, 137–139, 140–141. *See also* Post-tonality; Tonality; Twelve-tone system

Audience. *See* Listener; Music appreciation; Sensing subject

Authority, 19n12

"Autonomy principle," 3, 11, 40, 154

Babbitt, Milton, 113, 129, 152, 153; on Schoenberg, 134n43; self-reference concept of, 154; on Stravinsky, 144–145, 148, 150, 152

Bach, Johann Sebastian, 106, 107

Barthes, Roland, 98

Bartók, Béla, 102, 127, 129, 181, 206

"Basel" Concerto in D (Stravinsky), 174, 175–177; octatonicism in, 193, 194; rhythmic stutter in, 182; Russian-period motto in, 183–184

Beethoven, Ludwig van, 37, 38

Beethovens Neunte Sinfonie (Schenker), 75, 84–86

Berlioz, Hector, 202–205

Blacking, John, 38n59

Bloom, Harold, 160

Boretz, Benjamin, 67–68, 113, 142

Boris Gudonov (Mussorgsky), 215–216

Brahms, Johannes, 32

Burnham, Scott, 16–17, 19n12

Carter, Elliott, 205–206

Cassirer, Ernst, 22

Cello Sonata (Carter), 205

Music examples set by: George Thomson
Composition: Terry Robinson & Co.
Text: 11/13.5 Bembo
Display: Bembo
Printing and binding: Thomson-Shore, Inc.